Ex Libris
Douglas Joel Culver

WHAT THEY ASK ABOUT

THE CHURCH

WHAT THEY ASK ABOUT

THE CHURCH

MONSIGNOR J. D. CONWAY

FIDES · CHICAGO 19, ILLINOIS

Library of Congress Card Catalog
Number: 58-8341

NIHIL OBSTAT:
Rt. Rev. Msgr. A. J. Burke
Censor Librorum

IMPRIMATUR:
⊠Ralph L. Hayes
Bishop of Davenport, Iowa
December 23, 1957

Manufactured by American Book—
Stratford Press, New York, New York

55

Contents

Foreword

The Catholics who immigrated to the United States last century were the poor people of Europe. They were short of money, short of food and clothing and shelter. They were poor in spirit as well, illiterate or semi-literate for the most part.

The people who had immigrated earlier called themselves natives and looked on the later immigrants as inferior. They called them names (like wop for Italians) to express their feeling, and the vaudeville houses rang with laughter about Pat and Mike in the wonderland of America.

There was then a good deal of prejudice. Catholics were confronted with the straw men constructed by reckless charges made during the Reformation: the Pope is a bad man, the Mother of God should not be honored, Saints are silly, Purgatory isn't in the Bible, priests build arsenals in church basements, nuns are prisoners, and the like.

To puncture these little balloons, Catholics were provided with little answers in little books with arguments which were quick and to the point. The debates were often useless because the people who made the charges mostly did not really want information, and the people who gave the answers did so with resentment which sometimes mounted up to what was called "muscular Christianity."

Now there are millions of Americans who are willing to examine the credentials of the Catholic Church with intelligence and humility. The questions they ask are fairly similar to those their grandparents asked, but the attitude of those asking them has greatly changed.

Now, also, there are millions of Americans who are able

and willing to give the answers intelligently, and with congeniality and sometimes even with humor. The ambient air is of early morning in the spring.

Catholics and Protestants respect each other. They have mapped out areas of agreement and are working together in them to avert a common danger. They know the value of a better understanding of each other.

This book makes that understanding easier. Many of the answered questions appeared earlier in the *Catholic Digest*. They were actually asked by non-Catholics. We at the *Catholic Digest* know by means of continuing surveys that the seven million or so readers of the *Catholic Digest* regard them as the most interesting articles we have ever published.

PAUL BUSSARD,
Catholic Digest

1. *The Credentials of the Church*

The Church Is Christ. Is One
Church as Good as Another? Who
Founded the Catholic Church? "Ro-
man Catholic." The Faith of St.
Paul. The Primacy of Peter. Christ's
Mystical Body.

Q. Would you please quote a portion of the Bible, in either Testament, which proves that Christ was a Catholic?

A. Your question is like asking me to quote the Declaration of Independence to show that Christopher Columbus was an American.

What you need is a brief summary of religious history, so that you will get your horse, cart, and trailer in proper sequence.

1. Before time began, there was only God. He was always there. He is always everywhere.

2. God created the world. He probably began the job millions of years ago. It was quite a task. He had to make a few million stars and planets and scatter them carefully

1

through thousands of light-years of space. He had to design every atom and assemble its intricate parts from nothing. Quite possibly He made simple things, in the beginning, and let them develop, according to plan, into more complicated things.

3. Then God created man. It was His chief work, on earth at least. He created one man and one woman: Adam and Eve He named them. And after He got through making them man and woman, with life and intelligence and free will modeled on His own, He gave them a super-life which would permit them to live with Him forever in heaven. He gave them gifts to which they had no right by nature, gifts which made them resemble Him in most remarkable ways—so much so that He was able to adopt them, even as His own children and love them as their Father.

4. But God did not want to force these supernatural gifts on His children. They had no right to them. Neither were they compelled to keep them. He had made His children free. He would not force them. They could choose to keep His gifts or to throw them away. Adam and Eve chose to throw them away. And in doing so, they threw away their children's inheritance. If your father squanders his money you can never inherit it. Our first parents squandered God's great gifts—and their descendants were deprived of them and had no power to get them back.

5. God still loved his delinquent children. So He promised that He would one day get those special gifts back again for them. But it would take the greatest event of all time to accomplish it. He would have to send a Redeemer, to make up for the wrong of sin. And that Redeemer would have to be God Himself, because no less a person would be capable of the task.

2

6. With that solemn promise, then, God left man to his own ways, and man went deviously along them, mostly forgetting God's promise, mostly forgetting God Himself. That went on for years, and for centuries, with man's errors multiplying like his numbers on earth.

7. Then, at length, God decided to choose one race and nation upon whom He would keep His divine finger with special pressure. He would give this people a special revelation, teach them, make laws for them; He would choose and appoint their leaders, send them judges, kings, and prophets. In this way, at least one group of people on earth would know about the one God who created them, and would love Him—or lacking love, fear Him—and worship Him, and keep His commandments. From this, His chosen people, in due time His promised Redeemer would come.

8. Centuries went by—maybe twenty of them. The Old Testament tells us the story of those centuries. It is the history of God's chosen people, their crimes, infidelities, idolatries, and repentances; their wars, victories and defeats; their captivities and liberations; their lusts and loyalties; their worship, teachings, and laws. Through it all God is close to them, and there gleams the hope of the Promised One.

9. Then Jesus was born. The Promised One had come. The centuries of waiting were over. The Old Testament was ended. By His death, Jesus, who was God, made up completely for all sin, brought back to man the super-life which Adam and Eve had discarded and many of God's other special gifts to them. Men could now be God's own adopted children again. That super-life was the life of heaven—and those special gifts were a whole variety of divine helps to get man to heaven.

3

10. Not only did Jesus redeem man while He was on earth, He taught a beautiful, inspiring doctrine. He told the world about God, marvelous things which man could hardly have imagined. He told them of God's love for them, and of the love they should have for God in return, and of the love they should have for one another because of God. He gave them a new law of love, and seven sacraments to help them keep that law; and a new Sacrifice in which they would join Him in worship of God.

11. The death and redemption of Jesus were for the benefit of all men of all times and places. His teachings and commandments of love were for all men. His sacraments and Sacrifice were for all men. He wanted all men to get the life of heaven—His grace from Calvary—and to get all the helps He had provided to keep this life and live it fully. So he established an organization to give it all to them. We call it His Church. It is a sort of projection or extension of Himself through time and space—His own Mystical Body. He is its head, and in it we are all united to Him. Through it we hear His teachings, receive His heaven-giving super-life, and are brought into sanctifying union with Him.

12. He established that Church while He was on earth—about 1925 years ago. The Apostles, His closest friends, companions, and followers, were its first teachers, priests and bishops. St. Peter was their leader and head. This Church of Christ was very tiny in its early years, but it grew rapidly. It quickly took in thousands, then millions, first towns, then nations. In three hundred years it became the religion of the whole Roman Empire, which was nearly all of civilization. It was then that men began to call it the Catholic Church, because it was everywhere—

universal. It was the only Church there was—except for a few scattered heretical groups, which quickly died out.

It was more than a thousand years after the death of Christ before there was any serious permanent separation from His Church. Then, as a result of the Eastern Schism, in the eleventh century, the Greek Orthodox Church came into being.

It was almost another five hundred years—1500 years after the time of Christ—before Protestantism began, and a whole variety of little sects claimed to be the Church of Christ—or at least a part of the Church of Christ.

We cannot quote texts to show that Christ was a Catholic. But the New Testament has a variety of texts showing that Christ *is* the Church—its founder, its head, its life.

Q. In the office where I work the Protestants outnumber us Catholics four to one. In talking to us about religion they are accustomed to say: "Religion is religion; one is as good as another." Their manner is definite. What is the best thing for a Catholic to say? This is a very touchy subject. I have tried to say the right thing, but often feel that they think I consider myself better than them.

A. It is touchy. The bald truth may glisten brightly; but for all its sheen it may be rough and offensive. However, I believe that it is our manner of presenting the truth, rather than the truth itself, which gives the offense. The chip on shoulder or the jaw protruded invites a fight. The raised voice inflames but does not always convince. And by being on the defensive we invite offense, as counteraction.

We must avoid controversy, and simply explain our position calmly and confidently. If our faith is firm, our knowledge certain, and our charity warm, we will give no offense. If we are uncertain of our own belief, or of how to explain it, we are apt to be irritated with ourselves, and thence to transfer that irritation to our questioner, who caused our discomfort by bringing the subject up. And then we will surely give offense. Or if we are a bit prejudiced against Protestants, and actually do look down on them a bit, that is sure to show. And again we offend. If we are afraid of offending, our fear will cause us to stumble and apologize, and thereby justify itself.

With calm, friendly confidence, then, we try to explain our position: We simply cannot accept the idea that one religion is as good as another, for the following reasons:

1. Truth is factual, and our thinking or believing does not alter facts. It is important that we know and believe things as they really are: that black is black, and sin is sin. If my religion tells me that Christ was God, and your religion tells you that Christ was not God, then one or the other must be wrong. In a matter so vital to our salvation, it is important that we know which one is right, and not simply flip a coin.

2. We believe that Jesus Christ established a Church of His own, and required that all should believe in Him and belong to His Church. "Preach the Gospel to every creature. He who believes and is baptized shall be saved: but he who believes not will be condemned" (Mark 16, 15. See also Luke 2, 30-32; 24, 47; Matt. 28, 19-20; John 10, 16; 17, 20).

If Jesus Christ was God and established His own Church, then what right have we as His creatures and subjects to discard His Church and build a newer model of our own?

3. Religion is a relationship between God and man. It results from the fact that God created us. We as His creatures should adore Him. Surely God is entitled to a preference in the manner of this adoration. If He has indicated such preference we must follow His wishes. We have no right to reject them and substitute hobbies of our own. We believe that God has strongly indicated His preference: that He wants to be worshipped as His own Divine Son worshipped Him on the Cross—and that is through the Mass, the continuation of Calvary.

4. If religion were merely a source of personal pleasure,

7

edification, and instruction to us, then we might listen to the claim that one religion is as good as another. But it is much more than a diversion, something we do when we feel like it. Religion is a duty, and that duty is to God, and the rules for it are given by God. Indifference in religion often results from an egocentric idea of the universe: religion, like everything else, is for us; and we should be able to choose which brand is best for us—like we choose our cigarettes. Actually the universe centers around God, who made it, and religion is directed to Him. He is the one who chooses the brand—and in making the choice He knows with infinite wisdom what is best for us too.

5. If religion were merely humanitarianism—a sublime system of social service—we might listen judiciously to rival claims of philanthropic groups. This is a common modern concept of the Church, and its basic error is similar to the one above: it conceives of the universe as centered around man rather than God. It forgets the first part of Christ's command—that we love God above all things, with our whole heart, mind, and strength, and remembers only the second part—that we love our neighbor.

6. Religion is concerned with man. It is designed to lead him to God—to love of the Supreme Good and union with the divine source of our eternal happiness. God has designed and given us various essential aids to the accomplishment of that love and union. They stem from the Cross and reach us through His Church. They are the sacraments. We are not free to reject what Christ has required.

7. Our Lord has left Himself spiritually on earth in His own Mystical Body, the Church. It is the spiritual

8

vine giving life to the branches which remain united to it. We cut ourselves off at the risk of death.

8. Jesus Christ has taught. We are not arbitrary judges who pick and choose between His teachings. The Church which teaches part of His message can not be counted equal with His own Church, which He commanded to teach all of the message (Matt. 28, 20).

We can find other ways of saying it: There is only one true Church, and that is the one Christ Himself established. But no matter how we say it, our charity and understanding must be always evident. We must never question the sincerity and honesty of the person to whom we speak. We must recognize and admit his subjective right to follow his own firm conviction and formed conscience. We must realize that he probably loves God as deeply and firmly as we do, and that love is the vital source of sanctity (John 14, 21-23). In our own theological understanding we know that by his sincerity he belongs to the Church in desire—implicit, but real. However, we will probably do well not to taunt him with this fact. It is possible to explain it, however, in a very charitable and consoling manner.

Q. How can you prove that the Catholic Church is the one true Church when our Lord was a Jew?

Christ said to St. Peter "Upon this rock I will build my Church." He did not say "Upon this rock I will build the Catholic Church."

A. Our Lord Jesus Christ was God. That is the important thing. His nationality is incidental, except that God had chosen the Jews, many centuries before, to be His special people. Up until the time Jesus founded His own Church the Jewish religion was the true religion of God.

You admit that Jesus did establish a church. He called it "my Church," and Peter was the rock on which it was founded. All you need to understand is that the Catholic Church of today is exactly the same as that one which Jesus established 1900 years ago and called His own.

Certainly no church can be the one Christ established unless it is more than 1900 years old. You would laugh at a young lad of twenty who claimed to remember the Civil War. Yet there are young sprigs of churches, one, two, or three hundred years old which try to claim that they are the ones Christ established. The Catholic Church is the only one old enough to be Christ's Church. It was the only one around in the early centuries—the only one which stayed around for the first 1500 years.

Christ established His Church on the Apostles, whom He sent out to preach His Gospel to every creature. The

10

Catholic Church traces herself directly from those Apostles. Her bishops are their successors in office. She still teaches the same doctrines which the Apostles taught, and which the Master had taught them. She still has the same sacraments and devotions which they had; she has kept them and used them daily for nineteen centuries.

Christ used Peter for the rock foundation of His Church. The Catholic Church still rests on that same foundation. All other churches were established by moving off the old rock foundation. Peter, the rock, went to Rome, the capital of the world in his day, and the rock has remained there ever since.

Christ established a Church for all men—of every century and every nation. The Catholic Church was the only one trying to save the souls of our ancestors for fifteen centuries. It's a good bet that a few centuries from now she will be the only one left to carry on the work. The Catholic Church is the only one which has constantly tried to go to all nations and take the Gospel to every creature. It is the only one which has any reasonable representation in the great majority of nations today. Most Protestant churches are confined largely to one nation or to a little group of nations.

Christ established only one Church. He taught only one set of doctrines to be believed by everyone. The Catholic Church is the only one which teaches that set of doctrines in its entirety—teaches all of them the same everywhere, and has all of its members believing them just as Christ taught them.

Christ promised to remain with His Church always and to keep it from error, until the end of the world. The Catholic Church is the only one which puts reliance on

11

Christ's presence, to teach with His authority, under His infallible guidance.

Jesus Christ established His Church, which remains in the world today. It could not possibly be any other than the Catholic Church—the only one which has been around ever since.

Q. *Where in the Bible does it say that one must be a Roman Catholic?*

A. Among other places, in the concluding verses of the Gospel of St. Matthew (28, 19-20), and St. Mark (16, 15-16): "Go into the whole world and preach the gospel to every creature. He who believes and is baptized shall be saved, but he who does not believe shall be condemned."

Compare St. John, 10, 16: "And other sheep I have that are not of this fold. Them also I must bring, and they shall hear my voice, and there shall be one fold and one shepherd."

Of course the name "Catholic" was not given to the Church of Christ until after the time of the New Testament. It was commonly called merely "The Church" or "Holy Church."

There was no need to distinguish. There was only one Church.

St. Ignatius seems to have been the first to give the name "Catholic" to "The Church." He did this in a letter he wrote about the year 110, and in the course of the next two centuries the name caught on, and came into general use. By that time there were a few heresies in vogue, like Arianism, and "Catholic" became a name to distinguish the true Church from error and schism.

In the beginning the word "catholic" was simply an adjective meaning "universal." Then it came to have the meaning of "one and only" and to be used as an appellative—a "proper name" for the Church. This appellative use did not become common until the fourth century.

The Apostles Creed in the beginning had "I believe in the Holy Church." The word "Catholic" was inserted in the fourth century. Some Protestants have now thrown this word "Catholic" out of the Creed and frankly substituted the word "Christian."

As for the word "Roman," that is an Anglicanism—considered superfluous by all continental Europeans. It is like calling a man by his confirmation name, in addition to his baptismal and family names.

The word "Roman Catholic" really came from the legislative enactments of Protestant England. They tried to pretend that there was another "Catholic" Church, namely, the "English Catholic." Hence the name "Roman" was needed to distinguish the two. We still employ the consequences of their fiction.

Q. I am a convert and so do not know all of the church history I wish to know. Who was St. Paul and what did he do that made him as great as St. Peter, or at least got his name coupled with St. Peter so often?

A. St. Paul should be a favorite of converts. He was a sudden convert himself, and one of the greatest convert-makers the Church has ever known. Read all about him in the Acts of the Apostles.

Paul was a fiery young Jew at the time of his conversion —just a few years after Our Lord's Ascension. His name was Saul. He was well educated and a Roman citizen. He hated Christians and was active in persecuting them. Then suddenly Jesus appeared to him and won completely his great faith and love and zeal. He associated himself with the Apostles and was considered one of them. They evidently respected his learning and forcefulness.

Paul became the greatest missionary of the early Church. Accompanied at various times by Luke and Mark and Barnabas, he travelled repeatedly through Syria and Asia Minor, Greece, and Macedonia, and the islands of the Mediterranean, preaching the Gospel, making converts and establishing churches. He suffered great hardships on his trips and was often persecuted. Finally he was taken prisoner in Palestine and sent to Rome to be tried there as a Roman citizen. In Rome he found St. Peter and helped him establish the Church there. Both of them were put

15

to death in Rome—St. Peter was crucified head down; St. Paul's head was cut off with a sword.

In the course of his journeys St. Paul wrote many letters on doctrine and discipline to his various churches and to individuals who had worked with him. Fourteen of these are included in the New Testament—the Epistles of St. Paul.

Q. How can I explain that the faith St. Paul was spreading was the Catholic faith? My mother, a non-Catholic, thinks that could not be so, because the followers of Christ were called Christians and not Catholics. The answer seems obvious, doesn't it; but how can I make her see it?

A. The answer is so obvious to us that we find it rather hard to explain to someone who does not believe it. In the days of St. Paul the followers of Christ were not divided into different sects. They all believed the teachings of Christ as taught to them by St. Paul and the other Apostles. It is true that they were not yet called Catholics (see p. 13), but they were simply the only Christians in the world, and a little later the name Catholic came to be applied to them, without indicating any change in them at all.

By the time of St. Augustine (the end of the fourth century) there were some heretics about—like the Donatists—and St. Augustine insists that even these heretics have to "call the Catholic church Catholic," much as they would like to pretend that they were Catholics themselves.

In other words, all true Christians were called Catholics for more than a thousand years before any "reformer" had even dreamed about the various Protestant sects.

But, even so, names are not important. What does mat-

16

ter is that the Catholic Church is directly descended from St. Paul and St. Peter and the other Apostles. It has always kept, believed, revered, and taught everything they preached and wrote. The men they ordained were its early bishops and popes, and these ordained others, who ordained others, and so on, down through the centuries to the bishops and pope of the present day.

You must either admit that the Church of St. Paul was the Catholic Church or claim that the Church of St. Paul (and of Jesus Christ) promptly disappeared and was not found again for 1500 years or more. Isn't it strange how all historians have always thought that Europe was Christian throughout the long Middle Ages? But according to your mother, they couldn't have been really Christians; they were only Catholics. What happened to all the Christians? Seems they must have died with St. Paul and were only revived by John Wesley—seventeen hundred years later. Too bad the great Christian centuries of history were deprived of true Christianity.

Q. It seems to me that we non-Catholics have only one overriding question about the Church: "Is the Catholic Church the one and only true church of Jesus Christ?" If it is, then the answer to all other questions is simply: "The Church teaches that it is so."

The proof this overriding question revolves around whether or not the Pope is the direct and only successor to St. Peter. How can we be sure that St. Peter intended that the Bishop of Rome be his successor with all the authority given him by Jesus Christ? How can we be sure that St. Peter did not intend that one of the other bishops (earlier converted and established) or a council of bishops should have his authority?

If the Bishop of Rome was designated by St. Peter as his successor, why is it that it was several hundred years before a Bishop of Rome claimed this distinction? The fact that St. Peter died in Rome does not, I think, prove that the Bishop of Rome is the "Vicar of Jesus Christ and successor to the Prince of Apostles."

Please believe me that I am not asking this question with an antagonistic attitude. Nothing would give me greater peace of mind than to have this answered definitely, one way or the other. I married a Catholic, and my children are being raised as Catholics (with my permission). If the Roman Catholic Church is the "true" church, then I should be worshipping with my family. If not, then we should all be searching elswhere.

18

A. Your letter is logical and sincere. Jesus Christ was God who came to earth to redeem us and take us back to heaven with Him. He established a Church to continue His work of leading us to heaven; and He appointed Peter head of that Church. He made it clear that He wanted us all to belong to this Church. All these things you take for granted; and your conclusion is very sensible: If we find that the Catholic Church is the same Church Christ established, we should most certainly belong to it. If there is no way of finding which Church He established, then I don't see why we should belong to any, unless we specially like to listen to sermons or enjoy choir music.

I suppose you know that many people who are trying to find the Church of Christ do not take as many things for granted as you do. Your first point of concern is whether the popes of Rome are really the true and lawful successors to St. Peter. I don't want to disturb your more basic convictions, but I am sure you must know that some people have wondered whether Peter himself was ever Bishop of Rome—and whether Christ ever appointed him head of His Church—and even whether Christ ever established a Church at all.

So maybe we might briefly review these earlier questions. Since you already agree with us on them we will not go into detail, but simply indicate our line of reasoning.

First, Jesus Christ did establish a Church. One of the first things He did in beginning His public ministry was to select His twelve Apostles, and then for three years He taught and trained them carefully. He told them that they must go out and make disciples of all nations, "baptizing them in the name of the Father, and of the Son, and of the Holy Spirit" (Matt. 28, 19); and that they should go into the "whole world and preach the Gospel to every creature.

19

He who believes and is baptized shall be saved, but he who does not believe shall be condemned" (Mark 16, 15).

He gave them the power of binding and loosing, and made them shepherds of His flock (Matt. 18, 18; John 21, 16). He prayed for a united flock: "that all may be one, even as Thou, Father, in Me, and I in Thee" (John 17, 21).

He frequently compares this Church of His to a body, a kingdom, a sheepfold, and a city. Later, St. Paul calls it a body of which we are all members and Christ is the head (Rom. 12, 4; I Cor. 6, 15). And Jesus promised that He would remain with His Church "all days even unto the consummation of the world" (Matt. 28, 20).

Secondly, Christ made Peter the head of His Church. An organization was essential to the work Christ wanted done: teaching, baptizing, binding and loosing, and tending the flock. An organization was particularly necessary because this was a long-term work of tremendous extent and importance. It had to continue for centuries—twenty of them, at least. And it had to extend to every nation, and every creature. And heaven depended on it. Souls would be saved by it, or lost if it failed.

An organization was essential; but no organization can be effective or dependable or enduring unless it has a head. How would you hold it together and keep it united and stable and purposeful? If it had no head you could never tell which way it was headed! Feeling the need for authority and leadership, it would either have to grow its own head or else sprout a hundred little nubbin heads which would lead it off furiously in a hundred directions. And then how would Jesus ever keep His promise of remaining with His Church? Since it was divided, would He divide Himself? Would He give His divine blessing to each contradictory teaching as though it were His own Gospel?

Actually it is very evident from the Gospels and the Acts of the Apostles that Christ did give His Church a head, and that this head was Peter. You have to read the whole story to see how prominently and consistently Peter stands out. He is always the first named in lists of the Apostles— St. Luke even refers to the Twelve as "Peter and his companions" (8, 45; 9, 32)—and the angel at the tomb, after the Resurrection, told the women that they should "go, tell his disciples and Peter" (Mark 16, 7).

St. Peter is a natural leader, and takes his leadership for granted. The other Apostles accept it without objection, and the Master approves and confirms it. Peter was present at the Transfiguration and in the Garden of Gethsemane. He walked on the water. He took the miraculous catch of fishes, and was told that thenceforth he would catch men. He helped prepare the paschal supper, and was unfortunately prominent at the trial of Jesus. He was the first to enter the tomb on Easter morning.

The texts of Matthew 16, 13-20, and John 21, 15-17, are so well known and often quoted that we do not need to repeat them here. On the first occasion, Jesus received a profession of faith from Simon, changed his name to Peter, and promised that he would be the rock foundation of His Church, with the keys of the Kingdom and the power of binding and loosing. On the second occasion, after His Resurrection, Jesus obtained a profession of love from Peter and made him the shepherd of His flock.

The Acts of the Apostles tell us of many occasions on which Peter exercised his leadership in the early Church, especially in making important decisions on doctrine and policy. We simply haven't space to go into detail.

I don't believe there is any modern historian who doubts that Peter went to Rome and met his death there. So we

21

can take that for granted. You and I rather take it for granted, too, that he was in Rome as an apostle, doing the Lord's work—not merely as a tourist.

However, there have been some outstanding non-Catholic authorities, like Doctor Harnack and Bishop Lightfoot, who were not so sure. They readily admitted that Peter was in Rome and died there, but they either doubted or denied that he was bishop there. We can't brush aside eminent scholars like these and pay them no notice, but really it does seem that their arguments and claims are rather gratuitous, based on theories rather than historical evidence. We might take a brief glance at some of that historical evidence, especially that from the early centuries.

St. Cyprian was an Easterner, a Cypriot, who became Bishop of Carthage. He was a strong advocate of local authority and an outspoken critic of the Pope in certain matters. However, about the year 250 he wrote that Pope Cornelius had "succeeded to the place of Fabian, which is the place of Peter" (Ep. 55, 8).

Firmilian was a contemporary of Cyprian, and Bishop of Caesarea in Cappadocia. He was in violent controversy with Pope St. Stephen on the subject of the re-baptism of heretics, and he objected that Stephen claimed the right to decide this controversy because "he held the succession from Peter" (Cyprian's Ep. 75, 17). Firmilian would have been the first to deny this succession if he could have found any reason for doing so.

Tertullian, a great theologian and historian of the early Church, had become a heretic by the year 220, when he wrote (in *De Pudicitia,* 21) acknowledging the claim of Pope Callistus that Peter's power to forgive sin had descended in special manner on him. Like Firmilian, Tertullian would have preferred to deny this claim, and he

22

had been at Rome, where he would have found defects in the claim if any had existed.

There are other testimonies. But these which come from enemies of the pope or opponents of his policies have special value. In those early days, although you argued with the pope, you had to admit that he was the successor to Peter, the Bishop of Rome.

Now we come to a couple of points on which I may disagree with you a little. You rather take it for granted that St. Peter had the free choice of naming his successor or of deciding on the line of succession in the papacy. Maybe he did, but I am not so sure. Possibly our Lord, Himself, determined the manner of succession to Peter's office and power. Neither of us has positive evidence, but I believe my theory is as good as yours. At least we both know that there had to be a succession, that the authority and leadership had to continue—that there had to be a head. Where is that head?

If a head is going to be any good it must act like a head. It must lead. It must show its authority. Can you name anyone except the Bishop of Rome who even pretended to be a head during the first eight or nine centuries? A head is no good if it hides. Peter could hardly have left his authority in Jerusalem or Antioch. He still needed it after he left those places and went on to Rome. He gave it up personally when he died, and it is rather natural to suppose that his successor in office would take it up where he laid it down. Any other supposition would have to be proven; and there is no evidence. My own supposition needs to be proven too, and there is much evidence.

St. Clement was the fourth pope. Linus and Anacletus had filled in the years between Peter and Clement, who was a disciple of the Apostles. About the year 95 he wrote

23

an epistle to the Corinthians. He spoke with such a tone of authority that Bishop Lightfoot called it the "first step toward papal domination." So you see I can't go along with your supposition that the Bishops of Rome did not claim for several hundred years the distinction of being Peter's successors as head of the Church. Here is Clement, in the very first century, claiming that distinction and authority, and finding his claim accepted. His epistle was held in such reverence at Corinth that it was read in the churches like part of the Scriptures. St. John the Apostle was still alive at the time, and was certainly much closer to Corinth than Clement was. But here was a bishop of the West directly intervening in the affairs of an Eastern Church and claiming authority to settle the matter, saying that the "word of God comes through us . . . and the Holy Spirit speaks through us" (Clem. 1, 70).

St. Ignatius of Antioch wrote a letter to the Church of Rome, in the year 107, in which he acknowledged it as presiding over all other churches, "over the brotherhood of love." Remember that this same Ignatius was a successor of Peter, himself—in the see of Antioch. But he made no special claim to distinction for that reason.

St. Irenaeus was very close to the Apostles. He was a disciple of St. Polycarp, who had been named Bishop of Smyrna by St. John. Irenaeus wrote a great work against the Gnostics in which he appeals to the superior authority of the Church of Rome, which has "preserved the traditions of the Apostles" (*Adv. Haereses,* 3, 3, 2). He advises that Christians everywhere should conform to the traditions of the Church of Rome. And he also lists the popes by name from Linus to Eleutherius, pope at that time.

St. Victor (189–198) made the clearest assertion of papal authority of those early days. During his papacy there was

24

a violent quarrel between Asia Minor and the rest of the Christian world about the date of Easter. Victor stepped in to settle the quarrel; and when a certain Polycrates of Ephesus objected on the grounds that their local traditions came straight from St. John the Apostle, the Pope threatened to excommunicate him. St. Irenaeus intervened, and argued that the Pope should not cut off these churches in Asia Minor from the rest of the Church, because the subject under debate was not a matter of faith. So Pope Victor withdrew his penalty; but the force of his authority remained.

Much later, in the middle of the third century, about 257, St. Denis of Alexandria wrote to Pope St. Sixtus II, asking his advice and a doctrinal decision. At that time Alexandria was the most important see in the world, next to Rome, but there was never any evidence of a rival claim to authority.

In your letter there is a note of urgency and need. You want the proofs to solve your doubts. We can sympathize with you, but I doubt that we fully understand. We are relaxed about these historical proofs. Our faith in the supremacy of the pope is, in a way, independent of them. We know from the Scriptures that Jesus established a Church and made Peter its foundation and its head. The foundation must last as long as the Church which is built upon it; and if the Church were to lost its head it would certainly be a senseless organization. So Peter must still be there in his successor, and there is simply no question or doubt as to who that successor is.

Since we are sure of that already, we can examine the various proofs with relaxed interest, and note with pleasure how they confirm our faith. You need the proofs as a foundation for faith. We have the faith, and simply watch history back it up. Your sincerity makes us more appreciative of our own blessings, and we pray that in God's goodness you may share them.

Q. What is the Mystical Body of Christ?

A. It is the Church of Jesus Christ on earth. Its members are all those who have been baptized and profess the true faith. Once baptized a person remains a member of the Mystical Body until he cuts himself off by schism, heresy, or apostasy; or until he is excluded as punishment for grave fault.

The eternal Son of God created for himself a physical human body to be used as the means of our redemption. Then while He was living in that human body on earth He formed for himself a Mystical Body to be used as the means of our sanctification.

Cells of protoplasm grouped together into organs and limbs to form the physical body of Christ. Human beings such as ourselves join together into hierarchy, clergy, religious, and laity, to form the Mystical Body. And the Second Person of the Blessed Trinity lives in each member of the body.

The physical body of Jesus was tortured and torn by the Cross, the scourges, and the thorns. His Mystical Body is constantly afflicted by prejudices, persecutions, temptations and the varied struggles of human living. The divine person suffered in His physical body. The human persons who make up His Mystical Body continue His sufferings, in union with Him; and because of that union their sufferings are meritorious. Jesus gained unmeasured merit in

27

His human body; he shares those merits in such manner with the members of His Mystical Body that the very human acts of these members take on merit. The graces He gained through His human body so filled His human soul that they overflow through His Mystical Body and fill up those souls which love Him.

The Church is a body; St. Paul said so. It has many members, but they join together in unbroken unity, and they help one another, working together for the common good of each and all. The parts of the Church are not grouped in haphazard manner; they are united organically, one dependent on the other, each performing its own function—much like the parts of your own human body.

A body has the means of its own life, health, and growth. The Mystical Body has the sacraments: Baptism for birth into the life of the Body and union with it; Confirmation for strength; Penance to restore health and vitality; the Eucharist for food; Extreme Unction for critical needs of members; Matrimony to perpetuate the life of the Body in new members; and Holy Orders to provide those specialized members which feed the Body, guide it, see to its spiritual needs, and take care of its sacrificial requirements.

Not all the cells of a body are healthy. The Mystical Body has sinners amongst its saints. It keeps them in the Body to restore them to health, to heal them by charity, to give them new life by the grace which flows through the Body.

This Body—the Church—is rightly called the Body of Christ. He founded it. During His public ministry he prepared it and formed it by His teaching, His choice of the Apostles and training of them, by His establishment of the sacraments and his provisions for the Mass. Then on the Cross He brought the Church into being, gave it life; it
28

was born through the wound in His side, as St. Ambrose said.

This Church which Jesus prepared and established was finally strengthened and presented to the world on Pentecost, when it was placed under the protection, guidance, and inspiration of the Holy Spirit.

Christ is the head of the Body. St. Paul said it, and St. Thomas Aquinas explained it. He is the head by preeminence; His is the highest place. He rules and governs, guides and leads—all functions of the head. His teachings fill the Body with light; His grace gives life to all its members.

The head and the members must share the same nature if they are to form one Body. He became man that He might have the same nature we have; and He joined himself to us that He might communicate to us a share in His divine nature, distributing its life through His Mystical Body.

He is the Savior of the Body. He purchased its members by His own blood. He lets us collaborate with Him in Sacrifice. He intercedes for us with the Father; and He pulls us along with Him into His heavenly home.

This Body is called Mystical. It has to have a name which will distinguish it 1) from the physical body of Christ which walked the ways of Palestine nineteen centuries ago, died and was buried, rose transformed and now lives spiritualized in heaven; 2) from that same body in its Eucharistic form, as it now lives quietly and lovingly on our altars; 3) from any ordinary natural body; and 4) from a simple grouping of men together into a crowd—sometimes called a moral body.

In an ordinary natural body each member lacks individual subsistence; it is simply a part of the body. The

29

Mystical Body links its members together without destroying their individual personalities. In the natural body the members exist for the good of the whole body. The Mystical Body exists for the individual good of the members— to sanctify them and get them to heaven.

Men are grouped together in a moral body by common purpose or enthusiasm—by brotherhood and fellowship. But there is no organic unity, no functioning vitality. The Church is more than a religious society established to worship God. Even the fact that Jesus Christ founded her does not explain her complete nature. She is more than a distributor of graces, more than a teacher of revealed truth. She is a Body—a Mystical Body—Christ's Body.

St. Paul learned this lesson so forcibly that he never forgot it. Before his conversion he was persecuting the Church; and when Christ appeared to him on the road to Damascus, He greeted him: "Saul, Saul, why do you persecute me?" St. Paul asked: "Who are you, Lord," and he received the answer: "I am Jesus, whom you are persecuting" (Acts, 9, 4).

The frequent meditations of St. Paul on that truth show themselves often in his epistles: "You are the body of Christ, and severally His members . . . there are many members, yet one body . . . He hath subjected all things beneath His feet and given Him for supreme Head to the Church, which is His body, the fullness of Him . . . a husband is the head of the wife, just as Christ is Head of the Church, Himself being the savior of the body . . ."

This doctrine of the Mystical Body should make us realize that the Church is much more than a vast organization —Catholic and universal—comprising several hundred million people of all lands, united in astounding unity of faith and worship and government.

It is much more than a centuries-old society which dates essentially unchanged from the Apostles and teaches the truths of Christ with unwavering fidelity.

It is much more than a divinely established aid to salvation.

It is the Mystical Body of Christ, joined to Him in closest union, circulating His life through its spiritual veins, binding its members to the Head with firm bonds of faith, leading them to their promised goal by hope, and sanctifying them by love.

2. Sources of Life and Grace in the Church

The Divinity of Christ. The Role
of Mary. What Is the Mass? Where
Are the Sacraments in Scripture?
Baptism. Confession. The Holy
Eucharist. What Is the Bible?

Q. How would you prove to an unbeliever that Christ is God?

A. First of all, I would want to put the question on a discussion basis—one of serious, honest consideration, not of argument. Then I would want plenty of time; not just a few minutes, not just one evening. Then I would start praying. Because it would do me little good to simply convince him by logical proof. His final acceptance of Christ as God would be a matter of faith, and that is a free gift of God. He gives it in response to prayer, to those who really want it, whose good-will prepares them to accept it.

Then I would ask my unbeliever how well he knew the books of the Bible, and whether he accepted the four Gospels as good sound historical documents. If he did we could start from there. If not, I would have to spend some time proving to him that these Gospels were written by men who lived at the time of Christ and wrote shortly after His death; that two of these writers, at least, knew Christ well and personally witnessed the events they write about; that the other two were well qualified by close association with His Apostles; that they all wrote truthfully; and that their writings have come down to us complete and unaltered.

This proof that the Gospels are historical and reliable might take some time, depending upon my friend's knowledge of the Scriptures. But it is very important, because the rest of our proof will be based largely upon these Gospels. We would be wasting our time to build a beautiful house of proof without any foundation.

Next, I would go through the Gospels with my unbeliever, pointing out to him that they tell a beautiful and inspiring history of a most unusual man who lived in Palestine more than nineteen centuries ago, and has had a tremendous influence on all history since His time, and on the personal lives of billions of other men. This man certainly deserves some attention and study. Even the story itself is greatly worth our while.

The most unusual thing about this man, Jesus, as we find from careful reading of the Gospels, is His claim that He is God. He claims it by His words and by His action. His Apostles and early disciples made the same claim about Him, and his millions of followers have believed it ever since. He made these claims before the Jewish leaders, who accused Him of blasphemy for making them. He made these claims even when He knew He would die for making them.

Now we know that some fool or faker might claim to be God. But this man is evidently neither. Despite His quiet manner He attracts a great crowd of intense and faithful followers, so numerous as to threaten the leadership of the priests and Pharisees. That man cannot be called a fool whose doctrine has transformed the world. Nor does the faker die to uphold his falsehoods.

The fantastic claims of this man merit attention. Note how He claimed to be the Judge of all mankind: "The Son of Man (that is His favorite name for Himself) shall come in His majesty and all the angels with Him . . . and all the nations shall be gathered together before Him, and He will separate them one from another." (Matt. 25, 31-46). Only God can know the hearts of men, judge them and give them their deserts.

He claimed to be God the lawgiver: "The Son of Man is Lord even of the Sabbath." (Matt. 12, 8). He can change the laws God gave for the Sabbath. Then in His Sermon on the Mount he often repeats: "You have heard that it was said to them of old . . . *But I say to you*" (Matt. 5, 21-44). He gave His own laws, improving on the Ten Commandments given by God on Mount Sinai.

He claimed to be omnipotent, a divine person, the Son of God, equal to the Father: "All power is given to me in heaven and on earth . . . All things are delivered to me by my Father . . . No one knows the Father but the Son . . ." (Matt. 28, 18).

The Jews understood His claim that He was God. They often tried to stone Him or kill Him because He made these claims: "They sought the more to kill Him because . . . He said God was His Father, making Himself equal to God." (John 5, 17-21). When Pilate tried to set Him free, the Jews shouted: "We have a law, and according to that law He ought to die, because He made Himself the Son of God." (John 19, 7).

The Apostles and disciples understood His claim, preached it and gave testimony to it, especially after His death and Resurrection. But even before that, when Jesus asked Peter: "Whom do you say that I am?" Peter replied: "Thou art Christ, the Son of the living God." And Jesus said: "Blessed art thou, Simon, son of John, because flesh and blood has not revealed it to thee, but My Father who is in heaven." (Matt. 16, 13-17).

It was precisely for this claim that the Sanhedrin condemned Him to death. It was very early on Good Friday morning, and "the High Priest asked him and said to Him: 'Art thou the Christ the Son of the blessed God?' And Jesus said to him: 'I am. And you shall see the Son of Man sitting on the right hand of the power of God, and coming in the clouds of heaven.' And they rent their garments and said that this was blasphemy and "all condemned Him to be guilty of death." (Mark 14, 61-64).

Clearly then Jesus Christ claimed to be God and died rather than deny His claim. But you can't prove anything by claims. You have to back them up. You have to prove that the claims are true.

How did Jesus prove His claims? He worked miracles. He made prophecies. He rose from the dead.

How do these prove His claims? Only God can work a miracle. Only God can foretell with certainty free future events. Only God can raise the dead to life. Would God do all these things to back up the false claims of a fool or faker?

Jesus appealed to His miracles as proof: "The works themselves which I do, give testimony of me that the Father sent me." (John 5, 36).

Take a brief glance at those miracles. There are more than forty of them described in detail in the Gospels. They were facts widely known and accepted, which cannot be explained away. He healed the sick, the blind, the lame, the deaf and dumb, the epileptic. He did it by a word or a touch, and sometimes at a distance. He brought three dead persons back to life. He changed water into wine; fed five thousand people with five loaves of bread and two fishes; quieted the storm with a word; and walked on the water.

In His prophecies He foretold His Passion, Resurrection, and Ascension, and many things which would happen to His disciples and His Church. The fulfillment of these prophecies proves that His teaching had God's approval. But He taught that He Himself was God.

We have not the space here to develop the final and greatest proof which Christ gave of His claim that He was God. After His crucifixion and death He rose from the tomb and lived on earth for forty days, being seen often by His Apostles and by other disciples, and by as many as five hundred of them at one time. The Gospels, the Acts of the Apostles, and the Epistles of St. Paul all give testimony to the Resurrection.

If our unbeliever were familiar with the Old Testament we might show him how the Jewish people had looked forward for thousands of years to the coming of a Redeemer, whom God had promised to send them. We might point out the many prophecies which were made about this Promised One, particularly in the Psalms and in the books of Isaias and Micheas. And then we could show him how these prophecies and promises were fulfilled in Jesus.

The very character and personality of Jesus help to prove His claims to Divinity. He was known as the son of a carpenter; He had received no formal education. Yet He became the world's greatest teacher. He held men by His eloquence, astounded them by His knowledge, attracted them by the charm of His goodness. He was kind, friendly, courteous, and humble, but He was also firm and strong and full of courage and the strength to suffer patiently. He was merciful, quick to heal or forgive, but forceful and uncompromising in His attacks on sin and sham and scandal. He was a model of all virtue, in whom no evil could be found.

We might further urge as proofs the inspiring beauty of His teachings, the marvelous spread of His Church, His profound influence on the thought and living of men of twenty centuries, and the deep loyalty and worship He inspired in His followers, especially in those thousands who gave their lives for Him as martyrs, not only in the early centuries, but down to our own day.

Q. Just recently in our daily press I saw the announcement that His Holiness the Pope intended in the near future to declare the Virgin Mary as the only *mediator between mankind and God. Is this true?*

I am a non-Catholic myself but have been deeply interested in your faith for the last three years. I have all that time subscribed regularly to a Catholic paper, but have never seen any hint of this in your press, but neither has there been a denial.

If, therefore, it is true, on what does your Church base the assertion? It seems to me that it cuts out Jesus the Christ completely, and renders His self-sacrifice null and void. He was the one who devoted His life and gave it for mankind; surely then He is the mediator.

A. Someone has made a mistake. Your reporter has mistaken the Mother for her Son. It is not the Virgin Mary who is the *only* mediator between mankind and God; it is Jesus Christ, her only Son.

We do call Mary the Mediatrix of all graces. It is a title which stresses the intimacy of her association with her Son in that work which she brought Him into the world to accomplish: the redemption and sanctification of our souls. Some pope someday may declare it a doctrine of the Church that Mary is the Mediatrix in this sense; most Catholic theologians already hold it to be certain.

But you may be sure that such declaration would not

"cut out Jesus Christ completely." On the contrary, like all the mysteries and glories of Mary, it would add greatly to His glory, increase our love for Him, and draw us nearer to Him in profound adoration. Every doctrine of Mary is because of her Son, and for the sake of her Son.

Nothing is more distinctly Catholic than devotion to the Blessed Virgin Mary, and it is largely because of this devotion that Catholics remain deeply convinced of the divinity of Christ, and vividly conscious of His humanity. We are able to understand Jesus better, because we know His Mother so well. It is easier to know and understand her than Him. She is a human person—one of us. He is a divine Person. Of course, He does have a human nature, like yours and mine. But He also has a divine nature, entirely unlike anything we can ever imagine. A divine Person with two natures! How can we ever know Him and feel comfortable with Him? Thank God, we have His Mother. She brought Him to us in the first place, and she takes us to Him, and teaches us to know Him—and to love Him.

The early Christians, those of the first five centuries, found their knowledge of Mary very useful in clarifying their ideas about Christ. Right in the beginning they simply took Christ and Mary both for granted. The vision, memory, and love of their Savior so overwhelmed them that they did not stop to worry about the mysteries of His Person or His natures. Neither did they speculate about His Mother; she was simply there by His side at the crib of Bethlehem, at the foot of the Cross—and at the throne of heaven.

Never at any time did Mary occupy the middle of the stage; that spot was for her Son. But as those early Christians became more accustomed to the astounding fact of Christ's presence they began to inquire into the details of

39

His Incarnation, His Person, and His natures. And it was then that Mary helped them to understand rightly and avoid mistakes. Against the Arians, the Nestorians, and the Monophysites she guided them, through the Councils of Nicea, Ephesus, and Chalcedon, until those early followers of her Son finally had a clear grasp of the full meaning of His divinity and humanity, and the union of His two natures in one person. And as their knowledge of Him became more definite they understood her better, too.

After the Fathers at Nicea, in the year 325, had proclaimed the equality of Son and Father, it dawned fully on theologians that Mary was the Mother of a divine Person. The heretic Nestorius couldn't accept that. So it became necessary for the Council of Ephesus to declare that she really was the Mother of God, *Theotikos*. And then again, when the full meaning of that term had dawned, there came further disputes about the distinction of the two natures of her Son. Another heretic, Eutyches, failed to understand that if Jesus had a real human Mother He must have been a real flesh-and-blood human being Himself. But the Fathers at the Council of Chalcedon understood, and they declared definitely that the two natures, divine and human, in Jesus were complete and distinct, even though they were united in the one identical Person.

There is considerable evidence that veneration of Mary began even in the time of the Apostles, and her praises grew more frequent as the Christian community grew. Early writers like St. Ignatius, St. Irenaeus, St. Justin, and Tertullian, made explicit mention of her, right after the time of the Apostles. We have a second century picture of her in the catacombs. And even such unreliable apocryphal writings as the *Proto-evangelium of James* show how widespread was popular interest about her.

40

By the time of the Council of Ephesus, in the year 431, everything essential about the role of Mary had been firmly established as doctrine: There is only one person in Jesus Christ, and Mary is the Mother of that person; every privilege she enjoys, every title given her, and every honor paid her results from her divine maternity.

God's Mother is worthy of honor. He honored her Himself in choosing her from among all His creatures. We never forget the basic truth of our religion: there is only one God, and He alone is to be worshipped. But that does not mean that we are forbidden to pay reasonable, sensible honor to creatures. God explicitly commands you to honor your own father and mother. Is it then wrong to honor God's Mother?

From the beginning, the Church has given to Mary the highest form of honor that can be properly given to any creature. She is human, just as we are. We must never adore her; that is for God alone. But otherwise we cannot honor her to excess, because it is not possible to overestimate the privileges God gave her in making her His own Mother.

Most of the opposition to Catholic devotion to Mary results from a misunderstanding of the nature of that devotion. We do not try to deify Mary nor make her equal to God in any respect. We simply honor one of our own human race, in imitation of God who honored her first. We are trying to imitate Jesus Christ, who honored His Mother.

We hear complaints that there are too many Marian doctrines, some of which are not apparent from the Scriptures. They are all logical consequences of the divine maternity. First of all, there is Mary's virginity. The Gospels make it clear, as the Old Testament had foretold, that Jesus

41

was born of a virgin Mother. The Fifth General Council, in 553, and the Lateran Council, in 640, declared her virginity to be a matter of doctrine. It was necessary consequence of her divine motherhood, since the only Father of Jesus was God Himself.

Early Doctors of the Church, like St. Jerome and St. Ambrose, upheld the firm and constant tradition of the Church that the virginity of Mary was permanent. This was simply a fitting sequel of her divine maternity, since Christians from the earliest times had found it repugnant that other children should be born from the womb made sacred by the divine Child. Besides, this seemed the only reasonable explanation of Mary's statement, "I know not man."

The Immaculate Conception is a doctrine found in the traditional interpretation of certain texts: Genesis 3, 15 and Luke 1, 27. Mary is called "full of grace," and the doctrine of the Immaculate Conception simply takes those words without restriction. She was full of grace at every moment of her life: from the moment she began to live, from her conception. This privilege, too, is given her because of her divine motherhood: the flesh from which the innocent Body of Christ was formed should not be stained by sin. He who came to conquer sin was appropriately born of a sinless creature. Since He was God, He could keep her free from sin. So He did. Her sinlessness was the result of the Redemption; but it was by prevention rather than by cure.

The Assumption, defined by Pope Pius XII on November 1, 1950, is the most recent formal doctrine of the Church. But it is far from new. It is found in early tradition, and was commemorated in the first feast of Mary in the Church, celebrated since the fifth century. We do not find it directly mentioned in the Scriptures, but the Gospels and the Acts of the Apostles do present the Mother of God as always closely united to her divine Son, always sharing His lot, especially in His fight against Satan, which resulted in complete victory over sin and death—two words always joined together by St. Paul. The Assumption follows from her sinlessness, and that was because of her motherhood.

We honor Mary as the Mother of Men, our mother. She conceived her Son by her own free consent. And by that consent she accepted Christ whole and entire, not only the physical Christ, but also the Mystical Christ. And we are members of Christ, as St. Paul says, part of His Mystical Body. So we, too, were accepted by Mary, at the moment of the Incarnation, as her children, spiritual brothers of her Son. Her consent and acceptance of us was ratified, in the full realization of its burdens, at the foot of the Cross, when she united her personal sorrow with the sufferings of her Son for our redemption. We owe Jesus to Mary; and so, indirectly, we owe the grace of the Cross to her. This grace makes us children of God. So she is, indeed, the spiritual Mother of all men.

I am not avoiding your question about the Mediatrix. I have been trying to give it a background, so that my explanation will have more meaning. It is the common and explicit teaching of the Church today that every grace given to men comes to them through Mary. She is the almoner for her generous Son. She hands out His treasures, as a mother's right. Being mediatrix is simply a mother's privilege. She was intimately associated with her Son in everything pertaining to our redemption and salvation while they were both on earth. Why should He change the order of things now that they are both in heaven?

43

Jesus Christ is the only mediator between God and Man. He brought God to us when He became man. He takes us back to God with Him through His redemptive grace. He permits us to understand something about God, first, by bringing God down to the human level, in the Incarnation; and secondly, by giving us a bit of divine intelligence, in Faith.

Mary, the Mediatrix, brought Jesus to us, and brings us to Jesus. She permits us to understand Him, first, by making us realize how thoroughly He is one of us, as her own Son; and secondly, by reminding us that she, though human, is the Mother of God. Her Son is a divine Person.

No one who really understands Mary can misunderstand Jesus. But if we reject her, as many moderns have done, we will come to doubt the divinity of Christ, or the reality of His human nature, or the personal union between those two natures. Without her, we become confused about her Son, and if we are confused we may reject the true Christ. Let Mary, His Mother, lead you to Him and teach you to know Him completely and to love Him intimately. That is the way to become a saint.

Q. As a non-Catholic much interested in the Bible, my big question is: Why do you persist in saying Mass with a Latin Bible, so that nobody understands it? I believe that if the book were read in plain English it would promote the reading of the Bible, to the benefit of everybody.

A. I will preface my answer with a brief explanation of the Mass. Unless we understand what the Mass is we cannot possibly understand why it is said in Latin. And please don't consider my explanation a reflection on your personal knowledge. Most non-Catholics, and many Catholics, are rather vague about the real nature and the importance of the Mass. First of all, the Mass is a religious sacrifice. A sacrifice is the giving up of something for a purpose. A religious sacrifice is the offering of something to God, and giving it up to Him for His glory: as an expression of our love and submission, to give thanks to Him, to make up for our sins and offenses against Him, and to beg His further favors.

Religious sacrifices have been common in most of the religions of the world. In some of the primitive religions they were crude and revolting. But in the religion which God revealed to the Jews, sacrifices were used to express deep religious convictions, belief, and understanding. However, even the sacrifices of the Jewish religion had no inherent value. Their value came from the hearts of those

45

who offered them. God was pleased with their love and submission.

Our own religious sacrifice, the Mass, is different. It has value in itself. It is inherently pleasing to God.

The Mass has value in itself because it is a continuation of Calvary, a projection of the Cross down through time and space. It brings the Crucifixion to us so that we can have part in it. We have part in it by offering Christ's own sacrifice in union with Him. We have part in it by uniting ourselves to Christ as the victim offered, giving our love and the promise of our service to God. And we have part in it by receiving the benefits of Christ's redemptive sacrifice into our own souls. The Mass has value because Christ is in it, offering Himself to God in a sacrifice of love and adoration, and giving Himself to us in grace and sanctification.

It may not be immediately apparent to you how the Mass can be a continuation of Calvary. You probably consider it, instead, a memorial of the Last Supper. It is both. The two are but parts of our Lord's last day on earth as mortal man—the day devoted completely to the work of our redemption. The Mass had its beginning and institution at the Last Supper and received the full measure of its effectiveness in the Crucifixion.

The two events are close in time and sequence: our Lord went directly from the Last Supper to the Garden of Gethsemane, where He began those sufferings which were to continue without interruption until His death. But even more closely are these two great events united in meaning and purpose. They form one continuous project for the redemption and salvation of mankind. Note the words of St. Luke (22, 19), and St. Paul, who says (I Cor. 11, 24), "This is my body which shall be given up for

46

you"; and the words of St. Luke in the following verse: "This cup is the new covenant in my Blood, which shall be shed for you." (See also Matt. 26, 28).

Both St. Luke and St. Paul quote the words of our Lord, "Do this for a commemoration of Me." And St. Paul continues, "As often as you shall eat this bread and drink the cup, you proclaim the death of the Lord, until He comes."

Our Lord left us a memorial. But it is not a plaque or a monument; it is living and real. What He did we are to do in memory of Him; and our act is not an empty gesture of imitation: it brings Christ to us. The bread becomes His Body; the wine becomes His Blood, and the separation of the two on the altar recalls by effective symbolism the real separation of Christ's Blood from His Body on Calvary. He continues the sacrifice of the Cross and permits us to make it our sacrifice of adoration. And then He gives Himself to us.

So you see that the Mass is primarily an action, something which happens on our altar, in which we have a part. If it were merely a ceremony for our inspiration, a public prayer, and a collection of Scriptural readings for our instruction, then it should be in English by all means. Otherwise, it would lose its effectiveness entirely. But when we consider the great act of sacrifice and communion that the Mass really is, then the language becomes secondary.

When I say that the language is secondary, I do not mean that it is unimportant. On the contrary, the Scriptural readings, prayers, and hymns of Mass should serve as a means by which all the members of the congregation unite themselves with the priest at the altar and with Jesus Christ, the supreme Priest, in a collective offering. For this reason, many Catholics today, both priest and laity, hold it desirable that various parts of the Mass should be in English. But the Church is conservative, and moves slowly in making changes; and even the most impatient among us have confidence in her judgment.

In the beginning, the Mass was in Aramaic, the language of our Lord. But as the Church spread into the countries outside of Palestine, Greek became the language of the Mass. Even at Rome, Greek was used until the third century. But by that time very few Romans knew Greek; so the Mass was gradually changed into Latin, the language of the people.

Once the Mass got into Latin it stayed there. There are many reasons: Latin was in wide and general use, a language of antiquity and influence, of learning and literature, a common means of international communication. For many centuries, there was no other language to give it serious competition.

It is quite possible that the literary growth of English, German, French, and Italian, and the impetus of the printing press would have changed Latin to the vernacular languages in the Mass about the sixteenth century, had it not been for the Protestant Reformation. The reformers, generally, denied reality to the Mass. For many of them the Body and Blood of Jesus were not really present; and for none of them was the Mass a sacrifice, in the true sense. To them, it had lost its meaning as an act; its only purpose was to inspire and instruct. To accomplish that purpose, it had to be in the vernacular, so that the people would understand it, and thus have their faith enlivened—because it was only through faith that they could be sanctified.

Thus the demand for the vernacular in the Mass came to be associated with heresy. The Council of Trent found it necessary to condemn the proposition of the reformers that

48

the Mass must be in the vernacular. So we would not be far wrong in saying that the Protestant Reformation caused a delay of four centuries in the change of the Mass from Latin into English.

However, there are many other reasons why the Mass remains in Latin. Probably the most powerful reason is the inertia of custom. For about seventeen centuries, the Mass has been said in Latin in most of the Catholic world.

There are certain advantages in having a dead language for the Mass. It always remains the same, and does not need revision every few years. It avoids vulgar connotations. It has the same meaning in all parts of the world and in every century. It has evident advantage for both lay and priest travelers.

To most Catholics, Latin has come to be a symbol of the unity and universality of the Church. The language of the Mass is the same in India and the United States; the same in the ninth century and the twentieth. And it keeps the rites and ceremonies unchanged, just as the official use of Latin by the Church assures the integrity of her teachings in all ages and all lands.

In spite of all these reasons in favor of Latin, there is a growing feeling in the Church today that this dead language, generally unknown to the people except by sound, prevents the laity from participating as closely in the offering of the Mass as they should. Recent popes, beginning with St. Pius X, early in this century, have urged increased participation of the laity, stressing the unity of all members of the Church as living cells in the Mystical Body of Christ.

I should indicate a little mistake in your letter. The book we use for the Mass is not the Bible, though probably 75 per cent of it is taken directly from the Bible. We

49

call it the missal. And now most of the people have their own missals, translations of the one the priest uses. This permits them to follow more closely and intelligently. But since each one is reading his own little book rather than listening to the words of the priest, or joining with him, the desired unity of prayer and action is still lacking.

There are indications today that at least parts of the Mass will be changed into English in a few years. The Church has given encouragement and approval in recent years to a translation of the *Ritual*, the book used for the administration of the sacraments and for various blessings. But in a recent world-wide liturgical conference held at Assisi, official indication was given that the Church is not yet ready to permit use at the altar of a vernacular missal.

Of course, Latin is not essential to the valid celebration of the Mass. From the earliest times the Mass has been said in various tongues, and even today, in the Eastern (Catholic) Churches the Mass is said in Greek and Slavonic; in classical Armenian, Coptic, and Syriac, with parts in Arabic; in an old Ethiopian language called Ge-ez, and in an Indian dialect called Malayalam; in Rumanian, Hungarian, and Old Georgian.

But the vast majority of Catholics throughout the world belong to the Roman rite, and know the Mass only in Latin. Though we may discuss the matter freely and present petitions for a change, we are all, priests and laity alike, content to await the judgment of the Church. She has divine help and centuries of experience to guide her in the choice of those things which best serve the welfare of souls, for the glory of God.

Q. The Roman Catholic Church has seven sacraments. Most churches have only Baptism and Communion. Are there references in Scripture to these seven sacraments?

A. *Baptism:* "Go, therefore, and make disciples of all nations, baptizing them in the name of the Father, and of the Son, and of the Holy Spirit." (Matt. 28, 18-19). Cf. Mark 1, 6-8; 16, 15-16; John 7, 12; 3, 5; Acts 2, 38; Titus, 4-7.

Confirmation: "Now when the apostles in Jerusalem heard that Samaria had received the word of God, they sent to them Peter and John. On their arrival they prayed for them, that they might receive the Holy Spirit." (Acts 8, 14-15).

Holy Eucharist: "This is the bread that comes down from heaven, so that if anyone eat of it he will not die. I am the living bread that has come down from heaven. If anyone eat of this bread he shall live forever; and the bread that I shall give is my flesh for the life of the world . . . Unless you eat the flesh of the Son of Man, and drink his blood, you shall not have life in you. He who eats my flesh and drinks my blood has everlasting life, and I will raise him up on the last day. For my flesh is food indeed, and my blood is drink indeed. He who eats my flesh and drinks my blood abides in me and I in him." (John 6, 48-58).

"And while they were at supper, Jesus took bread, and blessed and broke and gave it to his disciples, and said,

'Take and eat; this is my body.' And taking a cup, he gave thanks and gave it to them, saying, 'All of you drink of this; for this is my blood of the new covenant, which is being shed for many unto the forgiveness of sins.' " (Matt. 26, 26-28).

See also Mark 14, 22-24; Luke 22, 19-20; 1 Cor. 11, 23-29.

Penance: "Receive the Holy Spirit; whose sins you shall forgive they are forgiven them; and whose sins you shall retain, they are retained." (John 21, 23).

Extreme Unction: "And going forth . . . they anointed with oil many sick people, and healed them." (Mark 6, 12-13).

"Is any one sick among you? Let him bring in the priests of the Church, and let them pray over him, anointing him with oil in the name of the Lord. And the prayer of faith will save the sick man, and the Lord will raise him up, and if he be in sins, they shall be forgiven him." (James 5, 14-15).

Holy Orders: "Do this in remembrance of me." (Luke 22, 19).

"And they chose Stephen . . . and Philip, etc. These they set before the Apostle, and after they had prayed they laid hands upon them." (Acts 6, 5-6).

"Take heed to yourselves and to the whole flock in which the Holy Spirit has placed you as bishops." (Acts 20, 28).

See also I Tim. 3, 1-13; 4, 14-16; II Tim. 5, 22; also Titus 1, 5-9; Heb. 5, 1-4.

"For every high priest is appointed to offer gifts and sacrifices." (Heb. 8, 3).

Matrimony: Study all the texts on the subject from Genesis to St. Paul, especially Ephesians 5, 12-33, where marriage is called a great mystery (sacrament) in reference to Christ and the Church. When you study them all to-
52

gether, e.g., Gen. 1, 27-28; 2, 18-24; Matt. 5, 31-32; 19, 3-9;
I Cor. 7, 1-7; John 2, 1-10, you will see how sacred and
sanctifying is the bond of marriage as elevated by Christ
to a life-giving symbol of His own vivifying union with the
Church.

Q. Why don't Catholics wait with Baptism until their children are old enough to know what is happening?

Surely they can be brought up with a strong faith in God and taught that after being baptized they are expected to live strictly according to the Ten Commandments. I don't think so many people would fall away from the Catholic Church if they weren't rushed into religion. It's hard to believe that God wouldn't let children into heaven just because they aren't baptized.

A. It may be hard to believe, but it is apparently the truth. The reason you find it hard to believe may be that you do not fully appreciate the soul-changing importance of Baptism. It is not a simple little rite of initiation into the Church; it injects a spark of divine life into the soul, lifts it up to heaven's height, and prepares it for heavenly living.

Maybe the reason you find it hard to believe is that you do not fully appreciate heaven itself, and what a tremendous thing it is for us to get there. Unless we stop to think, we may imagine our getting there as a sort of natural process: after death our souls hop across a vast abyss, and there we are, happy as you please, amid twanging harps, golden streets, and green pastures.

Actually it is much more complicated than that. Heaven is God's own home; we live in His presence as His own children. We see Him and understand Him, appreciating His unlimited perfections; and our overwhelming awareness of His goodness makes us love Him completely, so that we are simply filled with happiness. This state is entirely above our human nature, our human life, and our human capacities for knowledge, love, and happiness.

It is above our human nature. God is divine by nature. If He adopts children you would expect them to share His nature, to have something of the divine in them. We do not have anything of the divine in us naturally; if we are to get it God must give it to us. Baptism is the means He uses to give it to us.

Heaven is above our human life. We are adapted to life on earth. Our bodies are built for an atmospheric pressure of fourteen pounds per square inch, an oxygen content of 21 percent in the air, temperatures within reasonable range, and foods which have a caloric potential and vitamin content. If we were suddenly transported to Mars our problems of adjustment would be superhuman, unless we were provided with mechanical aids to create earth's atmospheric conditions artificially. The transition from earth to heaven will be infinitely more radical. It will require an adjustment far beyond the mechanical. We cannot live in heaven unless we have the life of heaven, and we must take it with us when we leave the earth; we cannot expect it on arrival. God gives us this life in Baptism.

Heavenly living is above our human capabilities. Philosophers like to speak of God as transcendent. It is a good word. It means that God is, by His nature, completely beyond us, so that we cannot really touch Him. Our minds cannot reach Him to know Him directly; and if we do not know Him, how can we love Him? And if we cannot love Him, how can we possibly be happy living with Him eternally? A plain human being in heaven would be more

55

unhappy than a horse at the opera, more out of place than a fish in the air. Completely out of his human element, he would not know what was going on.

If we are to see God in heaven and love Him happily, our human minds must somehow be stretched across that transcendental chasm which separates us from God. Our human powers of comprehension must be sharpened and extended to the point where we can know God directly and so appreciate His goodness that it will compel our love. Baptism performs this sharpening and extending. It gives our intellect the ultimate capability of knowing God, and gives it faith to train on. It makes our will radically capable of loving God personally and completely, and it gives us hope and charity to practice heaven's love and possession.

Maybe you think I am fond of hyperbole, or am injecting poetic aspirations into theology. Really, I am just trying to express facts which are plain but tremendous. God elevates us by Baptism to supernatural living on heaven's own plane. The supernatural life which we receive in Baptism we call sanctifying grace. It was first given to Adam, but was rejected by him and lost for all of us when he sinned. It was obtained for us again by Jesus Christ when He died on the Cross. He gives it to us in Baptism, and we keep it until we reject it by sin. If we have it at death we will sail smoothly into heaven. If we do not have it, we would be utterly lost in heaven even if we could get there.

Now do you see why we baptize babies? We want them to have this life of heaven in their little souls, and Jesus Christ has given us no reason to believe that they can get it in any other way. In fact, He has indicated that there is no other way: "Amen, amen, I say to thee, unless a man be born again of water and the Spirit, he cannot enter into the kingdom of God." We know that Jesus sent His Apostles out with the command that they baptize everyone: "Go, therefore, and make disciples of all nations, baptizing them in the name of the Father, and of the Son, and of the Holy Spirit."

We are conscious that heaven is a free gift of God—that He does not need to give it to anyone—that no one has a claim to it. We are aware of those words of St. Paul that because of Adam's sin "death has passed unto all men." And we are reminded by St. John that this death of sin can only be taken away by the rebirth of Baptism. With all these things in mind we would not dare take a chance of depriving an infant soul of Baptism, the very means Christ gave us to get that soul to heaven.

The early Fathers of the Church were insistent upon infant baptism. They understood Christ's commands to be universal: to apply to everyone. St. Irenaeus lived in the latter half of the second century. In his book against heretics he wrote that Jesus "came to save all who through Him are born again unto God; infants and children, boys and youths, and elders." Origen, writing in the first half of the third century, declared that infant baptism was an institution of Apostolic times and was necessary to cleanse infants from original sin. In the year 253, the Third Council of Carthage taught that children should be baptized as soon as possible after birth. The vigorous statements of St. Augustine in this regard are quite well known. Here is an example: "If you wish to be a Catholic, do not believe, nor say, nor teach, that infants who die before Baptism can obtain the remission of original sin."

From the very beginning then, Catholics have believed it necessary to baptize infants that they may receive the new life of sanctifying grace to take away original sin and prepare them for heaven. It is necessary to baptize adults, too, but a person who has grown up and attained the use of reason can have a Baptism of desire when it is not possible for him to receive actual Baptism with water. He can love God and that love will unite him with God, and from that union God's grace will come into his soul, sanctifying it.

Our Savior has spoken some comforting and inspiring words about this Baptism of desire. "A certain lawyer got up to test him, saying, 'Master, what must I do to gain eternal life?' But He said to him, 'What is written in the Law? How dost thou read?' He answered and said, 'Thou shalt love the Lord thy God with thy whole heart, and with thy whole soul, and with thy whole strength, and with thy whole mind; And thy neighbor as thyself.' And He said to Him, 'Thou hast answered rightly; do this and thou shalt live.' "

The person who loves in this way will live the life of grace, the life of heaven.

In speaking to His Apostles at the Last Supper, Jesus told them: "He who has my Commandments and keeps them, he it is who loves Me. But he who loves Me will be loved by my Father, and I will love him and manifest Myself to him." And again a moment later He said to Jude: "If anyone love Me, he will keep my word, and my Father will love him, and We will come to him and make our abode with him." When God loves us and lives in our souls He sanctifies us and prepares us to live with Him in love forever.

The infant is not capable of a voluntary act of love of this kind; so he cannot be sanctified by Baptism of desire. As far as we know, there is no way in which he can be

58

sanctified, and Catholic theologians have tried to find evidence of such a way in the words of Sacred Scripture, because they do know that the good God, in His great love for all mankind, desires the salvation of everyone. But in their search they always end up confronting these words of the Master: "Unless a man be born again of water and the Spirit, he cannot enter into the kingdom of God."

The fact that a person cannot enter heaven and live there in the knowledge and love of God does not mean that he is punished. His human nature makes no demand for such living; it is not even capable of it. He is not made sad when deprived of something to which he has no natural inclination. Is a dog sad because deprived of the power of speech? It is possible for an infant to be naturally happy—very completely and permanently happy—without being in heaven. Catholic theologians believe that this is what happens to infants who die without Baptism: they live happily forever in a place which we call Limbo. We know little about this place, actually; but we do know that God is good, and that His love and mercy will find more ways of expressing themselves than we can ever imagine.

If I understand your question rightly, I think you imply that we Catholics rush children into religion not only by baptizing them in infancy but also by force-feeding them on Catholic doctrine and practice during their earliest years. Maybe I am imputing to you an objection we hear often: "Why not let children grow up and choose their own religion?"

My answer to the objection of that question might be implied in another loaded question: "Why not let little children grow up and learn manners and proper behavior for themselves? Aren't we brainwashing them when we teach them how to behave? We are rushing them into

59

being polite. It isn't fair. We should give them an equal chance to be insupportable brats if they wish to be."

You admit that children should be brought up with a strong faith in God. But how are you going to do that unless you teach them definite and personal things about God? How can they believe in Him if they don't know what manner of being He is?

We Catholics are generally firm and sure in our own faith. It is something beautiful and precious to us. Naturally, we want to share it with our children, just as we want to share the good things of earth: the warmth of the sun, the beauty of the stars, the thrill of love, the security of a home, and the savor of food. What sort of unnatural parent would make no effort to lead his child to appreciate the good things of life?

We Catholics honestly believe that we have found the way to heaven. Jesus Christ has pointed it out to us, and He leads us lovingly along it. We want to point this way out to our children, and to train each to place his tiny hand in that of the Master, who will guide his toddling steps, with love, in the right direction. We would not put our children in a maze just to see if they could find the right way out by themselves. This is not a game they are playing. It is eternity's business.

We Catholics honestly believe that our Church was established by Jesus Christ, that it is the only true Church, and the only means of salvation which our Lord placed on earth. Can we possibly thus believe and be indifferent whether our children are raised in the Church or not? Can a good parent be content to see his child deprived of the God-given means of salvation?

We Catholics believe that our Church offers us means of grace and sanctification in the Mass and the sacraments.

60

Children may have only tiny sins to be forgiven; but if they do not learn early to use the sacrament of Penance they will be lost when they do need it because of serious sin. Holy Communion brings their innocent souls into life-giving union with the love of Jesus Christ. How could Catholic parents who appreciate the sanctifying value of this union keep their children from it until they find it, unaided, for themselves? Parents rejoice in teaching their children to talk; shall they resolutely refrain from teaching them to talk to God, in prayer?

Almighty God has taught us many great truths about time and eternity, about good and evil. The great philosophers of all ages have sought these truths with uncertain success. Shall we withhold them from our children lest we influence their little minds unduly, and let youngsters flounder in the painful game of finding truth alone? And what if they never find it? The school of experience teaches soundly—but not if each generation discards what it has learned.

Would you call it brainwashing to give your own children the loving benefit of your own life and experience, your own faith and convictions? Is it unfair to train them to the knowledge and love of truth and beauty and goodness? Is it despotic to guide their faltering steps away from the traps you have learned to recognize from your own ensnarement or from the warning of the Master?

A really good Catholic simply overflows with the knowledge and love of Jesus Christ, and it is inevitable that this overflow will seep into the minds and hearts of his children.

Q. My husband is a Catholic, and although I took instructions before we were married, there are still some aspects of the Catholic religion which I do not understand. Perhaps you can explain one for me.

As a Protestant, I was always taught that God knows what we think and how we feel. Therefore, if we sin and are truly repentant, will not God know that we are, and forgive us?

Why, then, is Confession necessary? Can we not ask God's forgiveness directly rather than confess to an intermediary?

A. Any Catholic will agree with you that God knows what we think and how we feel. He knows when we are truly repentant. We can certainly go to Him directly and ask His forgiveness, and He will be pleased with our confidence in Him.

If we love Him enough and are rightly sorry He will forgive us then and there. But if we are Catholics, well instructed, we will be reminded that this forgiveness is not independent of Confession. On the contrary, we are forgiven because we intend to confess, because of our desire to receive the sacrament which our Lord Jesus Christ gave us as the means of forgiveness.

This is very easy for the Catholic to understand; he is well acquainted with the sacraments as external signs established by our Lord to give us grace. This whole sacramental method is foreign to the Protestant concept of sanctification. So I hardly expect you to understand Confession unless I explain to you the idea of the sacraments in general.

Almighty God requires that we go to Confession for much the same reason that He demands we be baptized. "Amen, amen, I say to thee, unless a man be born again of water and the Spirit, he cannot enter into the kingdom of God" (John 3, 5). For a similar reason our Lord insisted that we receive Him in Holy Communion. "Amen, amen, I say to you, unless you eat the Flesh of the Son of Man, and drink His Blood, you shall not have life in you." (John 6, 54). Baptism, Confession and Holy Communion are external signs instituted by Christ to give graces to us, share His love and His life with us, and prepare us for heaven.

The Catholic Church teaches that Jesus Christ established seven of these sacraments, each one an external sign or symbol which effectively brings God's graces into our souls. The sacraments are effective because Jesus uses them as His instruments. You know that He became man to redeem us and sanctify us, so that we might get to heaven. He accomplished our redemption by His death on the cross, and He sanctifies us by sharing with us the graces which He obtained by that same death. These graces are His own; He was free to choose His own way of distributing and sharing them with us. He chose the sacraments.

Certainly our Lord could have decided to give His graces to us by direct spiritual contact, without any external signs. Apparently He chose the sacraments because He wanted to sanctify man in accordance with man's own nature, as a creature composed of body and soul.

63

Almighty God had created both our bodies and our souls, and the Scriptures indicate that He was pleased with the way He had made us (Gen. 1, 31). It would be rather surprising then if He had ignored our bodies and dealt only with our souls in the work of our sanctification. That would be treating us as angels, not as men.

Because God made us the way we are He knows perfectly well that the things which make an impression on us are the things which affect our senses. We have no way of acquiring knowledge, no way of being impressed, except through our sight, hearing, taste, touch, and smell. And you will certainly admit that our sanctification should be an impressive thing.

Jesus Christ was a Man. He knew human nature as the God who had created it and as the Man who lived in it. He used His human nature to redeem us, His body as well as His soul—His body even more than His soul, it would seem to a man at the foot of the cross. Should we then expect Him to ignore our bodies in sharing with us the graces He had won through the crushing of His body?

We know how illusory, uncertain, and undependable, subjective things are. We can never be quite sure of them unless we can hook them onto some objective testing point. We could never be sure of our own sanctification if we had no external sign to prove it to us and convince us that we were not imagining things, or following our feelings.

Confession then, and the rest of the seven sacraments, are the result of the decision of Jesus Christ to treat us as human beings in sanctifying us. They are visible signs which impress and convince us, and are at the same time effective because He made them so.

Jesus chose His signs carefully so that each one would clearly indicate the kind of grace it gave. The external washing of the baptismal water signifies the internal grace which cleanses the soul from original sin. The bread and wine of the Eucharist signify a nourishing grace that feeds the supernatural life of our souls. The solemn words of man and woman in marriage are a visible sign of the unifying grace which binds them together spiritually in their mutual sharing of Christ's life and love.

The sign chosen for the sacrament of Penance is equally appropriate. This sacrament gives the grace of pardon and acquittal: the forgiveness of sins. In human affairs a person accused of crime is tried in judicial action. Sins are crimes; so the natural sign for the remission of sin is a judicial action.

This sign appears doubly appropriate when compared to that judgment which awaits each one of us after death. That will be a judicial procedure; judgment will be final and irrevocable, and it will be based upon justice. In the sacrament of Penance we get a preliminary hearing before a tribunal in which mercy prevails. If we are pardoned in this sacramental judgment we have no reason to fear the final one.

In judicial proceedings you generally have someone who brings a charge or complaint, witnesses to present the evidence, and the accused person who will be convicted or acquitted. In Confession the penitent is his own accuser and the only witness. He enters a plea of guilty, testifies against himself, alleges sorrow and purpose of amendment as his only defense, and throws himself on the mercy of the court.

In judicial proceedings you have a judge who weighs the evidence, makes his judgment in accordance with the law, states his findings, and pronounces sentence. No judicial action is complete without this judgment, and no

65

judge can make a sound decision without evidence. In the sacrament of Penance, the evidence, by its very nature, can come only from confession.

At this point you might well offer an objection: a judge must have authority. He cannot condemn or reprieve in his own name. Where does the priest get his authority to act as a judge and forgive sins?

Rather than give you an immediate answer to this question I would ask you to review with me some events and sermons of our Lord's life. St. Luke (7, 36-50) describes a dramatic scene in the home of a prominent Pharisee where Jesus was a guest at dinner. A penitent woman, a notorious sinner, came to Him and bathed His feet with her tears. He forgave her gently, because she loved much. St. John (8, 3-11) tells us about the poor woman accused of adultery who was being stoned by her accusers. Jesus forgave her with the admonition that she should sin no more.

Particularly interesting is the case of that paralytic who was brought to Him at Capharnaum (Matt. 9, 1-8; cf. Mark 2, 1-12). When Jesus told this man publicly that his sins were forgiven the crowd murmured in protest, and the Master then promptly proved by a miraculous cure that He really did have the power of forgiving sins, as He had claimed.

Some of the best known of all the parables of our Lord proclaim His kindness, mercy, and readiness to forgive. On one occasion, when He was accused of welcoming sinners and eating with them, Jesus obviously compared Himself to the good shepherd who leaves the ninety-nine sheep and goes out after the lost one, bringing it back affectionately on His shoulders (Luke 15, 3-7). And then He followed this up with a story of more remarkable forgiveness: that of the prodigal son (Luke 15, 11-32).

These examples and parables of our Lord show clearly that He was always ready to forgive, that He had the power to forgive, that He used this power, and that His forgiveness was effective. Then after His Resurrection He passed this power of forgiving on to the Apostles: "As the Father has sent Me, I also send you. Receive the Holy Spirit; whose sins you shall forgive, they are forgiven them; and whose sins you shall retain, they are retained" (John 20, 21-23).

These words are clear and precise. Power was given, and it was a twofold power: of forgiving or retaining. A judgment was necessary: that judicial procedure which is the established sign of the forgiving sacrament. The judge must have the evidence, or his judgment will be arbitrary. So confession is necessary. And the judge has his authority; it is given to him by Jesus Christ. When the priest makes his judgment and pronounces forgiveness, Jesus stands by the bargain He made with the Apostles, and the sins are forgiven, as He said they would be.

Actually Confession is much more simple and personal, direct and informal, than our listing of judicial trappings makes it seem. The priest listens with sympathy to the penitent's secret story of sin and sorrow; he judges that Jesus in His mercy would certainly forgive this poor fellow; so he pronounces this judgment in the words of forgiveness, and by these words he administers the sacrament of Penance—that external sign which Jesus uses as an instrument for the forgiveness of sin. The sacrament forgives the sin because it was instituted by Christ for that purpose.

Again, if you are alert to trip me up, you will charge that I have made a tremendous twenty-century jump from the Apostles to the priest of the present day. Jesus gave the power of forgiving sins to His Apostles. How then does the priest get it?

In giving this power of forgiving sins to the Apostles, Jesus told them, "As the Father has sent me, I also send you." Jesus had been sent by the Father to teach, redeem, and sanctify men, to be the Truth, the Way, and the Life for them. He taught eternal truth. He opened up the way to heaven by the Redemption. He showed men by His own example how to travel that way to heaven. And He helps them personally, by His graces, every step along that way.

Only one phase of this work had Jesus completed: the Redemption of mankind. Atonement had been made for sin, grace had been merited, the gate of heaven opened up, and the way to heaven prepared.

But the rest of His work for individual men was only in the beginning stages: His truths would have to be taught to millions of men for many centuries; each one of these men would have to be sanctified, the sins of each man forgiven, and graces imparted to him; and each man would need personal help as he traveled along the newly opened way.

The Apostles were told to go out and do this work for men. They were sent to teach the truth: "Go, therefore, and make disciples of all nations, baptizing them . . . teaching them to observe all that I have commanded you." (Matt. 28, 20). They were told to sanctify: "baptizing them in the name of the Father, and of the Son, and of the Holy Spirit." And they were told that their work would go on until the end of time: "Behold, I am with you all days, even unto the consummation of the world." (Matt. 28, 20).

These were ridiculous commands if the twelve of them were expected to accomplish them all alone. They would never get the job done. They couldn't possibly reach all the nations of their own day. And what of the following centuries? How meaningless would be that promise of our Lord: that He would remain with them all days until the end of the world! In a few years all twelve of them were dead. If the various gifts of Jesus to His Apostles for the good of men were to make any sense and were to have any practical value, they had to be given to the Apostles and their successors in the ministry of teaching, baptizing, consecrating, forgiving, and variously sanctifying.

Sins need to be forgiven today as much as they did in the days of the Apostles. Sins need to be forgiven as much as preaching and teaching need to be done, as much as baptizing needs to be done. So the power of forgiving sins was given to the Apostles and their successors. And the bishops and priests of the Church today are the successors of the Apostles in the work of bringing Christ's truth and graces to souls.

Now let me sum this up. We believe that Jesus Christ established a sacrament for the forgiveness of sin: an external sign which would bring the grace of forgiveness into our souls and give us tangible, consoling assurance of forgiveness at the same time. This sign was a judicial procedure; the informed judgment of an authorized judge expressed in words of forgiveness. Only Confession can provide the evidence necessary to make this judgment sound and fair. Confession is necessary, then, because it is an essential part of the sacrament which our Lord established.

What would be the purpose of His giving us this sacrament if it were not really needed, if we were free to discard or ignore it at will, if we could get forgiveness as well,

69

or nearly as well, without it? It must be used as surely as Baptism must be used.

This does not mean, however, that Almighty God tied His own spiritual hands when He gave us the sacraments. For millions, there is no human possibility of receiving the sacraments. God can and does deal directly with the individual soul, sanctifying it by His union with it.

But His action is never independent of the sacraments in such a way as to make them unnecessary. Through love and faith a man can be sanctified before he is baptized, but this sanctification is by a Baptism of desire, and if that desire is explicit it must later be carried out, if possible. Similarly, an act of perfect contrition, which springs from love and faith, can result in the forgiveness of sins before Confession, but this contrition implies, at least implicitly, a desire and intention of making use of the sacrament later.

Confession is a very practical and useful thing, spiritually. It helps keep us from sin. It gives hope to us when we have fallen, and comfort when we have used it. It gives us a true sense and awareness of sin and adds firmness to our resolution. It makes us alert to the dangers of sin, points out the places of temptation, and helps us control our passions.

Confession gives the advice and encouragement of a prudent confessor, and lets us shift the burden of our troubles to his helpful shoulders. Above all, it gives us external, convincing evidence that our sins are forgiven, because we know from divine promise that this sign of the sacrament is sure and effective.

70

Q. Matthew 26, verses 26 and 27, reads as follows: "And as they were eating, Jesus took bread and blessed it, and broke it, and gave it to the disciples and said: 'Take, eat, This is my Body.' And then He took the cup and gave thanks, and gave it to them saying, 'Drink ye all of it.'"

Why do Catholics receive only the bread in the Holy Sacrament, while the priest drinks the wine? I never could understand that part and hope that you will explain this.

A. It is not possible to give a simple answer to your question. Before we can rightly understand the Catholic custom of receiving Holy Communion under the form of bread alone, we must review: 1) the basic beliefs of Catholics regarding the Eucharist; 2) the early history of Holy Communion in the Church; and 3) the authority of the Church of Christ in interpreting the commands of Christ.

First of all, we Catholics believe that our Lord is really, truly, and substantially present in the Holy Eucharist. At the Consecration of the Mass, when the priest, in the name of Christ, repeats the words of Christ, "This is my Body," "This is my Blood," the bread and wine are actually changed into the body and blood of Jesus. From that moment on it is not correct to call them *bread* and *wine,* even though they look exactly the same as they did before, because they are not bread and wine; they just seem to be. Our faith in the words of our Lord tells us that the same divine power which first created the bread and wine has

71

now changed them into something else: the living reality of Jesus Christ.

I stress this basic doctrine, because you will find that among those who accept it there has seldom been serious dispute about the manner of receiving Holy Communion. The only notable exception I can think of was found among the Hussites, in Bohemia, in the fifteenth century. They continued to believe in the true presence of our Lord, but insisted that the Catholic Church was wrong in permitting Communion to the faithful under the form of bread alone. However, the main opposition to this Catholic practice came with the Protestant Reformation. Most of the reformers denied the reality of Christ's presence in the Eucharist, but insisted that you must receive this unreality under the form of both bread and wine. For the Catholic, the main thing is to receive Jesus Christ, and the manner of receiving Him is secondary. For the person who denies the Real Presence, there can be no question of receiving Jesus Christ; so the form and symbol become the important things.

Once you fully understand that Christ is really present, you will grasp the fact that His being there is a present reality: He is there as He actually is—now. He is not a historical relic, but a living person. Once upon a time the body and blood of Christ were separated from each other, in death. But that separation ceased with the Resurrection. He is now very much alive, in heaven. A living person does not split himself into parts and remain alive. Where his body is, there his blood is also. And where his body and blood are, there his human soul is also. Separate them one from the other and you have a dead man. Jesus Christ died once, in that way; but He lives now, to die no more. He is alive in the Eucharist.

In saying that, we have not told half the story. Jesus Christ is much more than a living man. He is God too—a divine person. And you cannot split a living human being from his personality. So where the human body and blood and soul of Christ are, there also is the divine person who is Christ—the eternal Son of God to whom this body, blood, and soul belong.

Another great fact is that you cannot separate the divine person who is Christ from His divine nature—which is God. So where the human body, blood, and soul of Christ are, there you will find God Himself, specially present. A person is present in the Eucharist; and that person is both God and man.

Thus in the Eucharist we have the real presence of a unified Christ. Real: not a symbol or memorial of Him, not an instrument for bringing Him to us on a spiritual string. Unified: not the dead body of the Cross, preserved like a spiritualized mummy; but the living body and soul of a divine person.

Maybe I overstress these basic points, but if we once grasp them we can readily see their application in practice. The early Christians were very much aware of the reality and the living unity of Christ's real presence. They realized that when they received any particle of the sacred host, or a single drop of the precious wine, they received Jesus Christ. Period. Not His cold body; not His shed blood; not His disconnected soul. But Him.

Consequently the early Christians were not overly particular as to the manner of their reception. Ordinarily they received under both forms, of course. It was the Lord's supper, both food and drink. "Take and eat." "Take and drink." However, there were many occasions, from the

73

very beginning, when Communion was received under only one form or the other.

1. You are probably familiar with the custom which permitted the early Christians to take the Holy Eucharist home with them and keep it there for private Communion. Tertullian and St. Cyprian tell us that this custom was very general in Africa during their time—the third century. And St. Basil and St. Jerome tell us that it continued throughout the fourth century and was practiced in Rome. However, it died out generally in the West shortly after that, though hermits continued the practice in the desert until the ninth century. All indications are that the Holy Eucharist was thus kept and received in the home only under the form of bread.

2. We have many early testimonies which indicate that Holy Communion was given to the sick under the form of bread alone. For instance, St. Basil received several times on the day of his death (P.G. 29, 315 *), and St. Ambrose apparently received Viaticum in this manner on his death-bed. (P.L. 14, 43.) Later on, in 675, the Council of Toledo permitted the sick who were not able to swallow the host to receive under the form of wine alone.

3. It was a fairly common practice in the early Church to give Holy Communion to little children. St. Cyprian tells of its being given under the form of wine alone (P.L. 4, 484), and St. Augustine indicates that it was given under the form of either bread or wine (P.L. 33, 984; 45, 1154). It seems that in the East, especially, there was the custom of giving under the form of wine alone; but in both East

* My references in the following paragraphs are to Migne's collections of the writings of the Greek Fathers (P.G.) and the Latin Fathers (P.L.); also to the *Summa Theologiae* of St. Thomas Aquinas.

and West there are indications that it was given under the form of bread alone.

4. A solemn public Communion service on Good Friday, without an actual Mass, was rather common in the early Church, at least in the East, and it was a Communion service for the people. Its ceremonies provided for the distribution of Holy Communion only under the form of bread. Just recently, in 1956, the Church revived this early Communion service. We had always had the Mass of the Presanctified on Good Friday, but the priest was the only one who received Communion—under the form of bread alone. Now, as in the early Church, all the people may receive—just as they did then, under the form of bread alone.

5. There are various indications that as early as the fifth century, even in ordinary Masses, Holy Communion was often given to the faithful under the form of bread alone.

6. In the early Middle Ages there is evidence that Holy Communion was often given to the faithful by dipping the sacred host in the chalice, or moistening it with a drop of the precious blood. The Church never quite approved of this method, and often condemned it locally, or restricted it; and finally in the thirteenth century she forbade it completely in the Western Church. From that time on the custom became general of giving Communion to the faithful under the form of bread alone. St. Thomas Aquinas tells us that this custom was already observed in some churches in his time—after the middle of the thirteenth century (*Summa* III, 80, 12).

There were various reasons for the gradual growth of the custom of giving Holy Communion under the form of bread alone: the danger of spilling when it was given under the form of wine; the unsanitary and repugnant practice of all communicants drinking from a common chalice; the time-consuming process of distributing under both forms, which became quite impractical as the number of communicants increased and crowds filled the great cathedrals; and finally, the difficulty of reserving the Blessed Sacrament for Communion under the form of wine.

Hence, reverence, convenience, and practical necessity combined to urge the growing practice; and there was nothing to prevent the development, because everyone realized that the Holy Communion was complete under either form, and it had often been given under either form in previous centuries.

The reformers of the sixteenth century were much concerned about this practice. They were not concerned with the question of receiving Christ whole and entire. They denied the reality of His presence under either form or both. But they claimed that Christ had given a direct command that we should receive under both forms, and that if we receive only under the form of bread we were breaking His commandment. They found this direct order from Christ in the texts of Holy Scripture:

Matt. 26, 27: (The text you quote in your question).

John 6, 54: "Except you eat the flesh of the Son of man, and drink his blood, you shall not have life in you."

Luke 22, 17 and 19: "And having taken the chalice, He gave thanks and said: Take and divide among you . . . Do this for a commemoration of me."

As the sharp arguments of the sixteenth century proved, the full meaning of these texts—and thousands of others in Sacred Scripture—is not readily apparent. You can understand them one way, and find some good arguments for your opinion. I can understand them another way, and find arguments to refute yours. But then a friend interrupts our argument with a third opinion well bolstered with proofs. It is in questions like this that we need the Church of Christ to interpret the teachings of Christ. The words of a book are dead, even though they be the Word of God. They can't explain their own meaning to us beyond question or doubt. Only a living teacher, with authority, can do that. We believe that Christ gave us such a teacher: His Church.

Through the thirteen early centuries the Church did interpret the words of Christ regarding the Eucharist. This interpretation found expression in the constant belief in the real presence of Jesus Christ under the appearances of bread and wine—both or either of them. And it found expression in all those various early customs of receiving under one form only—either bread or wine—when convenience or propriety recommended it. The really essential meaning of Christ's command is that we receive Him —alive, unified, and entire. We can do that by taking a particle of the host or a drop from the chalice. When we receive His body His blood is in it. Thus we fulfill the command of John 6, 54.

If you insist on your texts of Scripture, we might quote back at you John 6, 52 and 59, in which Jesus tells us that "if any man eat this bread, he shall live forever." No mention of drinking from the chalice there.

The Church does insist that the separate consecration of the bread and wine is required for the Mass, and the priest must always receive under both forms at Mass. In this manner the Last Supper is recalled fully, and we fulfill the command of Christ that we do this in commemoration of Him. And at the same time the separation of the host and chalice on the altar recall that historical separation of the body and blood of Christ on Calvary.

We Catholics believe that the Church of Christ knows the practical manner in which Christ wants His commands carried out. He gave her authority to work out rites and ceremonies for the Mass and the sacraments. She cannot change anything that Christ instituted, or ignore any of His wishes. But she can work out, through centuries of experience, the most practical and reverent manner of permitting all her people to receive Jesus Christ frequently in the Holy Eucharist. This would be most difficult if everyone received Holy Communion under both forms.

Q. What is the real difference between the Catholic and Protestant Bibles? I have heard many explanations, but they all seem to disagree as to the main difference. Since I am not familiar with the Catholic Bible, I would like your explanation.

A. We can find about seven differences, but only two of them are of much practical importance. I will list the important ones last.

1. Our Bible and yours are simply different translations, made originally from different textual sources. Seldom will two men express the same idea in precisely the same words. So even when our Bibles agree thoroughly in meaning, their exact wording will be different; and because we are likely to be fondly familiar with phrases of our own version, a different reading strikes us as foreign and faulty.

2. The Catholic Old Testament has seven more books than Protestant versions. It also has a few extra chapters in Esther and Daniel.

3. The names of a few of the books are different, e.g. our I and II Kings are entitled I and II Samuel in Protestant Bibles, and III and IV Kings are their I and II Kings; our I and II Paralipomenon are their I and II Chronicles; our Canticle of Canticles is their Song of Solomon; and in the New Testament our Apocalypse is their Book of Revelation.

79

4. Various names of persons and places in the Old Testament retain a closer resemblance to the original Hebrew form in the Protestant versions. In our Bible these names have been Hellenized. Examples: Hosea becomes Osee, Isaiah is Isaias, Jonah is Jonas, and Obadiah is Abdias.

5. The Psalms are divided and numbered differently. We each have a total of 150 Psalms, but our ninth Psalm is divided into two, the ninth and tenth, in Protestant Bibles, and that makes the numbering different until our 146th and 147th are joined into one.

6. Bibles are usually published with abundant footnotes, explanations, and commentaries. In Protestant Bibles these notes are naturally slanted towards a justification of the Protestant position; in Catholic Bibles they give the Catholic interpretation. Seldom could any practical danger come to a Catholic from reading the text of a Protestant Bible; the danger is in the notes.

7. The real, fundamental difference is that the Catholic Bible is edited, printed, and issued with explicit permission of the Church: it has an Imprimatur. The Protestant Bible may be published on private authority, or by a Bible society, or with the authorization of a king or parliament. This is the important difference, because the Church could take the average Protestant Bible, add and subtract a few footnotes, indicate that seven books and a few chapters are omitted from the Old Testament, and simply publish it with her Imprimatur and thus make it her own.

If we are properly to understand and evaluate these differences, we should consider just what the Bible is and the manner in which its various English versions came to us.

We call it the Word of God, and all Catholics agree that it is inspired. It is, then, the result of a cooperative work between God and human writers. God chose the writers, gave them the impulse to write, and assisted them in everything they wrote. So we may rightly say that the Bible is God's book; He is the principal author. The sacred writers were His instruments; they used their own intellect, memory, and imagination; they chose their own words and expressed their ideas in their own personal style.

As you know, the Bible is not a single book, but a collection of seventy-two different books (sixty-five by your count *) which were written by dozens of different authors over a period of more than one thousand years, from Moses to St. John. It is a treasury of literature with inspiring examples of great writing in history, law, narrative, in poetry and drama, prophecy and parable. On its own merits as human literature and because of its venerable antiquity it is the world's greatest anthology. But the fact that it is God's own letter to His people puts it in a class entirely apart from all other writings on earth.

The thirty-eight books which we Catholics and Protestants have in common in the Old Testament were all written in Hebrew. Apparently the seven additional books which we have were not entirely Hebrew, but partly Aramaic or some other Semitic language; and two of them seem to have been written originally in Greek. All twenty-seven books of the New Testament, as we have them in both our Bibles, were written in Greek. There is good reason to believe that St. Matthew first wrote his Gospel in Aramaic; but if he did, it has been lost. We have only the Greek.

Collecting these books was a great task: writings of a

* Sometimes these numbers are given as seventy-three in the Catholic Bible and sixty-six in the Protestant Bible. This difference results from counting the Lamentations of Jeremias as a book separate from the Prophecy of Jeremias.

81

thousand years, found here and there (some of them even in Babylonia during the Captivity), scribbled by hand on leather, parchment, or papyrus; no vowels used, only consonants; no printing presses or photostat machines; and only a few people able to read at all.

Tradition has given the prophet Esdras credit for making the first collection of sacred books, about the fifth century before Christ. This is usually called the Palestinian collection, or Canon. It has the same thirty-eight books which now appear in the Protestant Bible. We have all of them in our Bible, too; and the Jews likewise have them in their Scriptures.

Generally speaking, there has never been much dispute about them, though the Samaritans rejected all but five of them, and the Jews had some warm arguments at one time about the books of Solomon, Esther, and Ruth.

By the middle of the third century before Christ, the Jewish people were scattered widely beyond the borders of Palestine. They had forgotten their Hebrew and were losing contact with their Scriptures and traditions. So a translation of the Old Testament was made into Greek, so that these dispersed Jews could read it.

It would appear that the Torah, or Pentateuch—the first five books—was translated about the year 250 B.C. and all the other books by the year 100 B.C. This translation is called the Septuagint, and it was the version of the Scriptures most widely known and used in the early days of Christianity. It had all the forty-five books which are in the Catholic Old Testament today. Apparently all these books were accepted by the Jews of that time, or at least by those who were responsible for the translation into Greek. And they were likewise generally accepted by the early Christians.

The seven books mentioned earlier have been the subject of much dispute. It began long ago, among the Jews.

Around the time of Christ the Pharisees had set up strict criteria for determining which were sacred books, and which were ordinary literature. For, of course, many other books were written in those early days. How could one tell which were inspired and which were not? Almighty God did not sign His writings; the Holy Ghost imprinted no visible seal. Anyway, the Pharisees rejected these seven books; and Jewish scholars generally followed suit. Among Christians, the great Scripture scholar of the fourth century, St. Jerome, was the first to arouse serious controversy about the inspiration of these seven books. But he was not alone; many early Fathers of the Church expressed doubt; and yet most all of them quoted these books; and St. Jerome even translated two of them into Latin to fit into his Vulgate. By and large, the Church accepted all of them, and as occasion arose she definitely declared all of them to be a part of Sacred Scripture, inspired by God.

For some reason, Luther rejected these seven books and put them in the back of his Bible, calling them Apocrypha. Other Protestant churches were for a long time uncertain or inconstant in their consideration of these seven books—which we call deutero-canonical, i.e., belonging to the Second Canon—but finally all rejected them as first-class Scripture. In England, the Puritans had much to do with the complete and final exclusion of these books from the Bible.

Maybe you are not familiar with these seven books. Here is a brief summary of them:

Judith. The story of a brave and beautiful Jewish widow who saved her people and her city by decapitating Holofernes, the leader of the Medes. It was written in a Semitic language. St. Jerome translated it into Latin from Aramaic.

83

Tobias. The story of the heroism, faithfulness, tragedy, and joy of a Jewish family in Babylonian captivity. This book was very popular with the Jews and existed in five languages before St. Jerome translated it from Aramaic into Latin.

Ecclesiasticus, also called *Sirach.* It is full of advice on wisdom and virtue, citing a list of national heroes as examples of various virtues. It was probably written in Hebrew, and was held in high regard by the Jews before the time of Christ.

Wisdom. This book urges everyone to cultivate true wisdom, which is the fear of God. It was written originally in Greek.

Baruch. This is an exhortation to the people in captivity to keep God's law and return to their homeland. It may have been originally united with the book of Jeremias.

I and *II Machabees.* These books are stories of the heroic battles of the Jewish people against the Syrians. Members of the Machabee family were the leaders, and they fought for liberty and the right to keep their true worship and the glory of their temple. The first book was written in Hebrew; the second in Greek.

The early Christians had practically no familiarity with the Hebrew Bible. They knew and accepted the Old Testament in its Greek version, the Septuagint, and from it made their translations into Latin. St. Jerome, who died in the year 420, was the first Christian scholar thoroughly familiar with the Hebrew Bible and various Semitic languages. His translation of the Bible into Latin came to be known as the Vulgate, and was for succeeding centuries the most common and authoritative version in use among Christian peoples. In the sixteenth century, the Council of Trent named it the official text for use in the Church.

84

Most of us know the Bible only in English; so when we speak of differences between the Catholic and Protestant Bibles we refer to differences between the English versions that are accepted by the two groups.

Today, in actual text, those differences are negligible. There is greater difference between Monsignor Knox's translation and the Douay Bible than there is between the Douay and the King James. Our main objection to most Protestant versions of the Bible would result from the explanatory notes they carry, and from the fact that they are published without authorization of the Catholic Church, the divinely appointed custodian of the Bible.

Historically, however, the differences between the Protestant and Catholic Bibles were more emphasized. These differences date back to two basic translations: the Catholic one known as the Rheims-Douay Version, and the Protestant one called the Authorized Version, and popularly known as the King James Bible. The Catholic translation was made in the latter part of the sixteenth century, and the Protestant at the beginning of the seventeenth. There had been various English translations before that time: Wycliffe's, Tyndale's, Coverdale's, Cromwell's Great Bible, the Geneva Bible, and the Bishops' Bible. But the Catholic Church found all of them objectionable, and the Protestants, too, found them unsatisfactory. In the sharp controversy of those days both sides quoted the Bible often; so it was important that they have reliable English texts.

The Catholics were at a disadvantage at that time; they were exiles. Because of persecutions at home many Catholic scholars left England and went to the Continent. There they established colleges and seminaries for the education of priests who would later return to England to work. The most famous of these English schools were in

85

Belgium, France, and Spain; and one of these was established in 1568 at Douay, in that part of northeastern France known as Flanders, and was transferred to the famous Cathedral town of Rheims ten years afterward.

An Oxford scholar, William Allen, established these schools; he later became a Cardinal, and it was he who inspired and financed the translation and publication of the Bible. The actual work of translation was done by another Oxford scholar, Gregory Martin, who sacrificed his health in the exacting work, and died within a year after he had finished.

Accuracy was the great aim of Gregory Martin and the men who helped him at Douay and Rheims. They sacrificed literary excellence for literal translation, which was made directly from the Latin Vulgate, with careful reference to Greek and Hebrew. The Old Testament was translated at Douay, but it was not published until about thirty years later, 1609. There were probably several reasons for this delay; one was lack of money. The New Testament was translated at Rheims and published there in 1582. Combined with a book written by Gregory Martin on "A Discoverie of the Manifold Corruptions of the Holie Scriptures by the Heretikes of our daies, etc." it created a storm of controversy.

The Authorized Version was prepared by the combined efforts of forty-seven scholars, appointed by King James. They worked in three groups at Oxford, Cambridge, and Westminster. They began their work in 1607, and completed it in about three years. It was published in 1611.

It was regarded as a literary masterpiece, and has exercised a great influence on the English language. The accuracy of some of its expressions was strongly challenged by Catholics, but for 270 years it remained, almost unchanged, the version of the Scriptures generally accepted by English-speaking Protestants. Since 1885 it has been partially supplanted in England by the Revised Version, and in the United States since 1901 by the American Standard Version. In 1946 the Revised Standard Version of the Bible appeared. It created sharp controversy in some Protestant areas but is apparently winning general acceptance in this country.

Meanwhile, the Douay Bible has undergone many revisions which have left it hardly identifiable with the original. The most important of these was made in the middle of the eighteenth century by Bishop Richard Challoner of London, who made two revisions of the Old Testament and five of the New. The Bible as we Catholics in America knew it, before our recent Confraternity edition of the New Testament, was basically Bishop Challoner's in form and expression. During the 1930's a group of American Catholic Scripture scholars completely revised the Rheims New Testament, and it was published in 1941 as the Confraternity edition. In 1948 a similar group of American scholars set to work on an entirely new translation of the Old Testament from the original languages into thoroughly modern English. Two volumes have now been published, Genesis to Ruth, and Job to Sirach.

As I indicated before, the only difference which is basic is that of the Church's authority and approval. How can anyone possibly know what books are in the Bible or how these books are to be interpreted unless the Church of Jesus Christ collects and preserves and teaches the Bible with divinely given authority? To explain this more fully I am presuming to paraphrase the words of a book written by the Reverend Konrad Algermissen and translated into

87

English under the title *Christian Denominations* (Herder, 1945).

Father Algermissen quotes St. Gregory the Great, who says that the Bible is a kind of letter written by Almighty God to His children in a strange land. The Church is with the children there in that land as their mother.

So the Father's letter naturally comes directly to her, that she may make its contents known to the children. As a wise and loving mother she acts discreetly. The younger children would not be able to understand all parts of the Father's letter; they might even be harmed by some of the passages in it.

She explains it to them in simple words, a Bible history. Even some grownups never get beyond the stage of children in simplicity. So the thoughtful mother satisfies them with easier excerpts from the letter. But she does try to get all of her children to penetrate more deeply into the knowledge and spirit of that letter, that they may come to greater religious maturity.

When the children are really grown up, the mother gives them the Father's letter directly and entirely. But even then she exercises vigilance that they do not damage the letter by tearing it up and throwing part of it away, or by misunderstanding and misinterpreting it.

The Church has always had the greatest reverence for the Bible. Her monks have copied it faithfully; her artists have illuminated its pages; her scholars have studied its manuscripts and versions. She has been careful that it should not be distorted or mutilated. And she has called on the Spirit of God to give her light and to guide her in interpreting its more difficult passages.

And in this spirit she rightly commands that the faithful use only authentic translations, inspected and approved by her. Thus we read the Father's letter with the heart of the mother.

Regarding the Father and the Father's house, the mother has much to tell the children which is not written in the letter. She has learned it from the Father, through his divine Son, directly and orally. This is Tradition. It permits her to know that the letter is authentic, that every page of it is genuine; and it permits her to understand the full meaning of every word the Father has written to his children.

3. Belief and Practice in the Church

How Are We Saved? What Is Sin?
Mortal Sin and the Ten Command-
ments. Hell. Purgatory. Limbo.
Heaven. Why Pray to Saints? The
Meaning of the Rosary. What Is an
Indulgence? Guardian Angels. The
Uses of Statues. Music in the
Church.

*Q. I would like to know what it takes to get to heaven.
A person told me that believing in God is enough. I told
her that keeping the commandments and doing good
works are necessary too. Am I right?*

A. You are right. At least you agree with Jesus Christ: "If
you will enter into life, keep the commandments." (Matt.
19, 17). "Go sell whatever you have and give to the poor
. . . and come follow me." (Mark 10, 21). "If any man will
come after me, let him deny himself, and take up his cross
daily, and follow me." (Luke 9, 23).

St. James the Apostle is very explicit also about the necessity of good works for salvation. The man who would be saved must be "a doer of the word" (1, 22). He must control his tongue (1, 26), visit the orphans and widows in their troubles, and keep himself unsullied from the world (1, 27). He must keep all the commandments, not just nine of them (2, 10-11). "What shall it profit, my brethren, if a man say he has faith, but has not works. Shall his faith be able to save him? . . . Faith if it have not works is dead in itself." (2, 14-17).

The idea that faith alone is sufficient for salvation comes from certain isolated texts of Scripture, often divorced from context and considered apart from other texts, like those quoted above, which complete and explain them. This idea comes from a failure to understand the complete plan of salvation, from a concentration of attention on one facet with forgetfulness of all others.

There are many partial truths about salvation. Of ourselves we can do nothing worthy of heaven. We are completely dependent upon our Lord Jesus Christ for the means of salvation. We get to heaven through Him, and by Him, and in union with Him. He gets us there by His redemption of us, His sanctification of us, His living within us. The Holy Ghost is the one who sanctifies us, and gets us to heaven, by living within us. It is by faith in Jesus Christ that we will be saved. If we wish to enter heaven, we must keep the commandments. Faith without good works is dead. There is no salvation outside the Church. Unless a man be born again of water and the Holy Ghost, he can not get into heaven. Nothing defiled can enter heaven. These statements are all true. We must put them, and other similar truths, together and consider them in the light of each other, if we want to get the complete picture.

Sanctification and salvation are not a simple process, no more than living in this world is a simple, unified action. You can not give a man the rules of correct human living in any one maxim. But it helps to understand that life is a simple, unit principle in itself. And it helps in understanding sanctification and salvation to know that they are a process of living, of supernatural living, of living for eternity.

God has destined man for heaven, which is life with Himself, a life of happiness beyond human imaginings. Living with God is not ordinary human living. It requires more than human faculties. Human intelligence is not enough for knowing God as He is. Human will is not capable of loving Him with the happy entirety of heaven. So God intends man to do something which it is impossible for man alone to do: live in heaven.

We are built to live on earth. With the lungs and heart we have we could not live or breathe on Mars or the moon. Spiritually we are built to live on earth too; to lead a life of natural human happiness here and hereafter. So if God wants us to live in heaven, He has to give us the life of heaven. He does just that. He gives us a life that is far above human life, a life that is very much like His own divine life in many ways. It raises us up above the human level. Even as human beings, we were made to the image and likeness of God. Now with this new life, we are much more like to Him, so much so that He is able to adopt us as His own sons and daughters, share His intimate and beautiful secrets with us, and let us enjoy life with Him in His own home.

When does God give us that life of heaven? Right now. Right here on earth. We call it sanctifying grace, or supernatural life. It is a sort of embryonic life now. We hardly feel its movements within us. But it is there, maintained by the intimate presence of God Himself, fed on the Body of the Lord, made to grow strong by the virtues He gives, exercised on good works, kept healthy by mortification.

Our principal human faculties are intellect and will. The principal faculties of our supernatural life are faith and hope and love. If we keep faith and let it grow, it will one day become the Beatific Vision. Hope will have its fulfillment in the happiness of heaven. Love will remain love forever.

God gave Adam and Eve that supernatural life when He created them. But He did not force it upon them. They could keep it or throw it away. They threw it away. God then became man to get it back. And He keeps on living in His Church to give it to each one of us.

God will still not force this life of heaven upon us. He gives it to us in Baptism; but we can throw it away, if we want to, as soon as we get big enough. If we want to keep it we must keep on loving God—and that means keeping His commandments. If we want to keep it we must remain united to Him, since it comes from Him. That means living as a part of the Mystical Body of Christ—in His Church. If we want to keep this life we have to nourish it, protect it, medicate it, warm it, exercise it. That is done principally through the sacraments, and through all those things which bring us into closer union with Jesus Christ: the Mass, our prayers and meditations, our good works, our penances and sufferings—all done for love of Him.

After writing all this I might answer your question in two words: *sanctifying grace*. If we want to get to heaven we must have sanctifying grace when we die. It is the life of heaven. God gives it to us here and now. If we keep it,

93

death becomes a birth; the embryo leaves the womb of earth and starts to see, and love, and laugh in heaven. If we lose it, we simply can not live in heaven; so we have to go elsewhere. And the choice is frightfully limited.

Q. What do Catholics consider a sin?

A. Sin is moral evil: an intentional violation of God's law. It is a rejection of God's love: the choice of some created thing in preference to His perfect goodness.

Sin can be committed by thought or desire (e.g. envy and lust), by word (e.g. blasphemy or a lie), an act (stealing), or an omission (sitting on the beach and watching a man drown when we could easily save him).

Sins may be serious, like murder, or minor, like a little white lie. The very serious ones we call mortal; the minor ones venial.

Mortal sin is a complete rejection of the love of God; the choice of something violently incompatible with His laws. It means the loss of that intimate, personal love of God which sanctifies us and prepares us for heaven. So it means the loss of heaven. And if you can't get to heaven there is only one other place to go.

Venial sin is a partial rejection of God's love; the choice of some petty thing which He has forbidden us. It lessens our bond of love with God, but does not break it. Venial sin deserves to be punished, but not in hell.

95

Q. Will you please list all the mortal sins under each of the Ten Commandments and the seven capital sins?

A. You want me to write a book instead of a column.

The seven capital sins are really bad habits or dispositions—vices which might lead to almost any sin. The usual mortal sins which result from them will be found in the following list, under the Ten Commandments. When we examine our conscience, the seven capital sins serve as a check-list of character traits. Are we inclined to be more proud than humble, more lustful than chaste? Does anger often ruffle our calmness and meekness? Are we more lazy than diligent, more covetous than liberal, more envious than loving, or gluttonous rather than temperate? We should check up on our inclinations, even though they have not led us into sin.

It is impossible, in this column, to list all the mortal sins under each Commandment. We will indicate the more common ones.

I. The First Commandment inculcates the virtues of faith, hope, charity, and religion.

We sin against faith by unbelief or by deliberate doubt. A person commits the sin of unbelief if he knows he ought to believe, but deliberately refuses to accept God's revealed truth. Deliberate doubt calls the articles of faith into question. Temptation to doubt is not a sin. Problems, troubles and difficulties are not sins.

96

We sin against faith by joining a non-Catholic church, or by taking active part in its worship—sometimes even by passive cooperation in its religious services (if there is not sufficient reason for it, or it gives scandal, or it is dangerous to our faith).

We sin against faith by indifferentism (holding one religion as good as another) or by exposing our faith to serious and needless dangers (e.g. reading books dangerous to the faith).

We sin against hope by presumption and despair, but these sins are rare. We often take foolish chances with our salvation—stupid, but not presumptuous. We often get deeply discouraged and melancholy, without giving up hope in God.

Any mortal sin is a sin against charity. So we can't break any commandment without fracturing the first one, too.

Sins against religion (under this commandment) are 1) neglect of divine worship, and 2) superstition. Seldom does either become a mortal sin for the average Catholic.

II. The Second Commandment lays additional stress on the virtue of religion, with reference to oaths and vows and respect for sacred things.

Perjury is a mortal sin. It is swearing to a lie or breaking a lawful promise made under oath.

Breaking a vow is a mortal sin.

Ordinary "swearing" or "cursing" falls short of being a mortal sin unless it is deliberate and malicious. If we have a bad habit of profanity and make no effort to correct it, we may be guilty of mortal sin.

III. The Third Commandment also has to do with the virtue of religion. The law of the Church makes its obligation explicit. It is a mortal sin to miss Mass (or a considerable portion of Mass) on Sunday, or a holyday, without sufficient excuse. It is a mortal sin to spend a considerable part (two or three hours) of Sunday or a holyday in needless servile work.

IV. Theologians call the virtue of the Fouth Commandment piety. We understand it better as "love, reverence, and obedience toward our parents and superiors."

It has a reciprocal obligation of parents toward children (and superiors toward subjects).

Mortal sins: severe hatred of parents, seriously wishing them evil or treating them very badly; using mean, insulting words to them; causing them serious and needless sadness; speaking serious evil of them; failing to assist them in their grave need.

Children who are minors commit mortal sin if they deliberately disobey the serious command of their parents in a grave matter (e.g. things related to morality, to their eternal salvation, to life and health, or to the proper governing of family life). The deliberate act of disobeying frequently or regularly in lesser matters might be a mortal sin too.

Parents sin mortally by serious neglect of their children's needs—health, education, religious training, discipline, and correction; by rejecting them or spoiling them, or giving them bad example.

We all sin by breaking the laws of the Church or the State. If the law is grave and the violation deliberate, the sin is mortal.

V. The Fifth Commandment imposes the virtue of justice with regard to our most personal rights: to life, health, and integrity of body and soul.

Suicide is a mortal sin, as is the serious neglect of our own health, or the serious endangering of our life or health.

Murder is a mortal sin, as is also serious, deliberate, unjustified injury done to another person.

Abortion and euthanasia are murder.

Deliberate and unjustified anger and fighting are mortal sins. Deliberate hatred, jealousy and envy may be, too.

Grave spiritual injuries (e.g. scandal, leading into sin) are mortal sins against this commandment.

VI. Any deliberate sin against chastity is a mortal sin. We sin against chastity when we seek illicit sexual pleasure, partial or complete, alone or with another, in thought, desire, or deed.

Serious, deliberate sins against modesty are mortal sins. We sin against modesty when we put ourselves in danger of sins against chastity, without sufficient reason. Modesty governs our thoughts, reading, looks, dress, touches, and embraces—the shows we see, the parties we attend, and the company we keep. The general rule is this: it is a mortal sin, without sufficient reason, to do things which tend strongly to excite carnal movements and cause the immediate danger of consent to the pleasure they give.

VII. Justice requires that we respect the rights of other people to property in the same way that we want them to respect our own.

It is a mortal sin to steal (or unlawfully keep) the property of another person, if the value of that property is sufficient to harm the individual seriously or the security of the social order. It would be a mortal sin to steal an amount sufficient to maintain a man and his family for a day. It would probably be a mortal sin to steal ten or fifteen dollars from anybody, however wealthy.

Destroying property in similar amount is a mortal sin. So is cheating and graft, breaking contracts unjustly, failing to make restitution.

VIII. Justice requires that we respect a person's right to his honor, good name, and reputation. A serious, public, unjust insult would be a mortal sin. You can often do serious harm by detraction or calumny; if you do it intentionally, you commit mortal sin. Ordinary lying is despicable, but is seldom a mortal sin. Ordinary gossip is shameful, but if it falls short of serious detraction, it is only the next-worst thing in the world, i.e. venial sin. Prying into other people's affairs and revealing their secrets are usually faults too petty and mean to be dignified as mortal sins.

IX. Deliberate thoughts and desires against chastity and needless, deliberate dallying with seriously suggestive thoughts are sins against the Ninth Commandment.

X. Mortal sins of thought and desire relative to property are probably rare, but you might feed your greed, encourage your envy and cozen your coveting until your fingers fairly itch as your mind reaches out to snatch the desired object.

A final note: even the worst thing mentioned above would not be a mortal sin for us if we did not understand it to be such, or if our doing it were not of our own will.

Q. If God loves a person so much that He knows the number of hairs on his head, how can He, even through justice, send him to hell? A mother, because of love, would not damn her own child, no matter how he damns himself.

A. Hell exists as a sanction—a reason for us to avoid sin and do good. Its force as a sanction would be entirely lost if God were to become sentimental and just not be able to stand it to see anyone go there.

What would God do with those who are so thoroughly vile and sinful that they would simply be intolerable in heaven?

We have a free will. God invites us to heaven, gives us the means of getting there, helps us with every step on the way there, picks us up when we fall and want to be picked up, forgives us as often as we honestly ask forgiveness; but he will never force us. If we persist in asking for hell, in spite of all His love, sacrifice, forgiveness, and help, then He will give us what we ask for—as He has promised. To do otherwise would be to force us into heaven against our will.

I wonder if you are not being a little sentimental about a mother's love. Will she actually endure everything from a rebellious, hateful, disobedient, and insulting child? Will she force him to remain in her home when he insists on leaving? Will she accept him back forgivingly a hundred times after his abuse and repudiation? Honestly now, does not God forgive much more, and more thoroughly and frequently, than any mother you ever knew?

Your comparison takes no account of the fact that salvation is a supernatural affair. Not only do we have no human right to heaven, but we can't get a step toward heaven by our own human power, and even if we got there we couldn't live in heaven with our own human life. We need to have that share in the divine life which we call sanctifying grace; and we need to have the momentary and constant help of God through His actual graces.

These things are gifts. We have no right to them; neither do we have to take them. It's an unsportsmanlike giver who forces his gifts upon someone by sheer strength or authority—even if he knows the gifts would be immeasurably good for the recipient. God tells us how good His gifts are for us. He demonstrated their precious value on the Cross of Calvary. He repeats His offer of them persistently. He invites us and even begs us with love to take them, but if we refuse He will not spiritually ram them down our throats. And without them we can't get to heaven—or even near it. There is only one place we can live: hell.

Q. I am an Episcopalian, and was taught that there is no purgatory. It was explained that a purgatory was not necessary because God is so merciful and forgiving that one has to be hopelessly wicked to be condemned to hell. Otherwise, if you have repentance you go to heaven—there is no in-between. Therefore: Can you justify for me the existence of purgatory?

A. From texts of Scripture alone, I doubt that I can convince you of the existence of purgatory. As an Episcopalian, you must know that Jesus Christ established His Church to teach His doctrine as He had taught it. Never did He promise that He would write out every detail of that teaching or have His disciples write it out completely.

But He did promise those He sent to teach that He would remain with them all days even to the end of the world, and that He would send the Holy Spirit, the Spirit of Truth, who would abide with them forever and teach them. In other words, He gave them assurance that they need not worry about the integrity or success of their teachings; He would be there, Himself, to see that they did the job properly, and the Holy Spirit would inspire and direct them.

Our immediate reason for believing in purgatory is that the Church of Christ teaches us, in our Lord's name, that there is such a place. In other words, Jesus Christ teaches us through His Church that purgatory exists. Since you are not a Catholic, you may not be entirely convinced by the fact that the Church teaches this doctrine today, or that she defined it clearly in the Council of Trent. But, as an Episcopalian, you do believe in traditional Christianity, and only a little investigation will make it clear that the Church has been praying for the souls of the dead since the time of the Apostles. She would not have prayed for them if she had not believed that they could be helped by her prayers. She knows that hell is eternal, that prayers won't help anyone there. She knows that the souls in heaven need no help; she has always prayed *to* them. If there were no purgatory, she would have wasted 1900 years of prayers.

The point of our investigation will be that the Church has held and acted on the idea of purgatory from the very beginning, and that she has taught it rather clearly from early centuries.

To be thorough we had better start from Old Testament times. It is quite apparent through all of Scripture that God imposes punishment and expects penance and reparation, even after the guilt of sin is forgiven. Adam was forgiven his original sin, but he still had to eat his bread in the sweat of his brow. Moses was forgiven his fault at the place of the Waters of Contradiction, but he was deprived of all but a glimpse of the Promised Land. David repented his adultery and murder, and God forgave him; but He still punished him by taking his child. But it is evident that not all of us are punished here on earth in proportion to our sins. Could the just God punish one sinner, and let the next one get by scot-free for the same offense? From God's ancient requirement that sins be punished even after they are forgiven, comes the need for purgatory, in order for that punishment to be equal and adequate.

We have definite evidence that the Jewish people, be-
104

fore the time of Christ, believed in praying for the dead. Our best information on this subject comes from II Machabees, 12, 43-46. Now don't shout at me that this is an apocryphal book. I know that, though I prefer to call it a book of the Second Canon. So I will not quote it to you as inspired Scripture; you would not accept my argument. But you certainly accept this book as good sound history. And on that basis we know that Judas, the leader of the Jewish armies, took up a collection after a battle, and "sent 12,000 drachmas of silver to Jerusalem for sacrifice to be offered for the sins of the dead . . . It is therefore a holy and wholesome thought to pray for the dead that they may be loosed from their sins."

The early Christians accepted these words as inspired by God, but even if they had not, they would evidently have found in them historical precedent for their own early practice of praying for the souls of the dead.

The New Testament has only a couple of texts which refer to purgatory, and they are a bit obscure, requiring the teaching authority of Christ's Church to settle uncertainties of their interpretation. One is from the Gospel of St. Matthew, 12, 32. Our Lord says that the sin of a person who speaks against the Holy Spirit "will not be forgiven him, neither in this world, nor in the world to come." Various Fathers of the Church, among them St. Augustine (*City of God*, 21, 24) and St. Gregory the Great (*Dial.* 4, 39), point out that these words would not have meaning unless some sinners were to be forgiven in the next world.

My other text is from St. Paul (I Cor. 3, 11-15). Every man's work will be tested, as by fire, and "if any man's work burn, he shall suffer loss; but he himself will be saved, yet so as by fire." Here again, the early Fathers, like St. Ambrose, St. Jerome, St. Gregory, St. Augustine, and

105

Origen, interpret this text as referring to the purifying fires of purgatory.

I don't want to bore you with a whole list of quotations from the early Fathers of the Church. But I believe it is important to indicate some of the historical sources of our information that the Church of Christ prayed fervently for the dead from the earliest times, and believed that their sins and debts would be forgiven after death, and that our prayers and sacrifices would help them to attain peace and rest. And that is the doctrine of purgatory, no matter what name you call it.

(The references in the following paragraphs are, again, to Migne's collections of the writings of the Greek Fathers (P.G.) and the Latin Fathers (P.L.). There is now a translation of most of these Fathers available in English, entitled *Fathers of the Church*.)

Tertullian was not always orthodox, but he is one of the best witnesses we have of second century customs. He died in 222. He once warned a widow that she would be guilty of infidelity if she failed to pray for her husband's soul, begging repose for him (P.L. II, col. 912).

Clement of Alexandria describes the process of purification of those who die without time for penance (P.G. IX, col. 332).

St. Cyprian forbade the customary prayers and Sacrifice of the Church for a person who died in defiance of Church law (P.L. IV, col. 399).

Origen teaches the doctrine of purgatory very clearly (P.G. XIII, col. 445, 448).

From the fourth century we have abundant evidence from the liturgy—the official prayers of the Church. Here is one of the prayers of that time; we could hardly improve on it today: "Let us pray for our brethren who sleep in

Christ, that God who in his love for men has received the soul of the departed one, may forgive him every fault, and in mercy and clemency receive him into the bosom of Abraham" (P.G. I, col. 1144).

If you want some real early evidence of the Church's custom of praying for the dead you should visit the Catacombs. There you often find the tombs of the dead inscribed with prayers that they may find rest and peace.

By the time of St. Ambrose and St. Augustine, around the end of the fourth century, the doctrine of the Church about purgatory finds definite expression. St. Ambrose preached a sermon for his friend and emperor, Theodosius, in which he prayed: "O Lord, give rest to thy servant, Theodosius, that rest Thou has prepared for thy saints . . . I loved him; therefore will I follow him to the land of the living; I will not leave him till by my prayers and lamentations he shall be admitted unto the holy mount of the Lord." (P.L. XVI, col. 1367). And St. Augustine points out that "some there are who have departed this life, not so bad as to be deemed unworthy of mercy, nor so good as to be entitled to immediate happiness" (*City of God,* 21, 24).

Maybe you and I will be in that class of men described by St. Augustine. I am sure that you do not expect to go to hell; I don't. If I did, I would be guilty of despair. I go along with your statement that God is so merciful and forgiving that only the hopelessly, unrepentingly wicked will go to hell. But I don't quite see how I could go along with you straight to heaven, immediately after death. I am aware of many things which I owe to God in justice as a result of my past sins, and also of a leopard's array of dark spots from present minor sins and from attachments to things which draw me away from God and prevent my complete and instant union with Him.

107

My idea of purgatory does not detract in any way from the effectiveness of the Redemption, or the completeness of God's forgiveness. It merely points out that God is just and holy, as well as merciful. God would not be just if He did not punish sin; it would mean that He condoned it; that He didn't really care whether we sinned or not. If He didn't have a purgatory He would be consenting to my rebellious spirit and my minor sins; He would let me get by with them.

God knows that the power of His love will not always keep us from mortal sin; so He adds the threat of hell. He knows just as well that His love will not always keep us from venial sin, either. Wouldn't you expect him to add a little threat of punishment there, too? That is purgatory.

If there were no temporal punishment after death, it would appear that God was arbitrary and unfair. He makes some sinners suffer here on earth while others escape; and He accepts the voluntary penances of some while others never think of reparation. Are all to be admitted to heaven equally? Purgatory is the great equalizer established by a God who is just and fair.

The doctrine of purgatory does not imply that God is harsh or vindictive, extracting so many ounces of pain for every sin. Rather does it demonstrate God's mercy, which finds a way to save us in spite of our sins, and to cleanse and purify us in spite of our lack of penitence.

It is true that many theologians and preachers have stressed the horrible punishments of purgatory, but it is equally true that others have pointed out the basic happiness that souls must enjoy there. They are saved; they can commit no sin; they can never go to hell. Surely, no impatience for heaven can stifle the joy of that security, nor any immediate pain obscure the awareness of God's love. For the souls in purgatory are His own chosen ones, His adopted sons, in the final stages of preparation for life in His own home.

Purgatory is not only a place for punishment, as demanded by justice; it is also a place of purification, to make us ready for heaven. I wonder whether many of us would be very welcome in heaven as we are right now, with our various rebellions against God's love and grace?

You point out that God forgives us when we repent. He forgives our guilt, which is the badness of our will. But sin creates evil outside the will; it throws the scales of justice out of balance. After the will turns back to good, and guilt is forgiven, there must still be penance, so that we do our part with Christ in righting the wrong done outside the will and in putting the scales back in balance.

Essentially, by our own efforts, we can never really undo the wrong of sin. Jesus Christ accomplished that by the Redemption. But God became man to do for man only the things he could not do for himself; He didn't exempt us from doing our part, in those things we can do. And we can do penance, for love of Him, and thereby cooperate in the work of the Redemption and in our personal sanctification. But suppose we refuse, or drag our feet. That's where purgatory comes in.

Here on earth we do our part in atoning for sin by performing the penances we are given in Confession; by doing the penances imposed by Church law, like fasting and abstaining; by accepting the sufferings sent by God, like sickness and troubles; and by our voluntary penances and good works. The Church helps us immeasurably through her power of binding and loosing. But even after all this we may well expect that we have not done enough when

109

we measure the smallness of our penances against the number of our sins. Purgatory lets us finish the job.

There are two points I would have you note particularly about purgatory. 1) The purifying and atoning process there is done entirely by the grace of God, without any meritorious cooperation on our part. So purgatory emphasizes in a special manner the redemptive power of the Cross of Christ. 2) Purgatory gives us here on earth a great opportunity to exercise the virtue of charity. The souls in purgatory cannot help themselves, but God permits us to help them by our prayers, penances, and sacrifices. It is the chief work of Christ's kingdom to spread love one for another, and to love each other for the love of Him.

Q. What is limbo? Do we have to believe in it?

A. The word limbo has two meanings:

1. The Limbo of the Fathers, where the souls of the just who died before the Redemption went for a temporary stay, while awaiting Christ's Ascension into heaven.

2. The Limbo of Infants, where unbaptized children will spend eternity. These children are excluded from the beatific vision because of original sin. They were born into the world without the supernatural life of grace, which is the life of heaven. So they are not capable of living in heaven—they have no supernatural eyes with which to see God. But they are not guilty of personal sin; they are as innocent as only babes can be. So they will be happy as they can be.

Both the Old Testament and the New teach clearly the existence of the Limbo of the Fathers. Those sons of Adam who died before Christ could not go to heaven. They had never received sanctifying grace, which is the life of heaven. This grace had been lost by Adam's sin. It was regained only by the merits of Jesus Christ. After His death Jesus went to limbo ("He descended into hell") to tell the "Fathers" there that they would soon be with Him in heaven.

The existence of the Limbo of the Infants is generally considered a "theological certainty." It is not in itself a matter of faith; there is no mention of it in the Scriptures, and apparently no clear teaching of it in earliest Tradition. But it is a direct conclusion from revealed doctrines, and most theologians think it is a necessary consequence of those doctrines. If you tried to deny it you might find yourself in trouble with such matters of faith as the necessity of grace for salvation and the necessity of Baptism as a means of conferring grace. And you would find yourself at variance with the attitude of the Church as expressed in her common teaching and in various pronouncements from authoritative and official sources.

We do know that God, in His love and mercy, wishes the salvation of all men, and that Jesus Christ died for the redemption of all. On the basis of this our sentiments may find hope that He has, without telling us about it, worked out some extraordinary means of conferring sanctifying grace on those infants who die without possibility of actual Baptism. But we must admit that such hope is not bolstered by the cold reasoning of most theologians, and it is rather shaken by statements like the one made by Pope Pius XII to a group of obstetricians on October 29, 1951:

"In the present dispensation there is no other means (except Baptism) of communicating this life to the infant, who has not yet the use of reason . . . An act of love can suffice for an adult to acquire sanctifying grace and supply for the lack of Baptism; to the unborn or newly-born infant this way is not open . . ."

Our soundest hope for these infants is that there is a place short of heaven where they can go and be happy—naturally happy, without the beatific vision. That place we call limbo. It is a funny old name for a beautiful, youthful place. The doctrine might be more appealing if we called it baby's paradise—or kiddie heaven.

112

Q. I would very much appreciate an explanation as to what the Church teaches concerning the beatific vision. I am a convert, but from my conversation with Catholics born in the Faith, I understand that pagans and those Jews who do not accept Christ will not behold the beatific vision, even though these people do attain heaven.

A. Heaven is the beatific vision, and anyone who gets there will have it. The problem of pagans will be to get to heaven; once they are there all problems will disappear. There will be no discrimination or segregation, no handicaps or disabilities. Everyone will see God directly and be united with Him in such intimacy as individual capacity for knowledge and love permits.

Since all those in heaven will see God directly they will see Him as He is, and He is a Trinity of persons. They may have had strange ideas of Him while they were here on earth, but in heaven they will see the actuality. And they will also enjoy the company and friendship of the Mother of Jesus and of all the saints, no matter how hesitant they were to pay them any honor while still on earth.

Our direct vision of God will result from the supernatural powers given to our intellect by divine grace—the grace we receive as a result of the Redemption. It is by sharing the life of God here on earth, in sanctifying grace, that we are made capable of sharing His life in heaven, in the beatific vision.

113

If we are to have any present appreciation of the complete happiness we will have in the beatific vision we must somehow bring ourselves to understand that God is all goodness, all perfection, all beauty—all of everything that makes for happiness—and that we will know and have Him with all the supernatural capabilities of our being, and that we will have the complete assurance of never losing an iota of it for eternity.

It helps sometimes to make an inventory of all the good things we enjoy in this life, of the thousands of bits of love and beauty which contribute to our partial happiness. Then stop and think that the good of all these things comes from God, that any beauty or perfection we see in them is but a reflected glint of His own complete perfection, and that in heaven we will have the unlimited Reality which gave all these things the power to exist in their own imperfect way. If these thousand bits of limited goodness give us intermittent happiness here, we might imagine them multiplied by a thousand, drained of their dross and satiety, and savored with supernatural zest. We would still be infinitely short of heaven's source of joy.

Q. I would like to know about praying to the saints. In the Roman Catholic Church, praying to a saint is just the same as praying to Jesus or to God. By praying to a saint, I understand, you pray to the soul of a pious person who lived in this world, died, and whose mortal body perished, but whose immortal soul lives.

We believe that God is omnipresent. We pray to Him in any place; He is there to hear the prayer. Do you mean to say that the soul of a pious person is omnipresent? Is this attribute of God applicable to every pious soul canonized as a saint by the Roman Catholic Church? In other words, is every saint of the Roman Catholic Church omnipresent? Unless this is so, how can all the prayers offered to them simultaneously, in different places, say America, Italy, India, China, and Japan be heard by them at the same time?

Do the saints of the Roman Catholic Church accept the prayers of Protestants? When Protestants pray to them for spiritual guidance or cure or mitigation of bodily ailments, are those prayers accepted, like those of the Roman Catholics?

Is this praying to the saints taught by Jesus anywhere? While Jesus says, "Come unto Me, follow Me, I am the way, ask in My name, etc.," He never points to anyone as a mediator. How did this belief creep into the Roman Catholic Church and become so popular while it is unknown in the Protestant Church?

A. The Catholic practice of praying to the saints is just as simple as your asking your best friend to pray for you, but you make it seem complicated. That is because you share several misconceptions which are quite common outside the Church. Therefore, in answering your letter, I think the first thing we should do is clear away the errors, so that we may have unencumbered space to establish our basis of understanding.

1. Praying to the saints is not at all the same as praying to Jesus or to God. We adore God as our creator; saints are creatures, like ourselves. We admit our total dependence on God, ask Him for divine protection and fatherly help, for grace and the means of salvation; we tell Him of our sorrow for our sins, because we love Him as the supreme Goodness and have offended Him; we ask His forgiveness. We don't say any of those things to the saints when we pray to them. When we pray to God we express our complete faith in Him, because He is Truth itself; we may reverence and admire the teachings of the saints, but we are critical and selective.

Jesus is God, and all the prayers we say to God in His divine nature we say also to Jesus in His human nature. In addition, we express our faith in His divinity; we savor and return the love which He has shown us by His human life and His death on the Cross. We accept His revelation of divine truth on His own authority; we ask Him for the grace to live by His teaching and example; we greet Him as our Redeemer, ask all favors through Him as our only Mediator, adore Him in His sacramental presence on the altar, salute Him as Man and God on the throne of heaven.

None of these things enter into our prayers to the saints. To adore them would be silly and sinful. The most they can do for us right now is to pray for us, and that is ex-
116

actly what we ask them to do. The example of their holy lives may inspire us, and in some things we may imitate them, but they are not the Way, the Truth, and the Life. They simply followed in the same wake we are trailing along in.

We never ask a saint to give us grace or forgive our sins. The only thing divine in them is the grace God gave them and the glory they share with Him. In our prayers to them we salute them as friends whom we love and revere; they plodded our own weary way before us, and some of them deviated from it, even as you and I. Because of their courage, sacrifice, and goodness, they are our heroes, and still our close friends in Christ. We ask them to pray to Him for us—simply that.

2. We do not mean to say that the soul of a pious person is omnipresent. This unique attribute of God is not applicable to any saint, whether canonized or not. The soul in heaven is a spirit and it probably has great agility; to be more accurate, we should say that it is independent of space. But it could never, by its own power, be in position to hear two prayers uttered simultaneously in America and Japan, or even in Minneapolis and St. Paul. A saint hears our prayers through God, who hears them everywhere at once by His divine power and presence, and transmits them without distortion.

3. The saints in heaven don't belong to the Roman Catholic Church. They graduated from membership at the time of their death. They belong to the Church Triumphant; Jesus Christ is the head of that Church also, and they are united to Him even more closely than we are. There is no prejudice among them—only charity. They are ready to hear the prayers of anyone—Protestant, Jew, or Moslem—who speaks to them in a sincere and friendly

117

manner. Even by earthly standards we would consider it rude and impolite to ignore the earnest words of an honest friend. Heavenly standards are higher.

4. Neither Catholics nor Protestants should expect miraculous cures for the asking. You can't put a saint on the spot by demanding a miracle. The best he can do is to pray to God for us, and the Lord in His wisdom will then decide what is best for us and for the world at large.

5. We have no words of Jesus Himself telling us to pray to the saints. But He does tell us that the angels take an interest in us: "So it is, I tell you with the angels of God; there is joy among them over one sinner who repents" (Luke 15, 10). And he tells us that little children "have their own angels in heaven" (Matt. 18, 10).

If the angels, who are creatures of a different order entirely, are concerned with the affairs of men, may we not presume that the saints, who are our brothers by nature and by grace, show interest, too, in their fellow men still on earth? If communication is possible between men and angels, it should be doubly easy between us and the saints. The angels never used an earthly language; some of the saints even spoke English.

6. Your final question is asked in reverse; in point of time and history it doesn't make sense. What you mean to ask is this: "How did this belief creep out of the Protestant churches and become so unpopular, after it had been the common belief and popular practice of all Christians for fifteen centuries?"

The Catholic doctrine of the intercession of the saints was stated by the Council of Trent: the saints in heaven do pray to God for us. So it is good and useful for us to ask their prayers. And any help they obtain for us will be
118

through our Lord Jesus Christ, who is our only Redeemer and Savior.

These three simple statements express the entire doctrine. The Council added nothing except to condemn the prevalent errors of that day—and this. It called impious the thoughts of those who: 1) deny that the saints are to be invoked; 2) claim that saints do not pray for men; 3) say that it is idolatry to ask the saints to pray for us; and 4) assert that it is contrary to the word of God and a dishonor to the Mediator, Jesus Christ, to pray to His saints.

The Bible frequently advises us to pray for one another, and to ask the the prayers of our friends. St. James says, "Pray for one another, for the healing of your souls" (5, 16), and St. Paul asks the Romans, "Give me the help of your prayers to God on my behalf" (15, 30).

Surely you believe that the saints in heaven are united to us by close spiritual bonds. They share the life of Christ, in His glory. We share the life of Christ, by His grace. We are both intimately united with Him, and through Him our union embraces each other. We are members of Christ, members of the Communion of Saints.

Surely you believe that the saints in heaven are alive and alert, interested in God and His creation, interested in Christ and His brethren, interested in their own fellow men stumbling along the path they once trod. Surely you believe that it is easily possible for God to let them know what happens in the world. And surely you believe that these live, alert, interested beings can express to God their interests and wishes. A heaven without facilities of communication would be a poorer place than earth.

We ask our friends on earth to pray for us; why not ask our friends in heaven? Angels pray for us (Zach. 1, 12); why can't the saints do it? Certainly the saints love us, for

119

the sake of Christ, who loved us first. Certainly the saints can expect a favorable hearing with God, whom they loved intensely and served faithfully, and for whom they sacrificed heroically. Is it then unreasonable to expect that they might put in an occasional good word for us with the Almighty, to whom they are so close?

For simple logical reasons like these, Christians, from the very beginning, have prayed to the saints and paid them honor. Many of the early Fathers of the Church give testimony to this belief and practice. St. Jerome sums it up beautifully: "If Apostles and martyrs, while they are still in the flesh and need care for themselves, can pray for others, how much more will they pray for others after they have won their crowns, their victories, and their triumphs? One man, Moses, obtains God's pardon for six hundred thousand armed men, and Stephen prays for his persecutors. When they are with Christ will they be less powerful? St. Paul says that 276 souls were granted to his prayers, while they were in the ship with him. Shall he close his lips after death, and not utter a syllable for those who have believed in his Gospel throughout the world?" (*Adv. Vigil.*, 6).

St. Augustine tells us that Faustus, the Manichean, accused the Christians of his day of idolatry because they honored the memory of the martyrs. "The accusation is not worthy of reply," wrote the saint (*Contra Faustum,* 1.20, *c*.21). He then explained that the Christians honored the martyrs so that they might imitate their virtues, share in their merits, and be helped by their prayers. Altars are built at their shrines, but the altars are built to God, and on them sacrifice is offered God. No bishop standing at the altar would think of offering sacrifice to Peter, or Paul, or Cyprian. We venerate the martyrs as we would

120

venerate holy men of God in this life, but with greater devotion and confidence, because they have gained their victory, while those in this life are still striving for it. So you see that by the end of the fourth century this belief had crept thoroughly into Christian devotion, and was already widely popular. It remained so for one thousand years before the Reformers, imitating Faustus the Manichean, again called it idolatry. They banned prayers to the saints, insisting that prayers be said to God alone. The result is simply that fewer prayers are said. Before, God was honored through His saints; now His honor is much neglected.

By praying to the saints we get acquainted with those who will be our friends and companions forever, in union with Jesus Christ, by whose grace and merits we hope to join them.

Q. What is the meaning of the Rosary, and what is "the story behind the story"? How long have Rosary beads been in use?

A. That's a nice, simple question; I wish I could answer it as plainly as you ask it. But the Rosary's history cannot be told simply; it is complex and diffuse. The Rosary is a prayer of many parts, and each part has its separate history of gradual development through many centuries, in various countries. And much of this history has not been neatly written; it is a story of the common people and their growing customs of popular devotion. We have to sift it from legend, and sometimes we must even keep the legend and assay it.

The Church did not invent the Rosary and impose it on her people; pious men and women found it bead by bead and came to love it. Then the Church saw that it was good and blessed it.

In studying the long centuries of the Rosary's growth we can learn much about prayer, man's age-old, humble effort to communicate with God. You must know the meaning of prayer and believe in it to understand the Rosary. It repels those who do not understand it, but fascinates those who do. By its own appeal it has become the popular prayer of millions, for both public and private use, and centuries of growing acceptance show that it is effective.

In his efforts at prayer man has sought to use all his human faculties: intellect and will, imagination, speech, and gesture. The Church has always approved this diversity of prayerful expression, because she teaches that man is made of body and soul and is most fully man when he uses both in unison and harmony. God created man's body as well as his soul. Why then should man try to worship his Creator with his soul alone, like an angel?

The proud and sophisticated have a tendency to discount the role of man's body, even his lips and vocal cords, in his worship of God. They consider genuflections, along with tribal dances and primitive prostrations, to be the superstitious gestures of simple people who are emotional and immature. And vocal prayer is, for them, hardly more elevated than physical contortions, especially if it is the reading or reciting of formulated prayers, or has any element of repetition in it. The only devotion to which such haughty souls attribute value is mental prayer or meditation; after all, it does exercise the mind and may produce new ideas, deeper understanding, and dynamic inspiration. If you pin the sophisticates down you will find that they don't really believe in prayer as a means of communication; they don't honestly think that they are getting through to God, or that He is interested enough to listen.

In the history of the Rosary, the voice, the body, and the mind all had a part. The favorite vocal prayer of the Church has always been the Psalms of David, all 150 of them. They have been variously read, recited, and sung down through the centuries, especially in the monasteries, constant centers of intensive prayer.

Uneducated lay Brothers in those monasteries, and the common laymen outside, did not know the Psalms by
123

heart. They could not read and they did not understand the Latin in which the Psalms were said. So they sought substitutes, and easiest to find was the Lord's Prayer (Matt. 6, 9-13), which was called the Pater Noster, from its first two words in Latin.

The monks frequently recited the Psalms, or sang them, as a penance or a prayer for a deceased person. Sometimes they said the entire Psalter of 150; very often they said a third of it, or fifty psalms. From this common custom each third part of the Psalter came to be called a *quingena,* from the Latin word *quinquaginta,* meaning fifty. To say a *quingena* for a penance or to promise a *quingena* for a special intention was routine.

The laymen followed this custom with their "Psalter" of Pater Nosters. Sometimes they would say 150 of them; often only fifty at a time. And then they naturally started looking for ways of keeping count. Probably they used their fingers at first, or pebbles, or pegs. But we find historical evidence that as early as the twelfth century people used a cord or string, possibly with knots tied in it; and soon beads were strung on it to replace the knots.

Since these strands were used for counting Pater Nosters, they came to be called paternosters; and the artisans who made them were called paternosterers. Apparently the manufacture of paternosters became quite an industry in the Middle Ages. In the heart of the old city of London there is a little street called Paternoster Row; before the blitz of World War II it was a publication center. In medieval times it had received its name from its trade; it was the quarter for the Guild of Paternosterers, the members of which made prayer beads and probably other articles of devotion.

The word "bead" comes from an old English word,

124

"bede," which meant a prayer. The strings of little stones used to count "bedes" came, like the paternosters, to be called the same name as the prayers they numbered.

Back in the Middle Ages, physical forms of prayer had their part in the development of the Rosary. Genuflections, prostration, bows, and other gestures were repeated in number and often combined with Psalms, Pater Nosters, or other prayers. And these, too, were counted carefully.

At least by the eleventh or twelfth century the greeting of the angel Gabriel to the Virgin Mary was in popular use: "Hail, full of grace, the Lord is with thee. Blessed art thou among women." (Luke, 1, 28). It was used as a fond greeting, which, like all expressions of sincere love, remain fresh and new through multiple repetitions. Then gradually there was joined to it the greeting of Elizabeth to Mary: "Blessed art thou among women and blessed is the fruit of thy womb." (Luke, 1, 42). They fitted naturally together by an overlapping of the words they had in common. And the idea was intensified that, if we greet Mary, she will greet us back; and look what happened to Elizabeth when the Mother of Jesus greeted her!

These greetings—"Aves," or "Hail Marys," as they were called—came to be said in definite numbers, often fifty or 150, just like the Pater Nosters or the Psalms. In this way there developed a "Psalter of Our Lady."

If we jump a few centuries in our history we find a "mystery" attached to each Hail Mary. By that time the name of Jesus had been added at the end of the greeting, and the mysteries, recalling events of our Lord's life, were joined directly to His name, something like this: "Hail, Mary, full of grace, the Lord is with thee. Blessed art thou among women; and blessed is the fruit of thy womb, Jesus Christ, whom thou, O Virgin, didst conceive of the Holy

125

Ghost." Other examples: "Who didst die on the Cross for us," or "Who will come to judge the living and the dead." And thus through 150 mysteries. This was the "Psalter of Our Lady" at about the fifteenth century.

In our brief story of the development of the Rosary we have not woven into the picture all the strands of its growth. In the development of these 150 mysteries there were two other medieval "Psalters" which had great influence. As the monks chanted the Psalms of David they noted that many of the ancient words applied to our Lord either in a prophetic or an adapted sense. So poets went on from there, using words from each Psalm to develop quatrains or stanzas pertaining directly to our Lord and commemorating mysteries of His life. These came to be known as "Psalters of Our Lord Jesus Christ." Later on, similar Psalm adaptations were made to apply to Mary: "The Psalter of Our Lady." Since these consisted of 150 stanzas they readily supplied material for 150 mysteries.

In those days when a different mystery was added to each Hail Mary it was necessary to read the Rosary, since memory could hardly keep 150 mysteries in order. This type of Rosary, "Our Dear Lady's Psalter," might never have become popular except that the printing press then came into use. Sometimes pictures were added to focus the mind on the mystery. Each meditation was brief—a flashing scene, a rapid recall.

This inclusion of mysteries, to be contemplated while the vocal prayers were repeated, marked a great change in the Rosary's growth. Repetition was relieved of monotony. The beads and the words became an accompaniment to mental prayer, an aid to concentration, something for us to do while we think. The man who fingers his beads now resembles the little old lady who sits in her rocking chair

126

thinking peacefully while her knitting needles work rapidly, or the busy executive who doodles idly to aid his concentration.

Gradually the number of mysteries came to be modified. First, fifteen Our Father mysteries were added to the 150 Hail Mary mysteries, and then gradually replaced them. There is evidence that these fifteen mysteries, the same ones that we use today, were used in Spain by 1488, when a woodcut was made of them. In 1490 an altar was erected in a Dominican church in Frankfurt which portrayed these fifteen mysteries. A Spanish Dominican, Alberto da Castello, gets most of the credit for popularizing these fifteen Our Father mysteries. In 1521, a year made famous by Martin Luther, da Castello published a book entitled *The Rosary of the Glorious Virgin Mary*. His combination of the fifteen Our Father mysteries and the 150 Hail Mary mysteries, so that they fit together neatly, is extremely interesting. In 1569 a Bull of Pope Pius V mentioned meditation on mysteries as essential to gaining the Rosary indulgences.

It was not until the middle of the sixteenth century that the Hail Mary was completed in the form we have now. To the confident greeting of Mary there was spontaneously joined a humble petition: "Holy Mary, Mother of God, pray for us sinners now and at the hour of our death." Prayers in the same spirit had been known and used for centuries; now they took a definite, widely accepted form, and were joined to the Hail Mary. In many places the Hail Mary mysteries were still said or read after the Holy Mary was added; but gradually they were discontinued, with only the Our Father mysteries remaining as subject for meditation throughout each following decade of Hail Marys.

The great benefit of the Holy Mary was that it permitted the Rosary to be recited by groups in alternation. It had often been used in public prayer before, but now everyone could take a more spontaneous and active part in it.

The Doxology, "Glory be to the Father, and to the Son, and to the Holy Ghost," is a very ancient prayer in the Church, dating from the third or fourth century, but it was never found in the Rosary before 1500, and then only in isolated instances. It was probably two hundred years later before it was in general use; even in the nineteenth century the Rosary was sometimes said without it.

Certain definite dates are important in the history of the Rosary. In 1470 A Dominican of Brittany, Alain de la Roche, founded the Confraternity of the Psalter of Jesus and Mary, which did much to spread the Rosary devotion as it was then known. On October 7, 1571, Don John of Austria commanded the fleet of the Christian League in a resounding victory over the Turks in the Battle of Lepanto; and credit was given to the devout praying of the Rosary throughout Christian countries. Two years later, in 1573, the Feast of the Holy Rosary was established by Pope Gregory XIII. In 1716 the widespread praying of the Rosary was given credit for another important victory over the Turks, by Prince Eugene, in Hungary, stemming their advance into Europe. After that, Pope Clement XI extended the Feast of the Holy Rosary to the entire world; before, it had been observed only where there were confraternities.

Modern popes, beginning with Leo XIII, have done much to spread the devotion of the Rosary. And our Blessed Lady, herself, in her two greatest apparitions of the past century, Lourdes in 1858 and Fatima in 1917, gave the force of her own encouragement to this popular prayer.

Now you can see that the Rosary is the prayer of the people; they developed it, they love it, and they use it. It serves the peaceful recollection of private devotion and the united worship of public prayer. Its heart and spirit consist in meditation on the profound mysteries of our faith, and the life and love of our Lord Jesus Christ; but at the same time it gives the complete man, body and soul, opportunity to worship his Creator, by honoring the creature He chose to be His Mother.

Q. I am an Anglican, but with an increasingly strong interest in the Roman Catholic faith. There are, however, certain phases of that faith to which I cannot become reconciled (probably through ignorance), such as the matter of indulgences.

I have seen Catholic prayers with the notation that, if they are said at certain times and under certain conditions, this will entitle the person praying to "one hundred days indulgence"—which I presume means "one hundred days less to spend in purgatory." I have also heard and read that these indulgences can be purchased or can be obtained by performing a specific penance.

There is, as far as I can discover, no basis in Holy Scripture for this practice. How can anyone be sure that God will allow "time off for good behavior" merely because a certain prayer is said or a certain act is done? Who composes these various prayers? Why should one prayer be more efficacious than another?

Even if one could be sure that God would, under certain conditions, reduce one's time in purgatory, who can decide by exactly how many days? Where and when did the idea of indulgences first originate? Isn't this practice a little like bargaining with the Lord, "If I recite this prayer or do this act, You will see that I suffer a little less than is my due in purgatory"?—or would it come under the "Act of Faith" category?

130

A. No single doctrine or practice of the Church has caused more fuss and furor during the last four centuries than indulgences. When we consider the word itself we wonder why. The original Latin word meant a kindness or favor. As used in reference to God it indicated His love and mercy. Why then should it have become a cause of strife?

In its technical, doctrinal sense an indulgence involves many other doctrines; it is complex and not easy to explain. Consequently there are many distorted ideas prevalent about it, and enemies of the Church have valiantly demolished dozens of straw men under its gentle name. Then, too, the practice of indulgences has had, at times, an unfortunate history, marked by scandalous abuses. Infuriated by those abuses, the Protestant reformers of the sixteenth century threw out the whole doctrine to get rid of the errors. Deep feelings were induced by the controversies of that agitated century, and to this day it is seldom possible for Protestants and Catholics to discuss the subject of indulgences without raising their voices, or even to think seriously of the question without tightening their vocal cords.

However, your question is presented in an objective, dispassionate manner, even though it does reflect various prevailing errors. I shall try to answer it with similar spirit and seek to eliminate the errors.

To clear the decks, we should first explain what an indulgence is not.

It is not permission to commit a sin. God Almighty couldn't give you such permission.

It is not pardon of future sins. No power in heaven or on earth can pardon those until they have become things of the past deeply and honestly repented.

It is not forgiveness of sin itself; it supposes that the

131

guilt of sin has already been forgiven through God's mercy combined with the sinner's repentance.

It is not an exemption from any law or duty; and, particularly, it does not exempt from the obligation of restitution or repair of damages.

It does not give security from temptation. Neither is it a guarantee of salvation.

It is not an automatic release from purgatory. It does not even imply that the Church has any control over purgatory, or any knowledge of which souls may be there.

It cannot be purchased. Any direct effort to sell or buy it would be a grave sin of simony, and under present discipline the indulgence would disappear once any money changed hands regarding it.

Now, having cleared away some of the debris, let us look at the positive side. Because the idea is complicated, I will break the definition into parts, and then take up each part, trying to weave the connected doctrines into a complete explanation.

1) It is a forgiveness, or remission,
2) of the temporal punishment
3) due to God's justice
4) for sin already forgiven
5) granted by the Church
6) through the power of the keys
7) by application of the super-abundant merits of Christ and his saints
8) for a just and reasonable cause.

1. The idea of forgiveness is not difficult. We might note here, though, that an indulgence has no immediate connection with any of the sacraments. Baptism takes away all temporal punishment at the same time that it removes the guilt of sin. The sacrament of Penance takes away the
132

eternal punishment of hell and much of the temporal punishment, too, especially through the penance which is given in confession. But there is probably a measure of temporal punishment remaining after confession and penance are finished. It is with this that indulgences are concerned.

Indulgences should not be confused with private penances, which are very valuable in removing temporal punishment: prayer, fasting, almsgiving, and sufferings willingly borne. These are effective through personal merit. An indulgence is effective through the merits of Jesus Christ and the saints.

2. The idea of temporal punishment needs explanation. God's justice requires that the sinner be punished. The threat of punishment is salutary; it helps keep us from sin when love fails. But the threat would be idle if it were not enforced. For grave, unrepented sin the punishment is hell—eternal punishment. For lesser sin the punishment is temporary, either here on earth or in purgatory.

Even when the guilt of sin is forgiven, punishment is not necessarily taken away completely. When mortal sin is forgiven the eternal punishment of hell is taken away, of course. It would be a cynical and meaningless Mercy which would say to the repentant sinner: "I forgive you; I restore you to my love and friendship, you are now my adopted son; but I am going to send you to hell anyway; you deserve it for the evil that you have done."

On the other hand, it is a just and reasonable Mercy which says to the prodigal son: "I am very happy that you have come back to Me; I know that your sorrow is sincere; and I forgive you completely. But look at the harm you have done by your sins: you have thrown my order of goodness out of gear, caused harm and suffering to my people, given bad example to my friends and aid to my

133

enemies. That harm is not automatically undone when I forgive you. Don't you think you should do some penance to make up for it? Do some good works to balance the bad? Undergo some sufferings to compensate for your sinful pleasures? Don't you honestly believe that some prayers and penances would do you good, keep you from future sins? And wouldn't the sight of your punishment be a warning to others, especially to those you have scandalized?"

It is, therefore, a teaching of the Church that temporal punishments often remain after the guilt of sin has been forgiven. Much of this debt can be repaid here on earth by penances, prayers, sacrifices, sufferings, the Mass and sacraments, and by generous works of love and goodness. Indulgences may well remove the rest. Otherwise, they carry over into purgatory.

I have oversimplified, of course, and it may sound to you as if we leave our divine Redeemer and His propitiatory sacrifice out of the picture. On the contrary, the doctrine of indulgences reminds us that Jesus Christ, by the infinite value of His sacrifice, made up entirely for our sins and earned complete forgiveness not only of the sins themselves, but also of the punishment due for them. Our voluntary penances have propitiatory value because they are performed in union with the sacrifice of Christ, and value is attributed to them through that union. An indulgence applies the satisfying merits of Christ's sacrifice to our souls.

3. I think we have explained why God's justice requires temporal punishment. We might just point out here that an indulgence does not do violence to that justice. It doesn't set aside the claim or let the sinner off without

134

paying his debt. It rather gives him the spiritual means of paying for it in full.

4. Sin must be forgiven before there can be any question of gaining an indulgence. The sinner cannot be released from the punishment due him while he remains unrepentant and unreconciled. Historians have found some honest confusion on this point from a faulty interpretation of certain documents in the Church's archives. However, various popes and councils have repeatedly made it clear that indulgences have nothing to do with the guilt of sin, but only with the temporal punishment which remains as a debt after the guilt has been forgiven.

5, 6. The Church's power to grant indulgences follows logically from the power given her to forgive sin. Our divine Savior gave this power when He said to the Apostles, "Receive the Holy Spirit; whose sins you shall forgive, they are forgiven them; and whose sins you shall retain, they are retained" (John 20, 23). This power is ordinarily exercised through the sacrament of Penance, and through it the guilt of all sin may be forgiven, and the eternal punishment of hell taken away.

But this sacrament does not remove all the temporal punishment. So the power of forgiving sins would be incomplete if it did not include the taking away of this temporal punishment. And wouldn't it seem strange that the power of forgiving the big things, of taking away the guilt of sin and the punishment of hell, were given, but the power of forgiving the minor remnants were denied?

Actually, this power was given very clearly and without restriction. First it was given to St. Peter. "Thou art Peter, and upon this rock I will build my Church, and the gates of hell shall not prevail against it. And I will give thee the keys of the kingdom of heaven; and whatever thou shalt

135

bind on earth shall be bound in heaven, and whatever thou shalt loose on earth shall be loosed in heaven." (Matt. 16, 18-20). Then, later, Jesus gave similar power to all the Apostles. "Amen I say to you, whatever you bind on earth shall be bound also in heaven; and whatever you loose on earth shall be loosed also in heaven." (Matt. 18, 18).

This grant of power is unquestionable, and no limits are placed on it. The Church uses it with simple trust in her divine Founder: that when she grants an indulgence loosing the repentant soul from punishment on earth, Jesus keeps His word and looses that soul also in heaven.

It might be well to note that the fact of granting an indulgence by the Church does not necessarily mean that it is gained by the soul. Effort is required, performance of the good works and prayers enjoined; and the soul must be rightly disposed, free of the guilt of sin, inspired by good intentions. Evidently, the Church cannot control these inner dispositions of the soul.

7. The Church's vision is broad. At one and the same moment she sees God's justice demanding reparation for sin and God's mercy ready to wipe out the debt. She is always aware of the overflowing abundance of Christ's redemptive merits, which are constantly available to sinners; and she is sharply conscious of her own mission of bringing these merits to individual souls. Inspired by God's own mercy she has tended to "loose" often and liberally, knowing that her spiritual treasury is overflowing and that souls have great need.

St. Paul wrote some startling words in his Epistle to the Colossians (1, 24): "I rejoice now in the sufferings I bear for your sake; and what is lacking of the sufferings of Christ I fill up in my flesh for his body, which is the Church." By his zealous works, fervent prayers, generous

136

sufferings, St. Paul made up for far more sins than he ever committed. The remainder he turned over to the Church to add to the accumulation in her spiritual treasury. The other great saints of the centuries, especially the martyrs, did likewise. And the Mother of Jesus never had any sin of her own to make up for; yet she exemplified all the virtues. Her satisfactions were all surplus; they go in with the rest. It is the Church's mission on earth to be the custodian, administrator, and dispenser of this spiritual wealth. She guards it carefully and gives it lavishly.

I am sure that you have no difficulty in understanding how the merits of Jesus Christ can be applied to your soul and mine to take away our sins and punishments. But a couple of points should be explained if we are to understand how the satisfactions offered for sin by one human person can directly benefit another.

First, we should distinguish two spiritual results of our prayers, good works, penances, and sufferings: one is the merit which God attributes to us because of them, because they are done for love of Him; and the other is the propitiation, or satisfaction, which they offer to the divine Justice to make up for the harm of sin.

Merit is for ourselves alone; we cannot share it directly. But the propitiatory effects can benefit someone else. This is because we are united to our fellow men spiritually in the Mystical Body of Christ, and to the souls in purgatory and the saints in heaven by the Communion of Saints.

I cannot hope to explain these two doctrines completely in the space I have here available. Yet they are essential to the understanding of indulgences. St. Paul proclaims the idea of the Mystical Body clearly in Romans 12, 5: "So we, the many, are one body in Christ, but severally members one of another." Jesus had proclaimed a similar notion in

137

His parable of the vine and the branches (John 15, 1-11). We share His life and merits because we are the branches united with Him, the vine. And we share with each other because, in the words of St. Paul, we are all living parts of the same body; and the head of that body is Christ, who gives life to all the members and meaning to their works.

8. The Church can grant an indulgence only for a good and just cause. She is not the absolute owner of her treasury, only the administrator. She must distribute her spiritual favors in accordance with the wishes of Him who does own them, keeping in mind both His mercy and His justice. Usually her good and just cause is the right disposition of the penitent combined with his prayers and good works. She uses indulgences to encourage repentance, self-denial, reception of the sacraments, good deeds, and various acts of devotion. For her more important indulgences, she usually requires a sincere confession and Holy Communion. For the lesser ones there must be a contrite heart, and then the good works or prayers for which the indulgence is granted.

My doctrinal explanation has been so long that I have left myself no space in which to trace the history of indulgences in the Church. That history is both ancient and interesting; it is also both edifying and scandalous. It begins with St. Paul (II Cor. 2, 5-10), who uses his authority to grant leniency and reconciliation to a sinner. It continues through the days of the persecutions and public penances, when the martyrs granted "letters of peace" asking that friends of theirs be restored to good standing in the Church; and shows itself through following centuries in the spirit of mercy, leniency, and mitigation which attended the penitential system of the Church.

Probably the Crusades gave the greatest impetus to indulgences, which were granted very generously as a spiritual encouragenment to volunteers. Abuses were numerous in following centuries, culminating in the great clash of the sixteenth century; and then the Council of Trent made corrections which practically eliminated all abuses of indulgences from that time on.

There is nothing so beautiful or sacred that man in his perversity cannot find a way to abuse it. St. Paul had to be very severe in correcting misuse of the Holy Eucharist (I Cor. 11, 17-34). Even the holy martyrs, while giving their lives in heroic sacrifice, were guilty of abuse in giving their "letters of peace"; St. Cyprian had to caution them (Ep. XV).

In the Middle Ages money was the root of most of the evils in regard to indulgences. Almsgiving is a generous and meritorious work; it seemed quite right that spiritual favors should be granted to those who helped the poor, endowed hospitals, and built churches. But it was easy for the alms to seem a price for the indulgence; and the granting of indulgences seemed enticingly easy as a way of raising money—for good causes.

Even if a pope or bishop were free of all guilt in granting the indulgence, there was opportunity for corruption among the agents who preached the indulgence and collected the alms. Chaucer's Pardoner is a prime example, with his bogus relics and false indulgences.

However serious and widespread were the abuses at one time or another, indulgences were still used piously and properly by honest Christians. The Church knew that indulgences were good and right and profitable to salvation; so at the time of the Reformation she determined to correct the abuses and keep the indulgences.

Oh, say, I almost forgot that "one hundred days less to

139

spend in purgatory." An indulgence of one hundred days doesn't mean anything like that at all. I don't know how they tell time in purgatory, which is more than halfway to eternity, but I am sure they don't have days or nights there. Besides, the Church has no authority over the souls in purgatory; it is her mission to look after the souls on earth.

The early Christians used to do public penances. Our modern "indulgence of one hundred days" replaces one hundred days of that kind of public penance, and takes away the temporal punishment which that amount of public penance would have expiated. Time in purgatory cannot be measured in earthly terms.

When it comes to the souls in purgatory, the Church can only pray for them. In her prayer she offers to God from her spiritual treasury the propitiatory merits of Christ and the saints, and begs Him to apply them to the souls who suffer. She has confidence that He will hear her and extend mercy as far as His justice will permit.

Q. I pray to my Guardian Angel daily, using the prayer I learned in school, and I often ask for guidance. I know that my Guardian Angel helps me a lot. Will you please give me a general outline of the Church's teaching on this subject?

A. The teaching of the Church is that God has deputized His angels to take care of human beings living on earth. We are in their custody. They look out for our welfare. In the words of Psalm 90: "He gave thee to His Angels in trust, that they may keep thee in all thy ways . . ."

You remember those words of Our Lord (Matt. 18, 10) when He cautioned us that we must not despise little children, because "their angels in heaven always behold the face of my Father in heaven." St. Jerome, after reading these words, exclaimed: "great is the dignity of souls, that each one has from its birth an angel to take care of it."

A traveler, who takes the trail through dangerous forests, who expects to encounter snakes or beasts, who tramps across vast deserts, or sails stormy oceans, who fords rapids, or scales steep and icy peaks, has need of a guide on his journey.

We are travelers on our way to Paradise. Our road is often hard, steep, slippery and dangerous. Robbers and demons hide behind every tree. Various vices entice us into luscious but lacerating traps. We can easily lose our way and end up in hell. But God gives us an angel to be our

141

companion, our guide, and our guard. You do well to pray to him daily. Keep close to him. He knows the road. He sees the traps. The robbers and demons fear him.

Every man, woman, and child, Christian, pagan, or Communist, saint or rascal, has his own special guardian angel. It is a good thing most of them enjoy the beatific vision and are incapable of sorrow; otherwise they would be a sad lot, looking after many of us. But they never desert us, even though we sometimes run a long way from them and try to shame them from us.

Their work starts when we are born. They stick with us to death. After that we don't need a guardian. Our angel becomes our pal in heaven; or else we trade him for a demon to torment us in eternity.

Q. I read an article saying that statues originated from Protestantism and that the Church frowns on them, since they distract from the Blessed Sacrament. One church I visit has twenty statues.

I also read that the altars in the first churches were all like tables, as we see them in pictures of the Last Supper.

A. Where in the world did you read that article about statues? Neither Protestants nor Catholics would be pleased with an article like that, and historians would sigh in despair. Would you obliterate the memory and the masterpieces of the great Christian artists of the Byzantine and Classical traditions, the profusion of statues which graced the Gothic cathedrals, and the Renaissance triumphs of Donatello and Michelangelo and Bernini? Would you in the same sweeping gesture wipe out from history the militant efforts of Calvin and all his iconoclastic and Puritan followers to purge Christianity of its Romanistic idolatry of these same statues?

No, statues are as Catholic as tradition and as old as the churches which they decorate. The Church has never frowned on them unless they are in poor taste in their profusion, or their arrangement, or their lack of beauty. They should serve as aids to piety; not distract or disgust.

I agree that twenty statues in most of our diocesan churches would be about eighteen too many. But I don't want to start an argument on the subject. I attempted to

143

count the statues in one of our churches and lost count at fifty. I know another church in which the transept resembles Madame Tussaud's—with plaster replacing wax. But some people like it.

Statues need not distract from the Blessed Sacrament. They may help to provide a proper setting and serve to focus attention. If they do distract they should be ejected.

You are right that altars in the beginning were simple tables. Then quite soon the early Christians began to build their altars over tombs of the saints, with the sepulcher under the table; so that the simple table became more like a chest of wood or stone. Later the front of this chest might be decorated, as with sculpture or mosaic, or covered with rich draperies. This was the antependium.

Later the altar was raised on a platform, with steps leading up to it. Then the custom arose of building a little raised ledge along the back of the table as a handy place on which to set the crucifix and candlesticks, with probably some flowers or relics. Later the tabernacle was placed on the altar and then the number of these raised ledges increased on each side of the tabernacle, and back of it.

Quite early, in the big basilicas, the altar was covered by a canopy and this served as a place on which to set or hang a variety of vases, crowns, and ornaments. In the early days, before the tabernacle was placed on the altar, a gold or silver dove was suspended from the center of this canopy. It was the pyx in which the Blessed Sacrament was reserved.

In the Middle Ages it became customary to place an altar-piece or altar-screen back of the altar and above. This might be a picture, a tapestry, or a cloth richly embroidered or ornamented. Soon afterwards this picture or drapery might be replaced with a structure in metal, wood, or
144

stone, which would often be richly painted or decorated with gold and silver, mosaics, or enamels, and fitted with ornamental panels, niches, and statues. This was the reredos, ancestor to the towering "backs" which we find on many of our altars.

The Church has looked with approval on these and various other developments of the altar from the simple early table, as long as they remain in good taste, enhance the beauty of the Church and serve the sacred function of the altar. The Tradition of the Church has always been a living, growing thing.

Q. Since I have become a convert I have often wondered why the Church does not have the congregation sing hymns. In the Protestant churches there are many pretty hymns. Where did they get these hymns? Would it be a sin if I missed these hymns and occasionally sang them while doing my housework?

A. We all wish that we had more congregational singing in our churches in this country. The main reason we do not have is that few of our parishes have the musicians and the choir directors to teach and lead the people in good singing; and we are unwilling to compromise with poor singing.

Nearly all the parishes which have a parochial school do have congregational singing at the children's Mass; and we all realize that grown-up children of all ages would profit by the same devotion. It would arouse interest and help avoid distractions. It would give hearty praise to God.

In many Catholic countries the Church does have congregational singing. And we are slowly working our way toward it here. It is the particular aim of many of our Catholic musical educators. Give them a few more years and the effects will be seen in your own parish.

It is most natural that you should miss the hymns that you were accustomed to in the Protestant Church. There is an attachment to them from habit and sentiment. There

146

is certainly no harm in singing them in time with the rattle of your dishes, or the swish of your broom.

These Protestant hymns came from every imaginable source. Luther himself, composed some good ones, and Wesley, too. Calvin hated all songs; but his modern followers have appropriated the works of their brethren. Many hymns are set to old popular tunes or melodies stolen from the music masters. And many of them have Catholic ancestry.

4. Law and Authority in the Church

Is the Pope Infallible? What Is Canon Law? The Church as Censor. The Indissolubility of Marriage. Should Children Choose Their Faith? The Marriage of Catholics and Non-Catholics. Excommunication.

Q. Just what do Catholics understand by the infallibility of the pope? This seems to be one of the things which non-Catholics find most objectionable in the Church. All men are capable of error. How can you believe that a mistake is impossible for any man?

A. Of course the doctrine of infallibility does not mean that the pope cannot make mistakes or commit sins. If it did we could not possibly believe in it, because history tells us of whopping boners some popes have pulled and of shocking sins a few of them have committed.

Infallibility does not mean that the pope is inspired as

148

were the writers of Sacred Scripture to express the word of God; neither does it mean that the pope has doctrines privately revealed to him. He must learn his doctrine even as you and I, by studying and meditating it; in doubt he must consult and seek advice; in expressing himself he probably furrows his brow and thumbs his dictionary and bites his pen like most writing mortals.

In a way infallibility is a negative sort of thing; it does not tell the pope what to say, but it keeps him from saying the wrong thing in the limited area in which it is effective.

But we are starting at this thing all wrong. The infallibility of the pope is but one phase or aspect of the infallibility of the Church. We must understand the broader doctrine first.

Isolated teachings of the Church do not always make sense when you pull them out of context. Truth is integral, and one doctrine supposes many others which explain it and on which it rests. So infallibility supposes:

1) that God became man to redeem and sanctify us,

2) that while He was on earth Jesus Christ taught us many truths about God and about ourselves, about our purpose in life and the means of achieving that purpose— truths that are of vital importance to our salvation,

3) that He established a visible church to bring knowledge of His teachings and the means of salvation to all men in all lands and all ages,

4) that He intended all men to belong to this Church and imposed on them the obligation of accepting its teachings (Matt. 28, 18-20; Mark 16, 15-16),

5) that He wanted this Church to be one in faith and worship, and prayed that it should have such unity (John 17, 11-20),

149

6) that He promised to remain with His Church all days even to the end of the world (Matt. 28, 20),

7) that He promised to send the Holy Spirit to abide with His Church and teach His followers to observe all the things He had commanded (John 14, 16-26), and

8) that He promised His Church that the gates of hell shall not prevail against her (Matt. 16, 18). The gates of hell are the forces of evil, and the greatest evil which can beset a teaching organization is that it be entangled in error.

Obviously I cannot at this time attempt to prove the truth of all these doctrines to you. Suffice to say that we Catholics hold all of them firmly and that in the light of them infallibility makes striking good sense. If you reject one or another of them you pull out the doctrinal foundation of infallibility.

As we see it, Jesus Christ was wasting His time in teaching the great truths of God and heaven if He didn't give us some assurance of getting His teachings straight and understanding their meaning. The things He taught could never be known except through His word; they cannot be verified experimentally, by observation or trial and error, like the truths of science. And they are so deep and complex that it is hard to understand them completely and surely.

It is true that many of His teachings were written down, with God's inspiration. But by the time they were written He was no longer on earth. So if there were no reliable teaching authority left on earth how would we ever know which books contained His true teachings and which were only imitations? And even if we did know which books were genuine, how could we be sure that they contained all His teachings, that everything essential was written down,

150

or that some books were not lost? And even if we knew we had all the books, how could we be sure that we understood their meaning properly? Actually men who reject such teaching authority disagree widely and bitterly on the meaning of Scripture.

As we see it Christ could never have required that all men belong to His Church and accept its teachings—as He did require (Mark 16, 16)—unless He gave some guarantee that this Church would teach the truth. Can you imagine the good and just Lord saying: "I suppose this old Church will get clear off the doctrinal track and teach you all sorts of errors, but still he who hears her hears Me, and he who believes not will be condemned."?

Can you imagine Christ remaining with a Church which was teaching things contrary to truth and goodness? And yet He promised "I am with you all days, even unto the consummation of the world" (Matt. 18, 20).

Can you imagine the Holy Spirit, the Spirit of Truth, living in an organization which was all fouled up in doctrinal errors?

Infallibility is a simple and natural result of Christ's remaining with His Church and keeping His divine hand on it.

Infallibility simply means that the divinely appointed teacher is doing a good reliable job of teaching.

Infallibility simply means that God, who became man to teach His doctrines and gave His human life to vitalize and sanctify His teaching Church, is now expending the minimum of divine effort required to prevent His teaching work from being a dismal failure.

Infallibility means that the universal Church of Christ is protected from teaching error in the restricted areas of

151

faith and morality. It means that the Church as a whole, at any given time and in all ages, has the true faith.

The divine care which results in infallibility is given primarily to the Church. The pope is infallible only because he is the visible head of the Church. The head leads the body. So if the pope were to head off in the wrong direction the whole Church would soon be astray. In a negative sense we might say that the pope is infallible so that the Church will be protected from him. In a complete sense, his infallibility is for the welfare of the Church—for its doctrinal security and integrity.

Papal infallibility is a restricted thing. It is effective only when the pope speaks *ex cathedra*—from the Chair of Peter, as it were. He does that when he teaches solemnly and officially as head of the Church, clearly defining or declaring matters of faith and morals in such way as to make his decisions binding on the whole Church.

Q. *What is canon law? Why does the Church have her own law? Isn't the law of the State enough?*

A. Canon law is the law of the Church—that law by which she regulates her own internal affairs. The rules are for her own members. It is neither in conflict nor in competition with the laws of the State. It is in another sphere, generally concerned with other matters.

Canon law is found in the Code of Canon Law. It is made up of 2414 separate canons, or laws, many of them subdivided. In its origin it goes back to the time of the Apostles. In its present form it was published in 1917 and became effective in 1918. It is in Latin, and there is no authorized translation. It is published only by the Vatican Press, but is available in bookstores all over the world.

Canon law has had a tremendous influence on the development of civil law throughout all of Western civilization. One of the highest degrees our civil lawyers receive is that of LL.D.—Doctor of Laws. Have you ever wondered why there are two L's or why "Laws" is in the plural? Originally one of the L's was for civil law and the other for canon law. A man was not a thorough lawyer unless he was versed in both laws.

We will understand better why the Church needs her own laws if we consider some of the subjects treated in the Code. Even a list, by name, of all the different subjects

153

would exceed the length of this column. We will try to give a brief summary.

The first part of the Code deals with a variety of technical subjects primarily of interest to lawyers, such as the nature of laws, their extent, force, promulgation, repeal, and interpretation.

The second part deals with persons. You become a person, under the laws of the Church, by Baptism, and your status may differ because of your age, sex, place of birth or residence, your relationships with other persons, or the particular rite to which you belong. All these things are here defined and determined.

Considered first among the particular classes of persons are "clerics." Their rights and privileges, duties and obligations, are defined: everything from regular prayer, meditation and confession, to tonsure, roman collar, and celibacy.

Clerics hold various offices or positions in the Church. So the law next determines their appointment or election to these offices (and that involves an entire set of laws on the subject of voting and counting votes) and their resignation, removal, or transfer from these positions.

The greatest of all clerics is the Pope. His authority and position are defined in the law.

The Cardinals form the Senate of advisors or aides to the Pope. Their number, rank, appointment, duties and privileges are defined.

The Roman Curia is the government of the Church. It has its various departments or secretariates (Congregations), its offices, and its courts (Tribunals). Most of these are headed by Cardinals and staffed by a variety of bishops, monsignors, priests, and laymen, flanked and aided by a battery of consultors (technical experts, professors, big-

154

name canonists, theologians, etc.) The constitution, authority, and duties of these various Congregations (eleven of them), Tribunals (three) and Offices (four) are defined in the law.

Then there are ambassadors (legates) or delegates of the Pope in various nations and for special events. There are Patriarchs in certain venerable sees, and Primates in some nations. There are laws about each of these.

The various territorial divisions of the Church are governed by archbishops, bishops, vicars apostolic, prefects apostolic, and sometimes by abbots, or by apostolic administrators. There are laws for each of these; and yet other laws to provide for the administration of their territories when they die or become incapacitated.

The archbishops, bishops, etc. have a formidable battery of aides and delegates to help them in the work of the archdioceses, dioceses, etc., e.g. the vicar general, chancellor, *officialis,* notaries, canons, consultors, deans. There have to be laws about all these: their appointments, duties, rights, resignation, removal and the like.

Then, of course, there are pastors, and their assistants, and various types of vicars. It takes many laws to define their rights and duties, and to lay down the terms of their appointment and tenure.

More than two hundred canons are required for the various religious orders and congregations of men and women, their provinces, monasteries, convents, novitiates, cloisters, churches, and chapels. The meaning of their vows is determined, their ownership of property, and the election and appointment of their superiors.

After all that, remarkably few canons are needed for the laity. They are rather free and unfettered by law.

Up to this point we have been dealing with persons. Now the law turns its attention to things.

First and most important in this section are the sacraments and the Mass. There are separate chapters devoted to each of the seven sacraments; the manner of their administration; who can receive them and when and how, at what ages and under what conditions; the materials to be used; the ceremonies; the minister; sponsors; records, etc. The Eucharistic fast, the seal of confession, and the rules for ordaining priests all have their place.

Marriage presents a particularly complicated set of laws, defining the form, the impediments, dispensations, and requirements of consent.

The part on the Eucharist is divided into two sections: 1) the Mass, and 2) Holy Communion. You may imagine the number of laws required for these.

Then there are the sacramentals: consecrations, blessings, and the like.

Also under the heading of "things" are holy places: churches, chapels, cemeteries. There are laws about how churches are built, consecrated and desecrated; about their altars and furnishings. There are the laws about funerals. And many such things.

Then there are holy times: feast days, fast days, days of abstinence.

And there is the whole subject of divine worship: the care of the Holy Eucharist, statues, pictures, relics, vestments, church music . . .

Then there are laws about preaching, teaching the catechism, and giving missions. Laws about seminaries, colleges, and schools. Laws defining the right of the Church to teach. Laws about books, their publication and censorship.

There is much more; but we will pass it by.

The fourth book, or section, of the Code deals with trials under Church law; the intricate legal machinery which the Church uses to see that justice is done. We cannot possibly go into detail here. There are 642 complicated canons, which only lawyers are expected to understand. Their most common application is in the trial of marriage cases.

Heresy, simony, bigamy, abortion, and a variety of other moral derelictions are classified as crimes under Church law; and the Church has provided certain punishments to fit the crimes, primarily for the purpose of reforming the criminals. The Church uses no form of corporal punishment. The best known and most serious of her punishments are interdict (which forbids divine worship in a certain place), suspension (for priests guilty of crime), and excommunication.

As soon as the criminal has repented and given evidence of reform he must be absolved from these punishments. The Church is not vindictive. She punishes with love.

Q. Isn't the censorship which the Catholic Church prac-tices over books, movies, and television an invasion of the God-given right of freedom of thought? Shouldn't people have the right to choose between good and evil (using as a standard the teachings of the Bible) instead of acting as robots, blindly obeying commands?

A. Do you really know any Catholic robots? Mind and heart are essential to a good Catholic, and a robot has neither. The Church wants no blind obedience to her commands; she expects and she generally receives a free and intelligent obedience, which is prompted by love and based on sound reasons.

Your question does touch on one of the sorest points of present-day friction between American Catholics and non-Catholics. In a way, it is rather hard to understand. The Church's laws and censorship are imposed on her own members, not on non-Catholics. Yet you do not hear Catholics protesting.

The conflict arises from a series of errors and misunderstandings on both sides.

First is a failure to understand the meaning of freedom itself and the natural limitations which must be placed on it to prevent its becoming anarchy. I hope I do not offend if I suspect you of this error. You write about "the God-given right of freedom of thought." There is such a thing, of course; but your expression has the familiar light-
158

ness of a cliché. It is well to tear these phrases apart and see what they really mean.

God has given you an intellect for learning. It is designed by its Creator to encompass truth; it is being misused when it gets fouled up in error. Every God-given power we have carries with it an obligation that it be used in accordance with its nature and purpose.

Your God-given intellect therefore, implies a God-given obligation of seeking the truth by using that intellect. If we keep this in mind we will understand better what we mean by "freedom of thought."

The obligation of seeking truth is entirely between ourselves and God. It comes from God and we are answerable for it to God. And we are free before God, in accordance with the dictates of our consciences, when those consciences are clear and certain. If a dictator tries to force our thinking by brainwashing he invades our freedom of thought. But if an honest and competent teacher tries to aid one's intellect by guiding it to truth that is no invasion. God does not leave us isolated to flounder unaided through errors on our way to truth. He has given us parents, teachers, and the accumulated experience of generations, to help us to greater freedom. And Jesus Christ has given us his Church for the same purpose.

I am afraid that we Americans sometimes get a hazy, sentimental notion of freedom. We consider it in the abstract and rate it as man's greatest good, his ultimate goal in society. Actually, while freedom is essential, it is only one of the contributing factors to man's happiness in his life with his fellow men. Truth, goodness, justice, responsibility, and a stable social order are other necessary factors. These and various other values, spiritual, intellectual, and

159

material, together constitute the common good of society. This common good is the ultimate goal of society.

Freedom must sometimes be restricted to protect justice or the social order. When one man's freedom comes into harmful conflict with another man's rights, it must be restrained, for the common good. Freedom is indispensable for man's happiness on earth, but society requires that it be a responsible freedom, considerate of the interplay of other freedoms, of the rights of other men, and of the common good of all men.

The average Catholic holds freedom in as much love and veneration as his non-Catholic neighbor does. He may possibly see freedom more clearly in the light of duty, but he will fight just as quickly if you try to restrict him. He loves the American Constitution and its Bill of Rights as much as you do. It should not be necessary to say this; but there are indications of skepticism on this subject.

The second reason for conflict arises from a misunderstanding of authority in general, and of the authority of the Church in particular. We seem to forget that in society authority is necessary to protect our freedom. Our freedom of thought may be a matter between ourselves and God, but our freedom of expression involves our fellow men. Socially, our rights are often restricted by the opposing rights of others; and when the rights of two people meet head-on we need authority to resolve the conflict.

Authority exists to protect freedom. Yet there is always a measure of conflict between freedom and authority, because to protect the freedom of one person or group authority must often restrain the freedom of another person or group. Sometimes a suspicious liberalist sees only the restraint and forgets the purpose and justice of it. The true liberalist sees the freedom protected and respects the authority which guarantees his rights. Authority is the necessary instrument of order, and order is essential to true freedom in society.

The authority which suppresses legitimate freedom is tyranny. And maybe we are suspicious these days because we have recently seen, and still see, tyranny exercising flagrant, cynical suppression. Maybe a taint of the Marxian theory that the ideal society will find authority superfluous has seeped down into our thinking processes. The only man completely free of social authority was the cave man; the only way we could hope to enjoy freedom without authority would be to return to the social status of the cave man. Even then, bloody fighting would ensue.

As regards the authority of the Church, I will not try, at this time, to prove to you that Jesus Christ gave his Church authority to teach his eternal revealed truths and to guide her members to heaven. I will simply state that the Church honestly claims to have that authority and that her members believe and accept her claim. So they recognize her use of this authority as legitimate, and consequently accept with due respect the acts which result from it.

A third cause of conflict is confusion between the Church's teaching authority and her jurisdictional, or lawmaking authority. The Church is known to be strict about several moral questions on which modern American society is largely at variance with her. In the face of growing trends, she loudly condemns divorce, birth frustration, sterilization, abortion, euthanasia, and various violations of modesty and chastity. As a result, many non-Catholics consider her a tyrant.

Actually, the Church is simply teaching God's law. In none of these matters does she make laws of her own. She uses no coercion, except that she does have a simple ex-

161

communication, reserved to the bishop, for those Catholics who attempt marriage in heretical fashion, or who procure an abortion. Surely it cannot be called an invasion of freedom to teach right and wrong, especially when the Church firmly believes that she was established by Jesus Christ for the purpose of teaching right and wrong, and that He remains with her constantly to see that she does it correctly.

It would eliminate some conflicts if non-Catholics understood that the Church does not make all these "offensive" laws. Should she pass the buck back to God, who does make them? But even that would not remove all taint of authoritarianism. The Church does censor books and movies, and it seems entirely probable, in view of the recent Encyclical of Pope Pius XII, *Miranda Prorsus* that she will soon be censoring radio and TV. Isn't that un-American, anti-intellectual, and despotic?

The answer depends very much on the purpose, method, and extent of the censorship and the legitimacy of the authority with which it is done. We have already discussed briefly the Church's authority. But we might add that her attitude in all censorship is that of mother and teacher. She seeks to protect her children with the loving concern of a mother, teaching them truth, averting the confusion of error.

As regards methods and extent of censorship, it may help to outline the Church's laws, and then to indicate some of the things which are done by the voluntary efforts of her members.

One of the requirements of proper censorship is that it be competent. In the censorship of books the Church remains carefully in her own field: in the area of revelation, doctrine, and morality. She is precise and juridical in her laws and her methods. She defines the competence of cen-

162

sors and the means of recourse from their decisions, and the extent of her laws and various exemptions from them.

When Catholic censorship of books is mentioned most people think of the *Index of Forbidden Books*. Actually, the *Index* is only a minor feature of the Church's general concern with books.

First of all, she reserves to her own inspection and approval all texts and translations of Sacred Scripture; books of theology, canon law, and Church history; prayers; treatises on the spiritual life, piety, and devotions; sacred pictures; processes of canonizations; books of indulgences; decrees of the Roman congregations; and liturgical books. These are her own books, in the subjects in which she is teacher. She is naturally concerned that they be accurate.

The Church does not try to exercise prior censorship over books on secular subjects written by laymen. However, all books written by her own priests and religious must be submitted for approval before they are published. These people write in her name, and she wants to see that they do not misrepresent her teachings.

This is the positive side of censorship. It results in the imprimatur, a permission from the proper Church authority for a book to be published.

The procedure in obtaining this imprimatur is to submit the manuscript to the bishop's office (either the author's own bishop or the bishop of the place in which the book is published or printed) with request for permission to publish it. The bishop has a priest appointed to be *censor librorum*—censor of books. He turns your manuscript over to this priest and you will probably not know who he is until after you have received a favorable reply. This prevents the exercise of any undue influence.

If the censor finds no errors or objections to publication

163

he will give a *nihil obstat*—nothing stands in the way of publication. The bishop will then grant an imprimatur, "let it be printed." If you belong to a religious order you will also have to obtain the permission of your own religious superior to publish the book. This is usually inscribed as *imprimi potest*—"it may be printed" or *cum permissu superiorum*—"with permission of superiors."

If there should be some minor objections, the bishop will either call in the author and talk these points over with him, or list the objections in a letter to him. In this case the imprimatur will be delayed until corrections are made.

In some cases it may be necessary to deny the imprimatur. In such case the bishop will generally let the author know the reasons.

The negative side of censorship has the *Index of Forbidden Books*. It is made up largely of deep and dusty tomes of theology and philosophy, books which misrepresent in an insidious manner the teachings of the Church, subtly undermine the faith of her people, or tend to pervert their morality.

For the rest, the prohibitions are in general terms. For most of them, no penalties are set for violations. You might say that the Church simply makes each of us his own censor, and carefully lays down the rules by which we are to do the censoring. Like a kind mother she tells us the things to avoid, and then leaves it up to our own consciences. These are the types of books she forbids.

Texts of Sacred Scripture edited by non-Catholics.

Books which teach heresy and schism.

Books which seek to undermine and overthrow all religion.

164

Non-Catholic books on religion, unless they are known to be correct.

Books which teach false doctrine, superstitions, etc.

All books of Scripture, theology, canon law, Church history, prayers, devotions, and the like, which are published without the proper authorization, i.e. without an imprimatur. Particularly condemned are unauthorized books about apparitions, revelations, visions, prophecies and miracles, or those which advocate new devotions.

Books against any teachings or laws of the Church, and books which insult and libel the hierarchy or the clerical or religious life.

Books which teach or advocate superstition, fortune-telling, spiritism, etc.

Books which uphold duels, suicide, and divorce; and those which uphold Masonic and other similar secret societies.

Books which are professedly obscene. (This includes modern books by the thousands. They are condemned by law just as forcefully as if they were named on the *Index*. Most of them are too trashy and ephemeral to be given consideration by the Holy Office. Only capable authors get on the *Index*.)

Unapproved liturgical books, or books of false indulgences.

When a book is prohibited, either by the general law or by the *Index*, it is forbidden to print it, read it, translate it, keep it, sell it, or give it away.

The Church has used a system of censorship for centuries. No Catholic gets excited about it. Anyone who has a good sound reason for reading forbidden books, and is qualified to handle them, can easily get permission. Nobody is hurt, and the unwary are protected.

165

In the United States these days the *Index* raises little fuss, compared with the furor over the Legion of Decency and the National Organization for Decent Literature. Now, these two groups are widely held to represent the authoritarianism of the Catholic Church, her intolerance of freedom, and her desire to impose her will on non-Catholics. The fact is that they have no connection with the authority of the Church, as such. The Church has no law regarding either the Legion of Decency or the NODL. They are simply voluntary organizations of Catholics who pledge themselves to stay away from morally objectionable movies, or try to persuade dealers not to show or sell offensive magazines of sex and crime.

The Legion of Decency is a pressure group only in the general sense that if enough Catholics stay away from a movie it will have a noticeable effect on the box office. A member of the Legion of Decency takes a pledge that he will not go to movies which are morally objectionable and that he will not attend those theaters which make a policy of showing offensive movies. He does not assume any new obligation by his pledge; he simply promises to do what he believes he is already obliged to do by the moral law of God. No law requires him to take the pledge, and no law of the Church requires him to keep it.

The NODL is likewise a voluntary organization of individual Catholics following their own consciences. It lists magazines and comic books according to its judgment of their moral fitness or their exaggerated emphasis on crime, sex, and varied violence. It urges Catholic people to follow its ratings when buying magazines; it urges merchants to be guided by its ratings in selecting periodicals for sale; and it urges its own members to exert their personal influ-
166

ence on merchants to recognize their public responsibility.

It is probably true that both the Legion of Decency and the NODL have been used at times to exert more direct pressure. Sometimes that use has been legitimate. You may have a right, according to law, to show an objectionable movie. But I also have a right, as a citizen, to speak out publicly and forcibly against your showing it, and to get my friends to protest, too.

In some cases, the advisability of either of us exercising our rights may be questionable. You would probably be smarter if you didn't show the picture. I might be well advised not to raise such a fuss, thus advertising your picture and stirring up religious prejudices. But the question in such instances is one of prudence, not of right. I am not being un-American because I stir up the ire of Catholics against the foul movie. I am not denying your freedom; I am simply exercising mine.

Local Catholic groups, guided by Legion of Decency ratings, inspired by zeal and urged on by oratory, may have used the picket line as a means of protest. Other local groups may have induced the police to use their NODL list as a guide in the enforcement of censorship laws. In doing so they may have acted unwisely, but they have neither violated nor threatened the freedoms guaranteed by the Constitution.

They have, rather, used those freedoms. If conflicts develop, they must be judged and solved in individual cases on the local level. My freedom conflicts with your freedom. If we can't settle it ourselves, authority must intervene, in the interest of personal rights and public order, and the freedom of one or both of us will have to be restrained. Neither the Constitution nor the Bill of Rights is in any danger.

167

I said earlier that present tension results from a series of misunderstandings on both sides. You must have noticed that my clarifications have been aimed mostly at one side. I think our Catholic mistakes have been mainly in prudence and far-sighted wisdom. We have been so sold on the rightness of our aims that we have failed to evaluate the attitude and temper of our non-Catholic neighbors and have not made proper efforts to sustain their support. In their beginnings, both the Legion of Decency and the NODL had encouraging backing from many non-Catholics. Now the opposition has become so bitter that some non-Catholic leaders seem tempted to recommend immoral pictures in defiance.

We should lower our voices, sit down together, and talk things over. It doesn't help for us to shout "prejudice" and for them to scream "authoritarianism." We are, all of us, Americans jealous of our rights and freedoms. We are occasionally in conflict, but more often in misunderstanding. And the conflicts do not so much involve fundamental issues as questions of method and prudence.

After all, many non-Catholic organizations, some of them representing churches, are as quick to use organized pressure as any Catholic group. They frequently try to influence legislation, e.g. prohibition laws. Personally, we may find the WCTU annoying, and the laws it induces may restrict our freedom. But we do not consider it un-American or authoritarian. So you may call the zealots of the NODL meddlesome pests if they annoy you. But it will help clear thinking if you remember that they are voluntary groups of Catholics striving for morality and decency in their homes and communities. They may try to wield influence, but they are not authoritarian, because they have no authority.

168

Q. I thought that the Catholic Church did not allow re-marriage after divorce. But a Protestant friend says she knows some Catholics who have been divorced and re-married and who still receive the sacraments. I told her that the Church must have given them an annulment. Or does the Church grant divorces in some instances?

Would you explain the different factors that would make a Catholic marriage invalid?

If a Catholic obtained a civil divorce, remarried with-out consent of the Church, and had children by her second husband, what would she have to do to be reinstated in the Church?

If my Protestant friend, who is divorced, were to re-marry, would she have to leave her second husband in order to join the Catholic Church? In case her first mar-riage had been annulled instead, what then?

A. I wish I could give a simple answer to each of your questions, but I cannot, because the subject is too compli-cated. As a general rule, a marriage, once validly con-tracted, lasts until one of the parties dies. But sometimes a marriage seems to be valid when it really isn't; and some-times even a valid contract of marriage can be dissolved.

So I am going to try to give you a summary of the laws of God and His Church regarding the indissolubility of marriage. However, I am going to ask you a favor: if you are not prepared to read this carefully, please do not read

169

it at all, because you would find that a casual reading would confuse rather than clarify.

We must start by giving some definitions and making some distinctions. We should clearly understand the difference between a declaration of nullity and the dissolution of a marriage bond. A declaration of nullity is simply an official statement of proven fact; it has no effect on a marriage bond, because no real marriage bond ever existed. The dissolution of a marriage bond does have an effect on an existing bond; it breaks and destroys it.

Declaration of nullity. It occasionally happens that a man and woman enter into an apparent agreement which looks like a marriage; but closer examination reveals that something essential was missing from their agreement, so that it never became a real, valid contract. We will later indicate and explain some of the things which might be missing. But suppose that the Church examines a seeming marriage of this kind and finds that it was never valid, never a real marriage at all; she will declare that fact as she finds it.

Dissolution of a marriage bond. There are a limited number of cases in which it is possible for the Church to dissolve the bond of a real marriage. In these cases, the bond, while real and valid, is not so sealed and ratified as to be absolutely indissoluble.

Some more distinctions and definitions are going to be necessary before I can expect this to make any sense to you. All marriages are made by contract. For baptized people this contract is also a sacrament. When husband and wife live together they consummate their marriage by physical relationship. All three of these elements, the contract, the sacrament, and the consummation, are required to make a
170

marriage completely ratified and indissoluble. Let us consider each element briefly.

1. As a contract, marriage results from an agreement between a man and a woman by which they mutually give and receive certain rights and assume corresponding obligations. Generally speaking, if an agreement is to make a valid contract it must be sincere and honest; it must embrace all the essential features of the contract; it must be made between parties who are capable of giving the rights involved and fulfilling the obligations; and it must be made with that external solemnity or formality which the law or the nature of the contract requires.

We believe that the contract of marriage was established by Almighty God and that it is by nature holy. It permits a man and woman to live together in chastity and fidelity and in mutual love and cooperation. It permits them to cooperate intimately with God Himself in the creation of a human personality, destined to eternal life.

Indissolubility is a natural feature of this marriage contract. This is true because permanency is required for the full development of marital love, for the security of the home and the welfare of children, and for order and stability in society. However, that marriage which results from a contract alone is not so absolutely indissoluble that God cannot permit occasional exceptions, as He did in Old Testament times, and as St. Paul indicates in I Corinthians, 7, 12-16. (I will quote these verses later.)

2. Our Lord Jesus Christ made the contract of marriage into a sacrament for Christian people, that is for those who have been baptized. I haven't the space here to explain what a sacrament is, but it does make marriage much more holy than it was before. It makes marriage a means of personal sanctification for the husband and wife. Because it

171

unites them in grace and supernatural charity as well as in their natural love, it makes their marriage more permanent and indissoluble than it would be if it were an ordinary contract.

3. Marriage, then, is made by contract, and further ratified by being a sacrament, but it is not completely sealed and consummated until husband and wife actually live together and by their union with each other give and receive the rights promised in their agreement.

Now, keeping these three elements of marriage in mind, we can make a firm general statement which can guide us through the rest of our discussion. Once a valid contract of marriage has been made between two baptized persons and has then been consummated by their marital life together, it cannot be dissolved by any power on earth. Such a marriage has all three of the elements discussed above: it is 1) a contract, 2) a sacrament, and 3) has been consummated.

Let us suppose, however, that one of these three elements of a complete marriage is missing. If the contract is missing or is essentially defective, there is no marriage at all and there can be no question of dissolving the bond, or of granting a divorce or an annulment. You cannot dissolve or annul something which does not exist; you can simply declare its nonexistence, its nullity. If the sacrament is missing, the contract can be dissolved under certain limited circumstances, as St. Paul tells us in I Corinthians 7, 12-16. And if the marriage has never been consummated, even though it is a valid contract and a sacrament, there is a possibility of dissolving it, even though such a dissolution may be very difficult to obtain.

In cases where the contract is invalid we have declarations of nullity. In cases where the sacrament is absent we may have the Pauline Privilege, or, in more general terms,
172

the Privilege of the Faith. And if it can be proved that the husband and wife have never lived together in marital relationship, we may have a dispensation from the nonconsummated bond.

It is highly probable that those Catholics known by your Protestant friend to have been divorced and remarried have received declarations of nullity from the Church. Ordinarily the Church will not investigate the validity of a marriage contract until asked to do so by either husband or wife.

Sometimes this investigation will be very difficult and complicated. It is always careful and thorough. It may reveal one of three general types of defect which would make the marriage null and void: 1) lack of form or defect of that form; 2) an impediment; or 3) lack of proper consent. We will take a brief glance at each of the three.

Lack of form. The law of the Church requires that a Catholic be married before a priest and two witnesses, and this is required under pain of nullity, so that if a Catholic tries to get married in some other way, e.g. before a minister, or a justice of the peace, his contract is invalid and produces no marriage at all. This law does not apply to non-Catholics when they marry between themselves (Canons 1094 and 1099 of the Code of Canon Law).

In cases of this kind the facts are usually easy to prove and the legal procedure for a declaration of nullity rather simple. A baptismal certificate will prove that a person is a Catholic and a marriage certificate will show that he was married by a justice of the peace. The great majority of declarations of nullity given by the Church in the United States are given because of "lack of form": A Catholic tried to get married "outside the Church," and his attempted marriage had no value at all.

173

In rare cases, even though a marriage takes place before a priest, there might be a substantial defect in the required formalities which would make the marriage invalid. This may be difficult to prove and the procedure for its investigation is long and complicated.

Impediments. There are thirteen impediments which not only forbid marriage between certain persons, e.g. cousins, but also make the marriage invalid if attempted in spite of the impediments. These impediments result directly from Church law, but some of them already exist from the law of God, from the very nature of things. In deserving cases, the Church will sometimes grant a dispensation from the impediments she creates by her own law; she cannot dispense from those which result from the law of God.

I cannot explain all thirteen of the impediments here; I will discuss only the ones which are better known or might occur more frequently.

1. Bond of a previous marriage. A man who has a living wife may not marry another. A woman may not divorce her husband and validly marry another man. Efforts to do so result in an invalid second union which may look like a marriage to the casual observer and may be recognized as a marriage by the state but is actually no marriage at all.

In these cases the second marriage can usually be proved invalid without too much difficulty. John and Mary are husband and wife, but John gets a divorce and goes through a marriage ceremony with Susan. Then Susan divorces him and meets a Catholic man whom she wishes to marry. She asks the Church to declare her marriage to John invalid, because John had a living wife. A few marriage certificates, divorce decrees, and identification papers, will probably provide the proof necessary.

174

2. Disparity of worship. A baptized Catholic is forbidden to marry a nonbaptized person; if he attempts to do so in spite of the law, his marriage is invalid. The Church will often grant a dispensation from this impediment if there are good reasons, and the required promises are signed.

3. Blood relationship. Unless the Church grants a dispensation, near relatives may not marry each other.

4. Impotency. By the very nature of things a person may not validly enter into a contract which he is incapable of fulfilling.

5. Age. A young lady may not marry validly until she is fourteen; a young man must be sixteen.

The remaining impediments which make a marriage invalid are: affinity, i.e. relationship resulting from marriage; public honesty; Holy Orders; solemn vows; kidnaping for purpose of marriage; crime; spiritual relationship resulting from Baptism; and adoption, where state law makes the relationship of adoption an invalidating impediment.

Lack of free and proper consent. There can be no real contract of marriage unless both parties give their consent freely, and honestly intend to contract marriage as God established it. If a person were forced into marriage or driven into it by unjust fear, his marriage would be invalid. If the parties, in contracting marriage, were to make an agreement between themselves entirely contrary to the purpose of marriage or directly opposed to its essential properties, their marriage would be invalid. You may find this statement complicated, but let me assure you that the problems involved are much more complicated. Proofs of nullity on these grounds are extremely difficult, and the process of investigation is long and exacting.

Here are some examples: John goes through a ceremony of marriage with Susan because her father is standing right behind him with a shotgun. Force and fear might well make this marriage invalid. In another case there is no shotgun, but John simply goes through the ceremony so that the neighbors won't talk quite so much about the baby Susan expects. He makes it very clear to her that he does not consider it a real marriage and does not plan to live with her. He has an intention contrary to the marriage itself.

In still another case, John and Susan make it perfectly clear that they will give marriage a trial, but agree that if they start fighting they will get a divorce. They have an agreement contrary to the permanency of marriage. In still another case, John and Susan might firmly agree that they would never have any children in their marriage. Such an agreement might well be contrary to the primary purpose of marriage, and so make it invalid.

The fact that John's marriages are invalid in these cases is one thing, but proving them invalid is quite another problem. Intentions are hard to prove. And the Church will not declare a marriage invalid unless it is definitely proved so.

Now suppose that a marriage is valid, a real contract, but is not a sacrament. The parties to the marriage are not baptized persons, or at least one of them is not baptized. Under ordinary conditions such a contract of marriage is indissoluble, but in certain limited circumstances it can be dissolved *in favor of the faith,* which usually means that the dissolution permits a convert to join the Church, receive Baptism, and practice the faith. In most cases the existing bond of marriage is dissolved by the Pauline Privilege, to which we have referred twice already (I Cor. 7, 12-16).

St. Paul has been explaining the command of the Lord that a wife must not depart from her husband, and a husband must not put away his wife. Then he continues: "If any brother has an unbelieving wife and she consents to live with him, let him not put her away. And if any woman has an unbelieving husband and he consents to live with her, let her not put away her husband . . . But if the unbeliever departs, let him depart. For a brother or sister is not under bondage in such cases."

This privilege of St. Paul, the Pauline Privilege, applies only to the marriage of two nonbaptized persons. It presumes that one of them has, since the marriage, become a Christian and received Baptism, but that the other one remains unbaptized, and refuses to be baptized. Furthermore, the nonbaptized partner must refuse to live with the Christian in peace and harmony. In this case, when all the facts are proved, the new convert may be permitted to marry a Catholic. This second marriage, which is a sacrament, dissolved the first marriage, which was only a contract.

Now suppose that the husband has been baptized, but the wife has not, or vice versa; their marriage is still not a sacrament. It is a valid contract, and it has been consummated, but the sacramental element is missing. And remember that general principle we indicated before: the only marriage which cannot be dissolved at all is the consummated bond of a true sacramental marriage.

In this case, John, a baptized Methodist (or Lutheran, or Mormon) married Susan, a nonbaptized person. They get a divorce; then John becomes a Catholic and wants to marry a Catholic. It is possible that his marriage to Susan

177

can be dissolved in favor of the faith. The same would be true if Susan were the one who became a convert.

A dissolution of this kind is rather difficult to obtain, however. It can be granted only by the Pope, and he will not grant it unless 1) the essential facts are clearly proved, especially the non-baptism of one of the parties; 2) there is a very good spiritual reason for granting it, e.g. it will permit a convert to practice the faith and the members of a family to be raised Catholics; and 3) no scandal or harm to religion will be caused by granting it—society in general must not suffer that an individual may receive a favor.

Now we come to the dispensation from a nonconsummated marriage. Two baptized persons have entered a valid marriage. It is both a contract and a sacrament. But the two have not lived together as husband and wife; their marriage has not been consummated. Such a situation is rare, and the fact of it is extremely hard to prove. But occasionally it does happen, and sometimes it can be proved beyond any reasonable doubt. In that case, if it is for the evident good of souls, the Church will dissolve the nonconsummated bond. Here again, only the Pope can grant the favor.

The dissolution of a nonsacramental bond, or of a nonconsummated bond is a kind of annulment. The Church, using the authority given her by her divine founder, Jesus Christ, nullifies the contract which exists. She considers this a favor, not a right; and she grants it only for the spiritual welfare of the parties involved. And again, remember this: the Church can never, under any circumstances, dissolve the valid marriage of two baptized persons who have lived together as husband and wife.

Q. A lifelong friend of mine, baptized and confirmed in the Episcopal church, married a good Catholic and had three children. She is now a widow. Almost from the start, she and her husband quarreled over their children.

Before they married, she had repeatedly told her fiancé that she could not, in conscience, agree to raise their children in his faith. Nevertheless, she did sign promises to do so, and after the children were born her husband kept reminding her of this. She realized that harmony was essential; so she reluctantly capitulated, and the children were being raised Catholic. But she felt resentful, left out. She wished her children to grow up tolerant, visiting other churches, respecting all sincere religions, and felt that her husband's Church rigidly barred such procedure.

After her husband died she moved back East to be near her parents, and suddenly the children were no longer attending a parochial school or going to Mass. They were attending an Episcopal Sunday school, finding a whole new outlook, and beginning to pelt her with questions. But now the oldest boy has begun to "investigate" Catholicism, and his mother is glad that he is having talks with a wonderful priest. They are now a very happy family— but the bitterness lingers on.

What right does any Church have to coerce any person into signing an agreement to raise any future children as Catholics? Isn't this contrary to the Constitution, which

179

guarantees freedom of religion? How can anyone be free if he is rigidly reared in one Church?

These arguments come from my friend. I cannot believe that there is any "ulterior" motive in the Church's insistence that children of marriages solemnized by the Catholic Church be raised in that faith. I know that the Catholic Church claims to be the one and only Church of God. My own children attend the Episcopal Church, but they must make up their own minds about religion when they reach the proper age. And as my husband says, if we give them a sound rearing in belief in God, they'll decide rightly.

A. Your question involves many problems. I readily distinguish five separate ones, all closely related.

1. Is the Church wrong in exercising authority, making laws for her people, apparently restricting their rights, and imposing duties on them?

2. Does this exercise of authority by the Church violate our American constitutional guarantee of freedom of religion?

3. Should children be raised to choose freely their own religion?

4. What are the consequences of the Catholic concept that there is only one true Church?

5. Is the Church tyrannical in requiring that the marriage promises be signed?

I shall try to propose some brief answers to each in turn.

1. Your question about authority, rights, and duties touches on the most frequent practical source of misunderstanding between Catholics and non-Catholics in America today. We all insist strongly upon our rights, but to the Catholic the authority of the Church is the means of pro-

tecting our rights, whereas to Protestants the Church appears as an authoritarian dictator infringing on liberties.

If we are to understand rights, we must know that they are not conferred on us by the government, nor granted to us by the Constitution. They are given to us by God. Since God gives them to us, we should exercise our rights in accordance with His wishes. Consequently, our rights are not unlimited. They are restricted by our duties, which result from the rights of others—God and our fellow men.

God had a purpose in creating us. Our rights fit into that purpose. God had a purpose in redeeming us, and in revealing truths to us. We have no right to violate God's laws, reject His teachings, and lose our immortal souls. Neither do we have a right to lead another person to hell, or to permit someone for whom we are responsible to lose his soul. The father of a family assumes certain obligations to his wife and children. He has no right to renege, to let his family starve, physically or spiritually.

In human affairs, the proper regulation of rights and duties often requires authority. We have our Constitution to guarantee that certain basic rights will not be infringed. We have a government to determine in detail what our rights are and to protect us in them, to determine what our duties are, and to see that we perform them. When the government uses its authority wisely and justly, for the common good, we certainly do not consider it inimical to our rights.

We have souls and are destined for heaven. So we have many rights and duties in the spiritual field. These come from God, too. But we frequently need an authority to determine them precisely and guide us in their exercise. We Catholics believe that our Lord Jesus Christ gave authority to His Church to protect our spiritual rights and

181

direct us in our spiritual duties. She exercises her authority in His name, not arbitrarily, but for the general welfare of His flock, to help its members live rightly here on earth and to get them safely to heaven. Her authority is in no way dictatorial; it is rather like the solicitude of a loving mother. She does not coerce, but insists on duties as a protection of rights.

2. We Americans often become confused on the subject of freedom of religion. Maybe one reason is that many of us have never read and understood the First Amendment to our Constitution. It begins, "Congress shall make no law respecting an establishment of religion, or prohibiting the free exercise thereof."

As traditionally interpreted by our Supreme Court, the general words of the Fourteenth Amendment, "No state shall make or enforce any law which shall abridge the privileges or immunities of citizens of the United States," prevent any one of the forty-eight states from making any law respecting an establishment of religion, or prohibiting the free exercise thereof.

So our American freedom of religion means simply this: There is no government church, no state church, no preferred church; and neither the United States government nor any of the states shall make a law which prohibits any person or group of persons from exercising their religion in accordance with their consciences.

It is because of the basic freedom thus guaranteed that Quakers are exempted from military duty as conscientious objectors, that Jehovah's Witnesses are permitted to annoy us with their phonographs and literature, and that the Catholic Church can refuse to grant a dispensation for one of her members to marry a non-Catholic unless the promises are signed.

182

Far from violating the "freedom of religion" clause of the Constitution, these promises are guaranteed and protected by that clause.

3. You can't raise children in a vacuum, or keep the child's mind carefully free of religious convictions and expect it to make an intelligent choice of religion. You show that you are more aware of this principle than you think. You are careful to give your children "a sound rearing in belief in God" so that they can decide rightly.

Now suppose that your husband were an atheist instead of a Christian. What would you do then? Would you be able to give the children a "sound rearing in belief in God"? Your husband would object. Or suppose that a husband were a bank robber who believed proudly in the skill of his lucrative profession and decided to train his children early in the fine art of safecracking. Might not his wife run into conflict there?

You see my point, of course. Where mother and father have different convictions, there is surely going to be conflict or confusion in the teaching of their children, unless previous agreements are made—and kept. You can raise children moral or immoral or morally indifferent. But you can't raise them without *some* attitude on morality. You can raise them as believers, atheists, or agnostics. Or you might confuse their minds hopelessly by mixing up all three beliefs. You can raise them as Protestants, Catholics, or religious indifferentists. But you can't possibly leave their impressionable minds uninfluenced.

It all depends on the point of the conflict. You would be greatly concerned if you were not able to give your children a "sound rearing in belief in God." You do not happen to consider any particular denomination to be of vital importance. The Catholic is greatly concerned if he can

183

not raise his children Catholic, because he does consider the faith a matter of vital importance.

4. And that brings us to a consideration of that basic Catholic concept which irritates non-Catholics very much: that the Catholic Church is the one and only true Church of Jesus Christ. Of course you don't agree with us, or you would be a Catholic yourself. So argue with us, if you will, and try to prove us wrong, if you can; but admit it to be a fact that we Catholics are absolutely convinced that ours is the true Church.

Now it is a logical consequence of this conviction that Catholics are strictly bound in conscience to raise their children Catholic, and they will know that they are guilty of serious sin if they neglect this obligation. Consider the point of view of a good Catholic father, like the husband of your lifelong friend.

He loves his children and wants them to be happy forever in heaven. He knows that the only means our Lord established on earth to get people to heaven is His Church. Can he be happy then if he sees his children outside that Church? Would he let his children risk damnation?

He believes that the Church is the Mystical Body of Christ, that it is the means of our intimate union with our Savior. Through it we receive a share in His divine life, His grace, which is the means of our salvation, the beginning of our life of heaven. Can he bear to see his children deprived of such benefits?

He has great love for the truths taught by Christ: truths of love and forgiveness, of redemption, and of union with God Himself. Can he be content to deprive his children of these inspiring truths? Or even of half of them?

He loves the Savior who died to redeem him. And he recalls many words of the Master similar to these: "I am the Good Shepherd . . . other sheep I have, that are not of this fold; them also I must bring, and they shall hear my voice, and there shall be but one fold and one Shepherd." Can he blithely close his ears to such an invitation of love? Missioners give their lives to heed these words.

He knows that religious indifference is one of the most dangerous spiritual epidemics of our time and country. As he sees his own children grow up without firm religious convictions, he knows that he is preparing them precisely for such indifference, and probably for a complete loss of faith.

Can a good father say, "I am going to be a Catholic and save my own soul, but let my children grow up and take their own chances. It is their life; they must be free. If they go to hell it's their own fault"? No, he knows that he will almost surely be there first to meet them when they arrive.

You believe in truthfulness, justice, and temperance; so you do not want your children raised as liars, thieves, or drunkards. Catholics believe firmly in God's Church; so a Catholic will not have his children raised as atheists, heretics or agnostics.

5. To understand the reasonableness of the Church in demanding that the promises be signed, we must first recall how strong is the opposition of the Church to mixed marriages. It is not because of bigotry or prejudice that she opposes them. It is because her long experience has taught her the dangers they present.

There is danger of marital unhappiness and complete marriage failure. Religion can be an inspiring source of unity in marriage when two people share intimately the same convictions, ideals, and aspirations, when they say their prayers together and make their sacrifices together,

185

for the love of the same God. Religion is then something shared, as all married life should be shared. But religion can be a profound source of division when convictions clash and ideals diverge. Statistics indicate that there may be four or five times as many divorces in mixed marriages as in unions between two Catholics or two Protestants.

There is danger that the Catholic party may lose his faith. He may succumb to indifference, compromise, lack of support, discouragement, and the fatigue of conflict.

There is danger for the faith of the children. They will be bewildered by indifference, insecurity, conflict, and divided loyalties.

The first duty of the Church, as a loving mother, is to guard the faith and morality of her children and get them to heaven. She wants to protect them from dangers. So she forbids mixed marriages. Her law is strongly worded. She intends it to be forceful.

Law is made for the general welfare. But a loving mother is always moved by exceptional needs. In a particular case, she judges that greater harm will be done to one of her children if he must obey the law; so she begins to think about making an exception for him. She knows that exceptions weaken the law, and that others will want exceptions, too. But still she can not forget the particular needs of this one person.

She would be a poor mother, however, if she simply excused her child from the general law and let him face all the dangers, unprotected. If she did that she would be forgetting her primary purpose of looking out for his faith and morality and his soul's salvation. So she tries first to remove the dangers, or to give him protection against them. She does that by getting the parties to promise that there will be no loss of faith; and before she grants

186

the dispensation she must have assurance that the promises will be truly kept.

If the Church did not insist on the obligation of Catholics to raise their children Catholic, she would have to deny that she is the one true Church, the Mystical Body of Christ.

If the Church were to grant a dispensation without requiring that the promises be signed, she would be giving formal permission for the children to be raised as pagans or heretics, or without any religion at all.

The Catholic has no quarrel with his Church in this matter. He knows that she is exercising her legitimate authority, as given her by her divine Founder, to protect his rights and his spiritual welfare. But what about the non-Catholic who is asked to sign? Is it not an imposition? Is it not coercion?

The Church has no law which touches the non-Catholic directly. Her laws are for the Catholic. She does not command the non-Catholic to sign. In many cases she would prefer that he refuse to sign. Then she could refuse to grant the dispensation.

Her law speaks to the Catholic party in this manner: You are asking that a dispensation be granted you, that you be exempted from the general law wisely made for the common good. Have you considered the dangers you will run if an exception is made? What assurance do we have that these dangers will not ruin you?

The Catholic party will reply: We have made very solemn promises, both of us, that my faith will not be endangered and that the faith of our children will be protected. You can believe us; we are very sincere about it.

It is only after the Church has assurance that the prom-

187

ises have been made and will be kept that she will grant a dispensation.

Is that coercion?

My word of advice to the non-Catholic: Don't sign, unless you fully understand those promises in all their implications and are sure that you can keep them. But once you have signed, keep them faithfully. Otherwise your betrayal of trust will guarantee the unhappiness of your marriage.

Q. I am a Protestant and plan to marry a Catholic woman fifty-three years old. What are the laws of the Church for our marriage? Please give all the details.

A. This is a mixed marriage. The difference of religion is an impediment. You will need a dispensation from this impediment. The priest will obtain it for you from the Bishop, who has special authority from the Pope to grant it, for sufficient reason.

Before the priest can ask for this dispensation, the following things are necessary:

1. You must take some instructions in Catholic doctrine, probably six. These are aimed at answering your questions and doubts, giving you a general knowledge of your wife's religion, of why she believes and does so many things which seem strange to you: why she won't eat meat on Friday, why she must go to Mass on Sunday, what the rosary means, the truth about confession, and purgatory, worship of the saints, and the price of indulgences! These instructions are not for the purpose of making you a Catholic (you would need five times as many instructions for that). But they let you know what you are getting into in marrying a Catholic, and they should eliminate many misunderstandings and arguments in your married life.

In the course of these instructions you will learn the Catholic teachings about marriage:

a. Its holiness. If you are baptized, it will be a sacrament

189

for both of you—a means used by Jesus Christ to give you the graces needed for a happy and successful marriage. Even if you are not baptized, it is a contract instituted by God to join you and your wife together for life, in a love which is based on His own love for each of you.

b. Its indissolubility. Neither of you can ever marry again while the other lives. Ordinary honesty and decency requires that you understand and accept your wife's convictions in this regard. She is marrying you irrevocably for life. It is not fair that you do less for her. Otherwise your contract would be one-sided, unjust and selfish. If you leave her, you leave her stranded on lonesome shoals for life.

c. Its unity. You must each be faithful to the other— forsaking all others, excluding all others who might detract from your mutual love and obligations.

d. Its primary purpose, which age will probably not permit you to achieve: cooperating with God in creating new life.

e. Its other purposes: Your mutual love, happiness, and help, physical thrills and comfort, intellectual companionship, emotional fulfillment and spiritual development, the working out together of your purpose on earth and your happiness in heaven.

2. It is only fair to you that you should have the benefits of these instructions, because you will be required to sign solemn promises before you can get that dispensation. You should fully understand what you are signing.

a. The first promise should offer no difficulty. It is simply that you will not interfere in any way with your wife's practice of her religion. Not by taunts and gibes, not by ridicule and mockery, not by sullen pouting or manifest

190

displeasure, not by unwillingness to provide transportation to church, or reasonable help, even in financial requirements.

b. The second promise offers no difficulty to you, either. In fact you will probably consider it a formality. But regardless of your wife's age and the improbability of your having any children, you must both sign promises that any children born of your marriage will be raised in the Catholic Church, taught Catholic doctrine, and trained in sound Christian morality.

3. Before your marriage takes place, the priest will ask you a number of questions to make sure that you are free to marry. He will ask the same questions of your fiancée. And you will both be expected to answer under oath. He will want to know the following points:

a. Were you ever baptized? The kind of dispensation needed will depend on this. If you have a baptismal certificate, he will probably want to see it.

b. Were you ever married before? If you were, is your wife dead? If you have a living wife, the Church can hardly permit you to acquire another—even though you may have a divorce from the first.

c. Are you entering this marriage with perfect freedom, intending that it should last until death?—intending faithfulness in your marital life, and without any intentions or conditions contrary to the purpose or nature of marriage?

d. Are you intending to observe the laws of God regarding proper marriage relationship? In your case there could hardly be reason to do otherwise and the question will probably be passed over as a formality. But in most mixed marriages, it is important to know that the non-Catholic intends to respect the conscience of the Catholic in such matters as birth control. Otherwise the Catholic's earthly peace and happiness may be forfeit and eternal salvation placed in critical peril.

It will take much less time for you to answer these questions than it does for me to write about them.

4. Now you are ready for the marriage itself. Ordinarily your marriage will take place in the sacristy or the rectory of the church. But if you, or your bride, want to have it in church, the Bishop will probably grant permission.

In any case, you must be married before the priest. Your marriage to a Catholic would be invalid otherwise. Usually that priest is the pastor or assistant in the parish where you are married. Any other priest must be delegated by that pastor or assistant—or by the Bishop.

Your marriage should take place in your bride's parish. If you want to be married somewhere else, she will have to obtain her pastor's permission.

There will have to be two witnesses at your marriage. They should be Catholics, but for good reason the Bishop will probably grant you permission to have at least one non-Catholic.

The ceremony itself will be very short and simple. Your bride may make you don tie and tails, if she wishes. The Church will gladly marry you in much plainer garb. In any case the acute stage of your agony will be quickly over —and then you will only share the chronic pains of other husbands.

All this must seem frightfully complicated to you. It really is rather simple. Just report to the priest in good time, at least a month before the marriage, and he will take it from there. You mostly remain passive—and that attitude may well continue for years.

192

Q. In your Question Box a few weeks ago you wrote about a Catholic girl converting a non-Catholic boyfriend. Just what does the Church say about mixed marriages? You used the word "forbid." Each day brings more Catholics in contact with this serious problem of mixed marriages. If we all were better informed we could face the problem much easier.

A. I can think of no better way of answering your question than simply to translate the law of the Church:

Canon 1060. The Church everywhere most seriously forbids marriage between two baptized persons one of whom is Catholic and the other a member of an heretical or schismatic church; and if there should be danger that the Catholic party or the children be led astray, then such marriage is also forbidden by the divine law.

Canon 1061. The Church does not grant a dispensation from this impediment of mixed religion unless:

1. Good and serious reasons urge it;

2. The non-Catholic spouse gives a pledge which will remove danger of the Catholic party's being led astray; and both parties give a pledge that all the children will be baptized and educated exclusively in the Catholic religion.

3. There be moral certainty that these pledges will be fulfilled.

These pledges shall ordinarily be made in writing.

Canon 1064. Bishops and pastors shall:

1. Keep the faithful from mixed marriages, as far as they possibly can;

2. If they can't prevent them, then they shall exercise every care that those marriages shall not be contracted contrary to the laws of God and His Church;

193

3. Keep a close watch on mixed marriages which have been celebrated in their own territory or elsewhere, to see that the parties faithfully carry out the promises they made.

Canon 1070. That marriage is null which is contracted between a nonbaptized person and a person baptized in the Catholic church or converted to the Church from heresy or schism.

Canon 1071. Everything which the law prescribes in Canons 1060–1064 for mixed marriages must be likewise observed for marriages which are forbidden by the impediment of disparity of cult.

Canon 1102. In marriages between a Catholic and a non-Catholic . . . all sacred ceremonies are forbidden; but if the Bishop forsees that greater harm will result from this prohibition, he may permit any of the usual ceremonies, except that in no case shall the marriage take place at Mass.

I will make a brief summary to clarify the above legal language:

1. Mixed marriages (between a Catholic and a baptized non-Catholic) are most severely forbidden.

2. Marriage between a Catholic and a non-baptized person is most severely forbidden, and is invalid. This is the impediment of disparity of cult, or diversity of worship.

3. The Church will not dispense from either one of these impediments unless the promises are signed and there is moral certainty that the promises will be kept.

4. Bishops and pastors are commanded to exercise their zeal and care to prevent mixed marriages, to see that they are contracted properly, and that the promises are kept.

5. In accordance with Canon 1102, the Bishop often permits that a mixed marriage take place in Church.

194

Q. I read that the Pope has excommunicated all militant communists: What will be the effect of this excommunication?

A. The Holy Office, acting in the name of Pope Pius XII, has imposed the punishment of excommunication upon all those Catholics who shall belong to Communist parties and make open profression of communistic doctrines, or shall teach these doctrines, or take active part in spreading or defending them.

The excommunication will be incurred *ipso facto.* Consequently it will not be incurred for past acts, but only for crimes committed in the future, with full knowledge of the penalty imposed. Those who have been members of the Party but give up their membership now will not be excommunicated. Those who have been active Communists but now cease their activity will not incur the penalty.

The excommunication is reserved "especially" to the Apostolic See. This means that only the Pope can absolve from the penalty, once it is incurred—except in urgent cases or in danger of death.

Excommunication is a personal punishment imposed by the Church for certain crimes against faith, or morality, or Church authority, or discipline.

In canon law there are many excommunications imposed as punishment for a wide variety of crimes. Here are a score of them:

1. Apostasy, heresy, or schism.

195

2. Editing, publishing, defending, reading, or keeping certain kinds of forbidden books.

3. Attempting marriage before a non-Catholic minister.

4. Entering marriage with an agreement that the children—any or all of them—shall be raised outside the Catholic Church.

5. Having one's own children baptized by a non-Catholic minister.

6. Permitting one's own children to be educated in a non-Catholic religion.

7. Desecration of the Blessed Sacrament.

8. Someone not a priest pretending to celebrate Mass or hear Confession.

9. Making, selling, or distributing false relics.

10. Selling Indulgences.

11. Recurring to the authority of the state to overrule the acts of the Holy See.

12. Making laws against the liberty or rights of the Church.

13. Making use of the state authority or police powers to prevent the Church from exercising her rightful authority.

14. Joining the Masons, or any other association of this kind which seeks to overthrow the Church or legitimate civil authority. (Canon 2335.)

Under this heading many authorities have claimed that members of the Communist parties were already excommunicated—long before the present decree of the Holy See. The Communist party certainly seeks the overthrow of the Church and the State.

It would seem that the Holy See wishes, by its present decree, to make perfectly clear that active Communists *are* excommunicated. There might be doubt as to whether

Canon 2335 applied to them. There can no longer be doubt that they are excommunicated.

15. Attacking, physically, the Pope, cardinals, bishops, priests or religious.

16. Stealing or unjustly appropriating property of the Church.

17. Priests attempting marriage.

18. Counterfeiting papal documents.

19. Being guilty of simony in appointments or promotions in the Church.

20. Engaging in various abuses in the administration of the sacraments or the exercises of ecclesiastical authority.

There are still others. All these excommunications are incurred *ipso facto*. But they are all medicinal punishments, imposed for the reform and cure of the criminal. Once the excommunicated person has repented and given evidence of reform, he can and must be absolved from the excommunication. But this absolution can be given only by the person to whom it is reserved.

Many excommunications are reserved to the bishop. He can absolve when the criminal has repented and reformed. Many others are reserved to the Holy See; in these absolution can be obtained only from Rome.

But the Church always provides for urgent cases, and particularly for the urgent danger of death. Any priest can absolve from any excommunication in danger of death. In more serious cases, if the person recovers, he must report the matter to the Holy See.

In general the effect of excommunication is to separate the person from "communion" with the faithful. The most important effect is that it deprives him of the right to receive the sacraments. He cannot gain Indulgences. He has no part in the public prayers or ceremonies of the

197

Church. He cannot vote in Church elections; he cannot obtain or exercise any office in the Church. But the ordinary excommunicated person may go to Mass, and of course he is personally obliged to do so. Excommunication does not take away the obligations he has as a Catholic.

5. *The Church and Non-Catholics*

Heretics and Heresy. Is there Salvation Outside the Church? Other "Catholic" Churches. How did Orthodoxy Begin? Are Anglican and Orthodox Orders Valid? The Church and Masonry. Inter-Faith Marriages. Catholic and Non-Catholic Cooperation. What Was the Inquisition? The Church and Freedom of Speech. Can Catholics Be Tolerant?

Q. What is your definition of a "heretic"? Frequently we read in Catholic publications that Protestants are heretics. This is offensive to Protestants, who are not conscious of any "heresy." But, aside from giving offense to our Protestant friends, is not the term "heretic" an exact, precise one which cannot be applied indiscriminately to non-Catholics?

A. My dictionary defines heresy as an "opinion or doctrine at variance with the orthodox or accepted doctrine of a church or religious system."

My theology book says that "propositions which are directly and immediately contrary or contradictory to Catholic faith constitute heresy."

Thus considered objectively, heresy is the rejection or denial of some doctrine or doctrines of the Church—believing something contrary to the Church's explicit teachings. And in that sense all those Christians who are outside the Church are heretics.

However, my theology book also distinguishes between "material" heresy and "formal" heresy. And that distinction is of great practical importance. "Material" heresy is the actual failure to believe all that the Church teaches, without any guilt. "Formal" heresy is the voluntary, intentional rejection of a doctrine of the Church. "Formal" heresy is a sin; it destroys the virtue of faith in the soul. "Material" heresy is simply a mistake, without guilt. It leaves faith intact, as a virtue.

In ordinary speech we would probably be more exact and felicitous if we reserved the word "heresy" for formal heresy, and called material heretics by some less offensive name. In their own mind they are not heretics. They see no reason why divergence from Catholic doctrine should be the norm of heresy. They don't like our smug way of dividing the whole world into Catholic and non-Catholic. Since they are honest and sincere we should respect their attitude and feelings. Charity is not served by insult; nor is good often accomplished by hard and offensive names.

Q. Can those outside the Church be saved?

The Catholic Church is adamant in its attitude that there is but one Church and that it is the weighty responsibility of everyone to belong to it. "Outside the Catholic Church there is no salvation."

Catholic priests whom I have asked concede that good Protestants will go to heaven as surely as bad Catholics will go to hell. The Baptism of desire, they say. Well, all of us desire to go to heaven.

Then, why all this bother about conversions into the Catholic Church and why all this worry about proselytism? Do not all Christians confess the brotherhood of man and the Fatherhood of God? Does this not make all religions the same?

A. As you imply, we Catholics are pretty sure that innumerable non-Catholics go to heaven. Your question then is: how do we account for their getting there, since we keep insisting—with St. Cyprian and the Fourth Lateran Council—that "outside the Church there is no salvation"?

We stress the fact that the Church is necessary to salvation precisely that we may avoid the conclusion you imply in the final paragraph of your letter: that all religions are essentially the same; boil them down to their least common denominator and take your choice. The Church would rather seem intolerant than give her approval to the proposition that error is equal to truth.

201

The doctrine of no salvation outside the Church is understandably offensive to those who are outside the Church. Their immediate impression is that we are condemning them, personally, to hell. And then, when we start explaining that we don't really mean them, individually, they decide that we are hedging and that, in our clumsy efforts to apologize, we contradict ourselves and fail to make sense. Actually, this doctrine is full of good sound theological sense, when we understand it as the Church has always taught it; and it need not give offense to anyone who grasps its full meaning and its logical necessity.

Nearly every priest in the United States has studied Tanquerey's *Dogmatic Theology* either as a basic textbook in the seminary, or as a book of reference. The two following statements are found within five pages of each other in his familiar book; they are stated as unquestionable dogmatic conclusions. The translation is my own.

Outside the Catholic Church there is no salvation.

They falsely expound Catholic doctrine who contend that non-Catholics, even though they be in good faith, are deprived of all hope of salvation.

At first glance these statements seem to be contradictory. If I keep shouting the first statement and you stubbornly repeat the second, we might each think the other a heretic. That we may thoroughly understand both of them, let us recall a few doctrines on which they are based:

1. Salvation is by the grace of God. Without sanctifying grace no one can enter heaven, or see God, or be united to God. Sanctifying grace is the supernatural life which makes heaven possible; it is the life of heaven.

2. Jesus Christ, true God and true man, obtained sanctifying grace for us by his death on the Cross. There is no

other grace available to man than that which Christ obtained by His merits.

3. Jesus Christ, now risen and immortal and glorious in heaven, distributes by His own hand, and through the means which He has chosen and established, the graces necessary to our salvation. No man can be saved except through the merits of Jesus Christ and by the graces which the same Jesus Christ personally distributes.

4. As the earthly means for bringing grace (and salvation) to all men, Jesus Christ, while still on earth, established His Church. To it He confided His doctrine, to be guarded without loss or change, to be taught to all nations, and to be believed by all men.

5. Jesus Christ, Himself, is the living head of this living Church, which is His own Mystical Body. The circulation of sanctifying grace (a part of His own divine life) is only through the organic structure of this, His Body—the Church.

6. Our Lord Jesus Christ gave a solemn command: "Preach the Gospel to every creature; he who believes and is baptized will be saved; he who believes not will be condemned . . . Going therefore teach all nations, teaching them to observe all things whatsoever I have commanded you." (Mark 16, 15; Matt. 28, 19-20).

These doctrines, and many others, lead us to the certain conclusion that outside the Catholic Church there is no salvation. It is the only way to heaven which Jesus Himself established. It is the only Mystical Body which He has. He commanded all to believe its teachings; he who believes not will be condemned.

Let us now turn our attention to another series of doctrines:

1. God is good and just and merciful.

2. He honestly desires the salvation of all men.

3. The just God will damn no man unless that man himself asks for it, by his own free will. No one will go to hell except for his own sin.

From these truths we rightly conclude that a wise and merciful God would not choose a means of salvation which would make that very objective absolutely impossible for a great majority of men.

The concordance of these two conclusions has been traditional in the Church at least since the days of St. Augustine, St. Ambrose, and St. Gregory Nazianzen (who wrote of his own father, a convert from paganism: "He was one of us even before he came into our church; his morality united him to us.")

As your priest friends have suggested to you, we can understand better how these two conclusions fit together if we recall the well-known teaching of the Church regarding Baptism.

Baptism is necessary to salvation; without it no one can enter heaven. But if Baptism be impossible for any particular man, he can be saved by a Baptism of desire. This implies an honest love of God, true contrition for sin, and a desire of salvation. Such implicit desire is possible even in those who have never heard the name of Baptism.

Likewise salvation is only through the Church. But if actual membership in the Church be impossible for some particular man, he can be saved by membership in desire. Baptism is the door to membership in the Church. Baptism of desire is the door to membership by desire.

And who will so limit God's mercy as to deny that some poor pagan, who never even heard the name of the Catholic Church, can be a member of that Church in desire? An honest love of God, as he knows him, a true desire for

204

salvation, and a faithful adherence to the natural law as known in his own conscience, are the means of such membership of desire—as St. Gregory said of his own father.

Pope Pius XII, in 1943, wrote an encyclical on the Mystical Body, in which he made clear the manner of salvation through the Church. He did not treat explicitly of those outside the Church, except to indicate the difficulties and uncertainties of their salvation, in spite of their disposition towards the Mystical Body by desire and longing—clearly implying the possibility of such salvation.

Pope Pius IX spoke twice, and very clearly on the subject, first in an address which he delivered on December 9, 1854, and later in an Encyclical, *Quanto Conficiamur Moerore:*

"We must hold as of faith that no one can be saved outside of the Apostolic Roman church . . . Likewise, however, we must hold it as certain that those who are ignorant of the true religion . . . are not charged with any guilt on this account in the eyes of the Lord. And who will arrogate to himself the power to indicate the limits of such ignorance? . . ."

Translating from Tanquerey again, these two axioms are stated as certain:

1. No one can be saved who remains outside the Catholic Church through his own fault up to the end of his life.

2. Those who through no fault of their own remain outside the Church can be saved through membership of desire in the church.*

---

* The new revision of the Baltimore Catechism states the same truths in these words:
167. What do we mean when we say, "Outside the Church there is no salvation"?
When we say, "Outside the Church there is no salvation," we mean that those who through their own grave fault do not know that the Catholic

Let me repeat myself, and try to say the same things in other words, for purpose of clarity.

Jesus Christ established only one means of salvation, His Church. He established no other churches as rivals or auxiliaries. And His Church is essential in his plan of sanctifying and saving men; not merely helpful, but necessary. He could have worked out a plan of salvation without the Church, but He actually chose to sanctify men in a unified group, using one to help the other.

We believe that the Church is the unique means of salvation because the New Testament and the early history of Christianity make it clear that Jesus established only the one Church.

We believe that the Church is the one means of salvation because our Lord yearned for unity (John 10, 16) and prayed for unity (John 17:20-21), because truth is by its nature exclusive and cannot be tolerant of error, and because Christ promised to remain always with his Church "even unto the consummation of the world." (Matt. 28: 19-20). It is this constant presence of Christ with his

---

Church is the true Church or, knowing it, refuse to join it, cannot be saved.

(a) "Outside the Church there is no salvation" does not mean that everyone who is not a Catholic will be condemned. It does mean that no one can be saved unless he belongs in some manner to the Catholic Church, either actually or in desire, for the means of grace are not given without some relation to the divine institution established by Christ.

168. Can they be saved who remain outside the Catholic Church because they do not know it is the true Church?

They who remain outside the Catholic Church through no grave fault of their own and do not know it is the true Church, can be saved by making use of the graces which God gives them.

The catechism also states that "persons who make use of the graces God gives them, even though they are not members of the true Church, actually have the desire to become members inasmuch as they wish to use all the means ordained by God for their salvation." (*New Baltimore Catechism, No. 3,* Benziger Bros., Inc., 1949, p. 93.

206

Church which makes it unique. He made no such promise to any other organization.

The Church would deny her very nature and divine institution if she were to admit rivals on equal or similar basis. It is her task to incorporate all men of all times and places into the one fold of the one Shepherd. How can she seek to embrace all, as her divinely given duty, if she recognizes a right of other churches to embrace some of them? There must be "one body and one Spirit . . . one Lord, one Faith, one Baptism; one God and Father of all." (Ephesians 4, 4-6).

This quotation from St. Paul suggests the principal reason for our belief that the Church of Christ is the unique and unified and exclusive means of salvation: it is the body of Christ. "For as the body is one and has many members, and all the members of the body, many as they are, form one body, so also is it with Christ . . . Now you are the body of Christ, member for member." (I Cor. 12: 12, 27).

If you try to split up Christians into many churches you seek to dismember the body of Christ. The Church hates heresy because it tears the body of Christ apart.

We are sanctified, each one of us, by membership in the Mystical Body of Christ. He is the Head of that body, and life flows down from the Head through the body to all its members. There is only one Redeemer, one Mediator, through whom we are saved. "I am the way, the truth, and the life. No one comes to the Father but through Me." (John 14:6). And we cannot come to Christ except through His Mystical Body, which is the spiritual extension of Himself on earth, and the only such extension of Himself on earth.

As long as we are speaking of institutions, this doctrine that "outside the Church there is no salvation" is rather

207

simple. We have already said and repeated it: Christ established only one Church; it is the only means He gave us for our salvation; and man has no power to create others. However, when we consider the people outside the Church as individual human persons, the problem of their salvation becomes complicated. We run into questions of moral guilt and merit, of firm conviction and inculpable error, of good faith and good living, of sacrifice and love and devotion. We must be psychologists as well as theologians if we wish to form any idea of the personal relationship between an individual man and his Maker. And even then it can be only a rough estimate; we can never know a man's will and conscience. It is not for us to judge.

This fact we do know: that the evidences for the one true Church are not so apparent and convincing that they command immediate acceptance, especially in the mind of the man who has been raised from childhood to regard the Church as an ancient ogre. It is entirely possible for him to be wrong without guilt. And the just God will blame him only for the things of which he is personally guilty.

Each man's salvation is his individual concern. The Church cannot save him in spite of himself. Even Almighty God will not do that. The Church is the means of bringing him to God, the instrument for bringing God's graces to him, but the rest is a matter of his own will. To her own members the Church brings the means of salvation directly and fully, but some of them reject her offerings. To those outside her actual membership the Church brings these same means of salvation indirectly and partially, and many of these good people accept all she brings, never suspecting that it is she who brings them.

If the Church is to distribute divine gifts to those who

are not her members there must be some connection between her and them. There is such a connection, though it is sometimes rather tenuous. It is the bond of implicit desire of membership, which is embedded in good faith and honest unawareness of error. Good faith is faith of a sort; and good intentions cover a multitude of faults.

This membership by desire is entirely subjective; it has none of the outward effects of real membership. But the Church, in her charity, fully recognizes its reality and effectiveness. She knows that it can often produce a devout and holy Christian life, and that saints and martyrs may result from it. She would have us regard our separated brethren with humility and charity, with tolerance and hope. But she does not want our charity to blind us to the importance of truth. There is danger that we come to imagine that doctrine doesn't matter, that sincerity and honesty are the only things that count. That is why she insists so strongly that she is the only source of salvation established by Christ.

Among non-Catholic Christians, membership in the Church by desire is often bolstered by various links of truth borrowed from her and by some powerful means of grace retained from their former membership in her. They believe in God, the Father Almighty; in Jesus Christ, His only Son; in the Redemption by Christ and our personal sanctification in Him; in a moral code based on justice and charity; and in an eternal life of reward or punishment. These great truths are terribly important, and they are all Catholic. The Church kept them alive for fifteen centuries to give them as a priceless heritage to those who deny her. Those who believe these Catholic truths have much of the Church deep in their souls.

Most non-Catholic Christians have also kept some of the

sacraments. Nearly all have Baptism. Some schismatics have the Holy Eucharist and Holy Orders, even Penance and the Mass. All have Matrimony, even though many may not recognize its sacramental character. We believe that an infant validly baptized in a Protestant church is an adopted child of God, filled with the grace which makes it heir to heaven. It is a little saint, and spiritually a real member of the Church. Its spiritual position deteriorates only as it learns and accepts false doctrines. Its direct and internal relationship with God changes only as it becomes personally guilty of heresy. If its faith remains honest, firm, and undoubting it may never become guilty.

Even the pagan has something of Catholicity in him. It may not have come to him directly through the Church, but it is one in substance with the teachings of the Church, e.g. that there is a Supreme Being, that man has an immortal soul, and that there is such a thing as moral right and wrong, with reward and punishment as sanction.

These people outside the Church, then, are saved by what is Catholic in them, not by anything non-Catholic in their position. Their rejection of Christ's Church would ruin their chances of salvation if they did it voluntarily and intentionally—if they were guilty of it. Their good faith saves them, and their good intentions provide a sanctifying link with the Church of Christ.

Pope Pius IX, in the Encyclical we quoted above, indicated that no one can know the limits of invincible ignorance. We might add in the same vein, and for similar reason, that none of us can presume to fix limits to the mercy and forgiveness of God. We do know that God wishes all men to be saved, and that to every man who has the use of reason He gives graces sufficient for salvation. Only a man who rejects those graces will go to hell. Only

210

God can read the heart of man. The theologian can define invincible ignorance, but he cannot determine its prevalence; neither can he measure the effects of divine love in the soul of a man. "He who has my Commandments and keeps them, he it is who loves me. But he who loves me will be loved by my Father, and I will love him and manifest myself to him" (John 12, 21). "If anyone love Me, he will keep my word, and my Father will love him, and We will come to him and make our abode with him" (John 14, 23). When God makes his abode in the heart of a man, that man is holy—ready for heaven.

Q. I have been reading a chart in my encyclopedia which lists 250 various religious denominations in the United States and gives their memberships. I am a bit confused over the different kinds of Catholic churches listed there. In addition to the Roman Catholic Church and some nineteen divisions of the Eastern Orthodox Church, the following classifications are listed:

Catholic Apostolic Churches—7, with 2577 members;

"Old" Catholic Churches—91, with 110,435 members;

"Liberal" Catholic Churches—14, with 4000 members.

Polish National Catholic Churches—146, with 250,000 members.

Are these churches a part of our own Roman Catholic Church? Is there any difference between their rites, practices, beliefs, etc., and ours?

A. The "Catholic Apostolic Church" is about as far from being either Catholic or Apostolic as you can get. It was founded in London in 1835 by Edward Irving, a Scotch Presbyterian pastor. It teaches that the charisms, or special powers given personally to the Apostles, still exist in the Church; these include the gift of tongues, the powers of prophecy, healing, and miracles, etc. Its members expect the second coming of the Lord any moment now.

The "Old Catholics" broke away from the Church in 1870, when the doctrine of papal infallibility was defined in the Vatican Council. The revolt against the proclama-

212

tion of this doctrine was led by a group of German professors and scholars, the best known among them being Doctor Dollinger, who was soon to become rector of the University of Munich. In doctrine this church might be classed with the Eastern Orthodox; it recognizes the first seven oecumenical Councils, and no more. It has real priests, but they are allowed to marry; it has abolished fasting and the confessional, uses the vernacular language in its Mass, and gives communion under both species—to Anglicans and Orthodox, as well as to Old Catholics.

The "Liberal Catholics" are a spurious off-shoot from the miscegenation of Old Catholics and Theosophists. This Church was established about 1915 in England, and soon split into two groups, since the Christian tradition and Theosophist ideas tended to separate like a mixture of oil and water. Its American headquarters are in Los Angeles, which gives a hint as to the depth of its theology.

The Polish National Catholic Church of America resulted from a revolt of certain Polish parishes and their priests against the authority of the Catholic bishops who were not Polish. The revolt took place at the beginning of the present century and was centered around Buffalo, Chicago, Cleveland, and various places in Pennsylvania. It goes farther than the Old Catholics in rejecting oecumenical Councils, accepting only the first four. It holds, with Protestants, that all men have the right to interpret the Bible according to their individual convictions and consciences.

From the above it is evident that none of these misnamed "Catholic" churches has any present connection with the Holy Roman Catholic and Apostolic Church which was founded by Jesus Christ.

Q. I came across the enclosed article in one of our New Orleans papers. Can you, in your column, clarify the claim it makes that the Episcopalians are "an integral part of the One, Holy, Catholic, and Apostolic Church, founded by Jesus Christ?" We know that only the Roman Catholic Church can make this assertion.

A. The article you enclose tells about five of your local Episcopal clergymen who were scheduled to attend the Catholic Congress to be held in Chicago (not to be confused with the ecumenical conference held at Evanston by the World Council of Churches. The words "Catholic" and "ecumenical" mean about the same thing. But the Evanston group made no claim to "catholicity" in the traditional sense of the word.)

That "Catholic Congress" in Chicago must have had some interesting delegates. They included the "prime bishop" of the Polish National Catholic Church, the "primate" of the Old Catholic Church, and "metropolitans" of the Eastern Orthodox Churches, besides our Episcopal brethren. In other words they represented all those lonely groups which long to be Catholic, but are a long way from being Catholic. They want the Church of Christ without the authority of Christ.

The Eastern Orthodox want to be Catholic without the Pope. The Old Catholics couldn't accept papal infallibility. The Polish National Church simply couldn't get
214

along with American bishops. And the Episcopalians—well it all started over a royal divorce case.

Those poor little catholic orphans who met in Chicago have a "branch" theory of the Church of Christ. According to them, the Mystical Body is like a tree. After all, didn't our Lord say that He was the vine and we the branches?

Now a tree that is nineteen centuries old has a big trunk, growing from firm wide roots. But no tree is complete without branches, some large and some small, but all an integral part of the tree. That old main trunk probably keeps right on growing up into the air, gnarled and proud. But it should not despise the branches which fork out from it. Some of the lower ones naturally got pruned off in the course of time. But up there about a thousand years in the air is a real, sturdy fork, growing eastward and pushing the old trunk to the west. Then on up another five hundred years comes that English sprig, and so on.

According to this theory one branch is as Catholic as another. They all grow from the same roots and have their life from the same source. The fact that a branch grew out late doesn't mean that it is less a part of the tree than the trunk.

The secret grievance of these various branches is that the old trunk won't accept them. She says they are not growing out from her, but have broken off from her. Recall again our Lord's story of the vine. If the branch breaks off, it is no good; it bears no fruit, but withers away and is raked up and burned.

The tree is a pretty good symbol of the Mystical Body. But we must keep in mind that a tree is a unit, a single living organism. All its branches have the same nature. An old oak does not sprout a maple limb to the north and

215

a persimmon to the south. If you find a cherry limb on a pine you rightly judge that someone has tried a graft; it didn't grow that way. And a graft, if successful, could change the nature of the entire tree. So it has to be cut off.

Most of the limbs cut off these past few centuries are content with their separate, withered growth. They figure that they retain enough of the sap of the old tree within themselves. They met in Evanston to bind themselves together like a bundle of twigs. They have little remembrance of the old tree-trunk and no longing for her. After all if you remain attached to a tree-trunk you have to stay in the same place. You can't follow your twiggy whims.

But those groups meeting in Chicago have read some history, and some theology books. They know full well that Jesus Christ established only one Church—that outside that Church there is no salvation. They don't dare be outside. Yet coming in is too hard. You have to accept authority and live by rules. So they try to convince themselves that they are in. That tough, proud old Roman Church doesn't know that they are in—will not admit their presence. But there they are, just as Catholic, and yet rid of certain annoying doctrines, unpleasant moral laws, pontifical authority, and clerical celibacy. And just a bit lonesome too, like orphans.

Q. Would you please give the reason or reasons, in your column, why the group known as the Orthodox Church separated from the Catholic Church?

A. You are asking for an historical survey covering many centuries. The great schism between the East and the West was a gradual estrangement. Its remote causes might be seen at work in the Easter controversy of the second century, and certainly it cannot be understood without going back to the establishment of Constantinople as the capital of the eastern part of the Empire, early in the fourth century.

There has always existed a certain cleavage between the East and the West, and its basis is rooted in a diversity of rites, languages, and customs. After the fourth century these diverse interests and sympathies grouped themselves around two rival centers of cultural and political influence: Rome and Constantinople.

We should start out, however, by defining our terms. The word "Orthodox" is the accepted name for a loosely joined group of about sixteen churches, most of which maintain at least a nominal union with the Patriarch of Constantinople (Istanbul). They use the Byzantine rite in their liturgy, but employ various languages for their ceremonies. And they form the largest Christian group in the world outside the Catholic Church.

The Orthodox are not the only Eastern Christian

217

Churches. There are various heretical churches of ancient origin: the Nestorians, Copts, Jacobites, Malabar Christians, and Armenians. These differ from the Orthodox almost as much as Protestants differ from Catholics.

Then there are the Uniates: Catholic Churches of the East. These are thoroughly Eastern in rites, languages, customs and discipline, but thoroughly Catholic in belief and practice. There is a Catholic Uniate Church corresponding to each of the Orthodox churches, and one to counter practically each one of the heretical groups.

As we said before, the separation of the East and the West was not a sudden event brought about by strong, clear-cut issues. It was rather a slow growth of centuries, caused by deep basic differences of interest, language, and tradition, which were later sharpened by rivalries, jealousies, ambitions, and personal hatreds, and were all ready to be set off by the clash of minor events or personalities.

So gradual and fluctuating was the separation of the Orthodox Church from the Catholic Church that only conventional agreement can set a definite date for the schism. Some might date it from the ninth century, when Photius tried to replace Ignatius as Patriarch of Constantinople and was repelled by Pope Nicholas I. But that schism was rather quickly healed. So most historians consider that the actual separation took place in the eleventh century, when Michael Caerularius, Patriarch of Constantinople, rebelled against the Pope, without much apparent or immediate cause, and made himself sufficiently obnoxious to get excommunicated (in July, 1054).

However, in another sense, this was not the final separation. The Fourth Crusade, at the beginning of the thirteenth century, contrary to the will of the Pope, captured Constantinople and tried to effect reunion by force. The net result was probably to make the separation more definite. At the Council of Lyons in 1274 there was a measure of agreement on reunion, and at the Council of Florence in 1439 there were even more hopeful negotiations. So we might say that it was not until the East had formally rejected reunion after the Council of Florence that the schism was complete; and even then many groups came back to union with Rome.

It is probably true to say that preliminary preparations for the schism began when the Emperor Constantine, in the fourth century, took over the ancient port of Byzantium and started building it into the thriving modern capital of his empire. The episcopal see of Constantinople was new then, and of minor importance; but with the Emperor's backing it started to grow in importance and influence—and ambition.

The growing position of the see of Constantinople in the Eastern Church was enhanced by the decline of the ancient patriarchal sees of Alexandria, Antioch, and Jerusalem, which were first plagued by heresies and then conquered by the Mohammedans.

Constantinople was a proud city: the capital of the Empire, the New Rome, the center of power and learning and art, the growing metropolis of a world which was otherwise in general decline. The bishop of the capital city became a patriarch; he was the Emperor's man, conscious of his strong political backing. His rapid growth made him ambitious. He would be in the East what the pope was in the West.

The see of Constantinople was established in 323. From that date until the time of Photius, who was the author of the first East-West schism, it was separated from Rome one year out of every three—or a total of more than two

219

hundred years in less than five and a half centuries. Ambition and rivalry were probably the basic causes, but Arianism, Monothelitism, Iconoclasm, and sundry similar conflicts had led the Emperor's bishop astray. It was not the kind of record to recommend him as leader of the East, but, unfortunately, by the time of Photius that leadership had been generally established. So, then, when the traditional bad-boy started acting up again he found many followers. He was accustomed to schism himself; now he was in position to take all the East into schism with him.

The final split cannot be explained by any doctrinal difference. In the beginning, at least, there was no heresy involved, and never, even up to the present time, has there been hopeless disagreement on matters of faith. It is true that Photius made much of the Western addition of the word "Filioque" in the Creed, and Caerularius ranted against the Roman use of unleavened bread in the Mass. But when the Council of Florence laid down the doctrinal basis of reunion, the primacy of the pope was the only serious point at issue. It was agreed that the Easterners might leave the word "Filioque" out of their creed, keep their leavened bread for the Eucharist, and retain their married clergy. About the only other point which might have required discussion was the doctrine of purgatory. Today we would have to add the Immaculate Conception and papal infallibility as points of dispute. Otherwise we might still have reunion on the same basis as in the fifteenth century.

Do I seem to be talking around your question? It is very difficult to give precise causes for a movement so vast in extent and so long in development. But at the risk of inaccuracy we might try this summary of causes:

1. The historic differences of language, culture, rites and customs between the East and the West.

Byzantine vs. Roman rites, leavened vs. unleavened bread, married clergy vs. celibates, icons vs. statues, whether Saturday should be a day of fast, whether the alleluia should be sung during Lent. These were unimportant but bitter points of conflict.

The language barrier was a real cause of misunderstanding and of failures in diplomacy. Latin was the language of the West; in general Greek prevailed in the East; at least no one in the Levant bothered to learn Latin. Even Photius, who was one of the most learned men of his time, did not know the language of the West. And neither side trusted interpreters. So there was lack of communication. It is hard to understand a man when you can't talk with him.

2. The political growth of Constantinople, and the increasing influence of its ambitious and political-minded Patriarch over the Church of the East.

3. The political and cultural decline of Rome.

4. The pride and ambition of the Patriarch of Constantinople, which resulted in rivalry, enmity, and frequent clashes with the supreme pontiff.

5. Minor issues and personality clashes which provided the spark to ignite dormant differences.

6. Stiff necks and hard heads which resisted compromise and understanding, and nullified efforts to mend the rift.

Q. Is there any doubt about whether Church of England bishops still have apostolic links back to Peter? I had thought the succession had been broken during the sixteenth century Protestant revolt. But lately I have heard that there is a possibility that the orders are still valid, since even the revolt does not take away a "revolting" bishop's right to consecrate other bishops and so pass on the ancestral apostolic authority. At what point in the English revolt was the apostolic succession severed? What event or events caused the severing?

A. No matter how revolting, a validly consecrated bishop can validly consecrate, and thus pass on apostolic authority. They do it every day in the Orthodox community. But in order to consecrate validly he must 1) intend to do so, and 2) use a valid rite of consecration.

In 1896 Pope Leo XIII had a careful study made of the validity of Anglican orders, and on the basis of the factual findings set forth in this study, declared that Anglican orders were not valid. In brief summary, back in 1550, the ordinal used in ordaining priests and consecrating bishops was so revised that it did not contain a valid ordination ceremony. And Archbishop Cranmer, who headed the commission which prepared the first Book of Common Prayer, made it very clear that the new ordinal was not intended to ordain a priest in the Roman sense, as one distinct from the layman, empowered to offer the sacrifice for him.

222

Presumably, Pope Leo would have been happy to find Anglican orders valid. It would have made reunion of Anglicans with Rome much easier. But he had to accept the facts as he found them.

Q. Has the Pope announced ex cathedra *that the Roman Catholic Church does not recognize the Anglican Church? The Greek Orthodox Church?*

A. What do you mean by recognize? The Church certainly recognizes these sects as existing, as schismatic, and as heretical. Of course she does not recognize them as forming an integral part of the true Church of Jesus Christ. They severed themselves from the living Mystical Body by disunion from the visible head of that Body (schism), and by rejection of some of the basic facts of its life (heresy).

The Bull of Pope Leo XIII, entitled *Apostolicae curae,* issued in September, 1896, is considered an *ex cathedra* *

* The Pope speaks *ex cathedra* when he speaks officially and formally as the shepherd and teacher of the entire Church, in defining a doctrine of faith or morals, making it clear that he is speaking with his supreme Apostolic authority, and giving a definite and final decision to be accepted and held by the entire Church.

Theologians distinguish 1) the direct and primary object of infallibility, i.e. revealed doctrines, and 2) the indirect or secondary object, which includes theological conclusions and dogmatic fact. When the Pope solemnly defines a teaching of the Church as a doctrine revealed by God there is no doubt at all that he is making use of the divine assistance promised him in St. Peter and is protected from error, as for example, when Pope Pius IX defined the doctrine of the Immaculate Conception. But when he makes pronouncements on dogmatic or moral conclusions which are deduced from revealed doctrine, as understood in the light of reason; or when he states facts connected with doctrine, e.g. that certain errors are contained in a particular book, or certain essential features are missing in an ordination book, it is not always quite so clear that all the conditions are fulfilled to make it an infallible declaration. That is why I say that *Apostolicae curae* is *considered* an *ex cathedra* pronouncement.

223

pronouncement regarding the invalidity of Anglican orders. It was not a definition of dogma, of course, but it was a solemn, official pronouncement and declaration, which gave a final judgment on the question at issue. It stated a dogmatic fact. There can be no further argument. It declared that the sacrament of Holy Orders as given in the Anglican Church is invalid. Consequently Anglicans have no real bishops; no real priests.

There have been whole series of papal documents issued about the Orthodox Church, from the days of Alexander II, in the eleventh century, down to the present time. Some of these would be classified by theologians as *ex cathedra*. One of the more recent and best known is the Encyclical of Pope Leo XIII, entitled *Praeclara gratulationis,* issued on June 20, 1894, in which he invited and urged the Orthodox to return to the true Church—to union with Rome. He stressed the fact that there are no great dogmatic differences keeping them away, and that Rome would recognize and sanction all their legitimate customs and practices, such as married priests, unleavened bread in the Eucharist, Greek and other languages in the Mass, etc. Various groups from the Eastern Churches have come back to Rome. They keep all these customs. Externally it is often hard to tell them from the Orthodox.

The Church has never questioned the validity of the Orders or of the other sacraments given by the Orthodox. They have real bishops, real priests, true Mass and Holy Communion. About all they would have to do to become Catholics would be to make a profession of faith. They would keep their churches; their priests and bishops would carry on as before, but under direction of the Pope.

224

Q. I have been told that at one time the Masonic organization was Catholic, with the Pope as its head. I was also told that when the Catholic Church condemned the Masonic fraternity and Catholics were forbidden to belong, the Pope permitted paid-up insurance members to belong, but they could not attend meetings, etc. Is this true? What caused the break from the Church? Why is the Church so opposed to the Masons? Doesn't the Knights of Columbus have a secret initiation ritual, etc.?

A. People sure tell you a lot of things, don't they?

1. The Masons were never Catholic. They like to trace their origins back to medieval guilds and the Knights Templar, to Noah and Adam, and even to God, the Great Architect, who founded their order before He created the world.

Such claims are not history. They are rather fables, usually not told seriously, but sometimes credulously accepted.

Actually Masonry began with the establishment of the Grand Lodge in England in 1717. It opposed the Catholic Church from the beginning, and was first condemned by the Church in 1738—twenty-one years after its foundation. By that year it had already been condemned by three Protestant governments—Holland, Sweden, and Geneva—and since that time the condemnation of the Church has been repeated in at least seventeen different decrees or laws. These condemnations are based on four principal reasons:

225

1. Masonry fosters religious indifferentism, and consequently creates contempt for orthodox doctrine and Church authority. It reduces religion to those basic truths "on which all men agree"—just as they all agree on the square, the level, and the plumb as basic instruments of the mason's trade. All that is necessary is to believe in God and obey the moral law—to avoid being a "stupid Atheist" or an "irreligious Libertine." The Grand Orient of France even held that belief in God is not essential. The moral law is diluted to mean "to be good men and true."

2. Its deep secrecy and ever-changing disguises throughout the years have given it the character of an undercover, subversive organization.

3. Its oaths of secrecy and fidelity are unjustified and sacrilegious in scope, object, and form.

4. It is a danger to religion and public order—to the Church and the State. Right now Masonry, in most countries, is not subversive of State authority, but its secrecy of organization is a model for dangerous groups which wish to elude the due process of law, both ecclesiastical and civil.

In the United States most individual Masons are no more enemies of the Church than any other non-Catholics. But even here Masonic groups fight the Church on certain questions, e.g. the parochial school.

Occasionally, when a man quits the Masons to become a Catholic, the Church will permit him to retain such passive membership as may be necessary to avoid loss of insurance benefits. Such permission is seldom requested.

The only secret about the Knights of Columbus is their initiation ceremony. Any good club or fraternity has similar secrets. It would spoil the fun and the lesson of initiation to reveal them.

Q. Is inter-faith marriage advisable? What are the advantages and disadvantages of inter-faith marriages?

A. This question was asked by a non-Catholic. The answer is directed to the questioner.

Inter-faith marriages are definitely not advisable. Success and happiness in marriage depend largely upon unity or harmony of interests, beliefs, purposes, and convictions. Differences of race, nationality, religion, cultural background, education, social standing, or economic status are dangerous to this unity and harmony. Some wag has said wisely that in ideal mating the only difference between husband and wife should be that one is male and the other female.

The Catholic Church has always strongly opposed the marriage of Catholics to non-Catholics. In general non-Catholic groups have been similarly aware of the dangers of such marriages, and today some Protestant churches, particularly the Lutheran, are quite as forceful as the Catholic in forbidding them.

Young people are generally religious and interested in religion, but they can not have that deep appreciation of the importance of religion to life which comes from long experience. Religion is much more than a belief, or a prejudice, or church-membership. Religion is a way of living. It is intimately interwoven with tradition, custom and cul-

227

ture, and is the very thread from which conscience weaves its fabric of character and forms its patterns of action.

Religion can be a great source of unity in marriage. Deep convictions held firmly in common, high ideals giving mutual inspiration, prayers murmured in unison, sacrifice shared for the same God: these can give harmony and solidarity. These can give mutual peace and happiness, dissipate conflicts, and form a strong support in adversity. Religion is something shared, as all married life should be shared.

Religion can also be a great disrupting influence in marriage. When deep convictions clash, high ideals divide, prayers become an annoying mumble, and sacrifice seems a shame, then even sacred things can cause dissension. They can cause trouble and breed mutual ill-will, create conflicts, and precipitate quarrels. Religion is then something which divides where there should be union.

Opposition to mixed marriage is not bigotry or prejudice. It is sane judgment based on experience, observation, and even some statistics. The figures available—too limited to be conclusive—indicate that the failures and divorces in mixed marriages may be four or five times as numerous as in marriages between two Catholics or two Protestants. Even if figures exaggerate, the danger is great.

The problem of mixed marriage requires clear, cool thinking, and that is often a bit difficult in the midst of that emotional agitation called love. The following questions should be frankly asked and honestly answered.

1. How great is the religious difference? The difference between two Protestant denominations may not be important. But the difference between Catholic and Protestant is very important and vital.

2. How much does your religion mean to you? Are you

rather indifferent? Do you consider denominations unimportant? Do you call yourself broad-minded? Or is religion a matter of firm conviction with you? Or deep prejudice? Is it an essential part of your daily life? Are you determined to convince others, and have them agree with you?

3. What about the Catholic you plan to marry? Is he a good Catholic, strong in his faith, firm in his principles, and faithful in the practice of his religion? Is he tolerant and considerate?

4. Would religion be a point of disagreement and conflict between you? You can't really answer this question of course. Love makes the ways seem smooth ahead, and you have never yet encountered the serious problems.

5. Have you talked about religion between yourselves? Do your argue? Do emotions surge? Have you worked out coolly a firm and honest plan of agreement and of settling disagreements?

6. What about the children? They can't belong to two religions. You can't raise them with no religion. You know about those promises you will have to sign. Are you signing them freely and willingly, and without reservation? Will resentments grow up later because you consider them unfair? What about parochial schools? How will you feel when your children study their catechism, learn their prayers, recite their rosary, make their first Communion, show you their holy pictures and crucifixes, jabber about the saints, and eye you critically because you are a heretic? Can you stand being left out like that?

7. What about birth control? Good Catholics are awfully stubborn about that. They think it is a mortal sin. Are you prepared for all the consequences?

8. What about divorce? Catholics are firmly old-fash-

229

ioned about that too. Of course the question will never come up in your marriage—but if it should, what then?

9. What about your family—and your Catholic in-laws? What is their attitude toward this mixed marriage? How much trouble might they cause? There is a theory that in-laws are the biggest single danger in mixed marriage.

10. What about marriage before a priest? And the instructions you will have to take—six of them, probably?

11. Do you think you might ever become a Catholic? Don't do it unless you are thoroughly convinced and have the Faith. Conversions which are not sincere and thorough may breed resentments and rebellion and cause more danger to the marriage than plain religious differences. But it might be worth investigation. A few instructions wouldn't hurt.

12. Do you have an idea that you might draw the Catholic away from his or her religion later? Better not give it another thought. You might just do it; but you probably would not have a happy marriage as a result. If the religion means anything to him or her, you would only create an uneasy conscience, remorse, and resentments.

13. Can you face facts? Catholics are absolutely convinced that the Catholic Church is the only true Church of Jesus Christ. You can't change them. They firmly believe that they are bound under serious sin to raise their children in the Catholic faith. You may foil them, but you can not change their conscience. You are not asked to agree with Catholics on these points. You should recognize the fact of their convictions.

14. Just how deeply in love are you? Can you possibly break away from this Catholic without fracturing your heart?

230

Q. In Time *magazine recently I read about an answer given by Father Connell in the* Ecclesiastical Review *to a question about religious cooperation. The question supposed that a Baptist church had burned down on Friday and that a Catholic organization had promptly offered use of its hall for the Baptist Sunday services. The question was: Did this Catholic organization do right in offering its hall? Father Connell is reported to have answered, without hesitation, that they did wrong.* Time *says that non-Catholics find this attitude scandalous, and I must admit that I cannot understand it myself.*

A. I certainly do not want to get into public argument with Father Connell. First of all, this column is not the place for theological controversy. Secondly, he is generally recognized as one of the outstanding moral theologians in the United States. And thirdly, his answer does, as he claims, represent the traditional solution of Catholic moralists to this question.

However, it might be useful and interesting for us to review some of the principles involved in cooperation with non-Catholics, since our daily activities require the application of these principles. We should remember this too; the principles are firm and certain; all theologians agree on them. But their application in a particular case often requires an estimate of causes and circumstances; and in this estimate we can disagree.

231

The basic truth which we should keep in mind is that our Lord Jesus Christ established only one Church, and gave us only one method of worship of the one true God. Any other church exists in factual defiance of the one Church of Christ. And any other method of worship is false, simply because it is not the true method designed and authorized by our Savior.

In this country, where we live in the midst of a variety of religions, all equal before the law, we must be careful to avoid the error of indifferentism, which would consider one church to be actually as good as another—man's church as good as Christ's. Indifferentism sees a hundred roads leading to heaven, and the choice of a particular path or highway is up to the individual. Let each man choose the one which suits his taste, and then follow it faithfully, and we will all meet eventually at the same terminus.

Father Connell's objection to the action of this Catholic organization is that it gives scandal by encouraging both Catholics and non-Catholics in this attitude of religious indifferentism. He definitely does have a strong argument there, and we will think more about it later.

In this country of ours we live on a basis of friendship and close association with our non-Catholic neighbors. Very often they are our bosom buddies or our close relatives. Morally, in what measure are we permitted to cooperate with them?

In non-religious matters, e.g. in business, politics, sports, and science, we generally cooperate with them without awareness of religious difference. Now and then we may run into barriers which result from differences of moral attitude in some professional or personal matters. And in social matters young people can not disregard those factors which lead to mixed marriage. But in general we are all

Davenporters or Iowans, Democrats or Republicans, bricklayers or physicians; and seldom does religious difference separate us.

In those matters which pertain directly to religion, however, the problem is much more complicated. If we are to think clearly we must distinguish between the private devotions of individuals or groups and that public worship which is official in a particular denomination. We must distinguish formal participation from material presence, passive from active, and immediate from remote. Here are some examples:

1. In private prayer we may join with our non-Catholic friends without hesitation, e.g. in night prayers, or grace before meals. Even when large groups meet for civic functions the prayers they say together are private, in this sense: they are not the official worship services of some church.

2. There are some limitations in our permitting non-Catholics to take part in our Catholic religious services. They are always welcome in our churches, to attend Mass, or hear the music, or listen to the sermon. But they cannot receive the sacraments or take part in the ceremonies at the altar.

3. We can never take immediate active part in the religious services of non-Catholics, join with them in church worship, play the organ or sing in their choir for religious functions.

4. Sometimes, when there is good sound reason for it, we can be present for non-Catholic church functions, without taking active part in them, e.g. at the marriages or funerals of our friends or relatives, or for special civic occasions.

5. Remote active cooperation can sometimes be per-

233

mitted, if there is good reason for it. By remote cooperation I mean those acts of ours which contribute to non-Catholic religious functions, but are not a direct participation in the services. These might include building the church, renting your building to the church, cleaning or repairing the church, fixing the organ, supplying hosts or wine, and various things of that kind.

My designation of this type of cooperation as *remote* may cause confusion. The accepted term is *mediate*. We want to avoid confusion here, because this loaning of the hall to the Baptists is precisely this type of cooperation, and Father Connell calls it "very proximate."

My term "remote" might seem to contradict him; I don't mean to do that. It is very close cooperation, but it is not immediate—like singing in the choir. Before deciding to cooperate in this way we must consider two factors:

1. The action itself must not be sinful. In this case, letting someone use your hall is not a sinful thing in itself.

2. There must be a good reason, serious enough to justify us in permitting those dangers and evils which might follow our action. The more serious the evil effects might be, then the more serious must be our reason for our action. In this case, community spirit and cooperation, sympathy, generosity, and fraternal charity form the positive reasons. Avoidance of hatred, bigotry, and factions in the community form the negative reasons. They are good sound motives.

In our act of loaning the hall it is worthy of note that our Catholic organization is not cooperating in the formal sin of anyone. The people who will use the hall are sincere and in good faith. They think that they are doing something pleasing to God by holding services. Their sin is only material, and it is much easier to justify our cooperating with material sin than with formal sin.

The Baptists with whom we are cooperating, in this case, are not bringing direct harm to anyone. It would be much harder for us to justify our cooperation if they were engaged in robbing people or destroying reputations. If you reply that they are giving scandal by their false worship, I would agree with you in theory, but would require a survey of the actual bad effects, before admitting any practical value to your argument.

Really, about the only serious evil which we foresee from our cooperation is the scandal we may give by our unintentional encouragement of religious indifference. But scandal is a serious thing. Better a millstone about your neck. So we had better assay this danger before we loan the hall.

1. There is no scandal to our non-Catholic neighbors. They are already confirmed in their doctrine of indifferentism. Rather would they be scandalized by our refusal to let them use the hall. It would be proof to them that we are devoid of that charity taught by Christ, that we are narrow and prejudiced, hateful separatists, intolerant bigots. Explain all you will; the impression remains with them. Actions out-shout explanations.

2. There is real danger of scandal to Catholics. But that danger varies greatly between different localities. In most of the towns of our diocese, where a dozen Catholics live in close daily contact with a hundred non-Catholics, custom has removed the danger from many of those things which might thoroughly scandalize a strong Catholic community. Consequently many acts of remote religious cooperation are tolerated in our Iowa towns which might be quite wrong in cities of the East. Custom alone provides a reason; and custom, too, diminishes the danger.

235

Some cynic might say that we are already so infected with religious indifference that we can loan our hall to the Baptists without danger of becoming more indifferent. I don't think so. It is a matter of attitude, not of conviction. We do not push from sight our firm belief in the one true Church. We simply live and let live. We are tolerant. We think it is just as important to practice the charity of Christ as to insist unwaveringly on the truth of His teachings.

So I have come to a conclusion. At least in our typical Midwestern towns, I believe that the Catholic organization might very well permit the use of its hall as a gesture of charity and friendship toward their stricken Baptist neighbors. I don't think the Catholics should be too impulsive about taking the initiative. Why stick your neck out? But if a request is made, or if circumstances strongly indicated the advisability of the offer, I believe that impulse of charity should be followed. It will help make the town a happy, friendly place to live. It will increase the Christian spirit. And I doubt very much that it will detract from the integrity of Christian faith. A little sermon in the parish church on Sunday might thoroughly eliminate the scandal of indifferentism—the only possible bad result.

Q. I am a recent convert, but my question comes from my non-Catholic relatives. There are many restrictions in the Catholic religion that I don't understand yet, either. Why can't a Catholic participate in a Protestant wedding as long as he or she isn't the best man or maid of honor? Also, why aren't Catholic children allowed to sing with a choir for a Protestant service? I have had a hard time try-

ing to explain to relatives why I can't attend a special church function with them.

A. Your problem is a common one, and often a difficult and delicate one. I am sure you understand that the Church's restrictions in matters of this kind are not made from caprice or prejudice, or from mere stubborn opposition to non-Catholic churches in general. A real moral problem is involved; and often so many variable factors and circumstances appear that it is hard to weigh them all accurately, and balance them precisely against each other. For this reason practices are not always uniform in different places, and answers given by priests or bishops in similar cases may not seem consistent.

The contradictory elements of the problem are clear. On the one hand, we must not do something wrong, like giving erroneous worship to God, encouraging that worship, or contributing to religious indifferentism. On the other hand, we must be considerate of our non-Catholic neighbors, especially when they are close friends or members of our own families. We must not cause enmities, nor contribute needlessly to the impression that Catholics are bigoted, narrow-minded, and supercilious.

The principles are clear, too. We may never take active part in the public worship-services of any non-Catholic church. We may join with non-Catholics in private prayer and worship; and we may sometimes be present in a passive manner at non-Catholic church services, but only with a very good reason.

First, let me explain why we cannot take active part in public religious services. As you know, Catholics firmly believe that Jesus Christ established the Church, the Catholic Church, and remains with her constantly and every-

237

where, as He promised. The Church is His own Mystical Body, the means of sanctification of all those on earth, and Jesus wants all men to belong to His Church. For the public worship of God He gave His Church a method which He designed Himself; it is centered around the Mass, which is His own sacrifice of the Cross. It is not a matter of indifference to Him whether His own method of worship be used or another be substituted.

We all know that during the last four centuries there have grown up in the world many dozens of other churches which claim, in one way or another, to be the Church of Christ, or a part of the Church of Christ. And each one has its own method of worship, largely centered around the Bible and augmented by hymns, prayer, and sermons. They are almost unanimous in rejecting the Mass.

According to our Catholic concept, these various churches are in rivalry and contention with the true Church of Christ. To give them positive signs of formal encouragement or approval would be morally wrong. And though Protestant services may be beautiful and edifying, by the very fact that they are conducted they supplant the true worship designed by Christ; and their claim to be that true worship makes them false. God is undoubtedly pleased when that worship is offered Him by sincere Protestants, and we respect their good faith; but if we joined them in offering that same worship we could not be sincere—unless we were very ignorant of Catholic teachings. We would know that we were offering false worship to God.

Private, unofficial devotions are different. It is quite proper for us to say our morning prayers or our prayers before meals with our non-Catholic friends. We can even join with them in prayers at civic gatherings or patriotic functions. These devotions do not represent any church;

nor do they imply the rejection of any church. We express together the faith we do have in common, and ask for the things we all need. Such prayer is not sufficient for our religious lives, but it is not harmful to them unless it should generate indifferentism.

That word "indifferentism" indicates the main reason why we must be sparing in our passive attendance at non-Catholic services, and must have good reason for such attendance. Because of the number and diversity of churches today, especially in the United States, there has grown up a notion that any one church is essentially as good as another. If Christ established a Church at all, it was, many people think, a vague, spiritual thing, without any visible, external organization; and consequently all those who believe in the Lord Jesus Christ are members of His Church, and all the divergent sects merely represent a variety of helps for people with different tastes and needs. Since the Holy Spirit directs each one of us in our interpretation of Christ's message, our internal faith is the important thing in our religious lives; so it makes no profound difference what we believe, in the opinion of these same people, as long as we are sincere, firm, and faithful in our belief.

None of this fits into the Catholic concept of faith and religion. It is directly contradictory to our belief in the one true Church established by Christ, the infallible teacher of a doctrine clearly and objectively revealed by God. We hold it vitally important that we rightly understand eternal truths. We cannot countenance indifference to these truths; neither may we do anything to encourage an indifferent attitude towards the true Church of Christ.

Yet our frequent attendance at non-Catholic religious functions would do just that. Not only would it bolster religious indifferentism among our non-Catholic friends;

it would foster the same attitude in ourselves, and tend to spread it to our fellow Catholics.

The Church has a law on this subject; it is found in Canon 1258 of the Code of Canon Law. The first part of that Canon states firmly that it is not right for Catholics to actively assist in any way or take part in the religious functions of non-Catholics. The second part indicates that passive attendance, or mere presence at funerals, weddings, and similar functions may be tolerated for reasons of civic duty or to pay honor or respect, provided that the reason for being there is serious; and in case of doubt the bishop is the one who must evaluate reasons. And it is noted that you may not attend if there is danger to your own faith, or danger that you will lead others astray.

You would take active part in non-Catholic religious functions if you were to share the pulpit with the minister, sing in the choir, or play their organ as an integral part of their services. Suppose that they had a ceremony similar to our Mass—you would take active part by being a deacon or altar boy at that service.

You would be present passively at a Protestant religious function if you simply sat quietly in the pew. But you need not be motionless to be passive. You could, if you had no sense of propriety, run up and down the aisle during the service. You would be very active, but you would take no part in the religious functions. And besides, not everything which is done in a church is religious worship. Conceivably, the congregation might hold a community sing in the church, and for good reason you might join in with them and take active part in the festivities.

Now what about bridesmaids, attendants, ushers, at a wedding? Is this a religious ceremony, and do they take active part in the religious features of the ceremony? Or are their activities strictly social or civic in nature? Can they perform these accessory functions and remain passive as regards any religious part of the ceremony? These questions are important in a solution of your problem, because you will remember that Catholics may not take active part in the religious services of non-Catholics. If a bridesmaid or an usher is passive as regards the religious features of the ceremony, then a Catholic might perform these functions, if he had a very good reason and gave no scandal.

According to Church law, as indicated above, it is the bishop who decides in cases of doubt. He must first decide whether the functions in question are active or passive as regards the religious services. Then if they are passive, he must see whether the reasons for assisting are sufficient; and he must weigh the danger of scandal, which in these cases is usually the danger of contributing to religious indifferentism.

These are difficult decisions to make with fairness, and circumstances are seldom the same in any two cases. If one person gets a Yes and another a No, there is sure to be dissatisfaction and a charge of discrimination. So some of our bishops have decided that the best solution is simply to forbid any direct participation in such marriage ceremonies.

They realize that they are causing hardship to some deserving persons, particularly converts like yourself, who may have cogent reasons to take part in the marriages of immediate members of their families. But laws are made for the common good, and they usually work hardship on some individuals. Where there is such diocesan law, of course, it must be observed.

In many dioceses there is no law on this subject, and each case is settled on its particular merits, in accordance with the general law of the Church, Canon 1258. For the benefit of people in these dioceses, I give my own views on the subject. Your pastor or bishop may not agree with me, because some of the distinctions involved are rather fine, and the evaluation of many and varied circumstances must have something of the subjective in it. Your pastor knows your local circumstances much better than I do, and is in better position to judge your particular case. And the final decision is up to the bishop. If the question is taken to him you must be willing to accept his decision—and don't quote my opinon at him, please.

What do ushers do at weddings? They show people to their seats, look dignified, smile graciously, and wear boutonnieres. These are not strictly religious functions, even though they are done in church.

What do bridesmaids do? They look pretty, with gossamer glamor and satiny sweetness. They smile self-consciously, strangle a tiny bouquet, and feel the admiring gaze of every eye upon them. Nothing very religious about that.

But what about the maid of honor and the best man? Are they an essential part of the religious ceremony? Is their presence required by this particular Protestant church in order to make the marriage valid before the church? Do they participate in religious activities, as such? This question is often hard to answer. And because of the doubts involved, many pastors and bishops may tell you that you should not be best man or maid of honor, lest you take active part in a non-Catholic religious service.

Personally, I believe that in most non-Catholic churches even the best man and maid of honor do not perform functions which are essentially religious. Their presence is necessary in order that the ceremony be valid civilly. Social
242

custom demands that they be there. They contribute to the show and prestige, but they are not directly engaged in the worship of God or sanctification of souls.

With due respect, we might inquire whether the wedding ceremony in some churches is a religious service at all. It is not considered a sacrament; it is clearly distinguished from a worship service. The marriage might be contracted with equal validity before a justice of the peace. But the church offers a more glamorous setting, the minister has greater dignity and reads the words more expressively; and then there is the organ—and the vocalist (some persons think that a wedding is really drab without a selection from *Lohengrin* and "I Love You Truly"). There may be a passing reference to God in the ceremony, and a blessing may be given. The rest is pomp and sentiment.

Now let us sum up our conclusions. Canon 1258 requires a grave reason for a Catholic to simply sit in a pew a non-Catholic funeral or wedding, or similar church service. In our country there is no doubt about attending funerals; the good reason is always there when we go to pay our respects to a friend, relative, or prominent citizen who has died. The same is almost equally true of weddings where the courtesy of our presence is expected and our absence would be offensive.

But what about making a public spectacle of our attendance by flouncing down the aisle to Mendelssohn's melodies or preening at the altar in pastel splendor? That certainly requires a much more serious reason. I would say that close friendship combined with insistent invitation would justify your being an usher; your refusal would be offensive and embarrassing. For you to be a bridesmaid or attendant there should be a more intimate friendship, relationship, or definite social obligation. And you should not

243

consider being a maid of honor or best man except for a very close relative, like brother or sister, or in special circumstances, for your very best lifelong friend, roommate, or shipmate.

Remember that if there is serious danger of scandal you may never take part at all in these functions. I cannot imagine any danger of scandal where a funeral is concerned; but for weddings much depends on the community. In a strong Catholic community your activities as a bridesmaid might not be understood at all and might seriously trouble the consciences of Catholic people. In one of our little Midwestern towns which have a few Catholic families scattered among friendly Protestants the problem is quite different. Here your participation would be taken as a matter of course, and your refusal would cause misunderstanding and prejudice. But even here we must not forget the danger of contributing to religious indifference.

Something depends on the nature of the ceremony, the solemnity of its celebration, the religious functions associated with it, and the attendant publicity.

I think you see now why Catholic children are not allowed to sing with a choir for a Protestant service; that would be taking an active part in the service itself. On the other hand, I think you can sometimes accompany your own immediate relatives to a special church function. Your attendance is passive, and there is excellent reason for it. Such attendance should be rare, however, and the occasion should be really special.

Q. When speaking with others we Catholics are often reminded of the cruelties of the Inquisition. Just what is this all about, and how much of it is true?

A. The Inquisition was a medieval system of judicial procedure for the apprehension, trial, and punishment of heretics. Usually by that name we understand the papal Inquisition which began before the middle of the thirteenth century and was used intensively to wipe out the Albigensian heresy in southern France, against the Waldensian heretics of northern Italy, and rather generally throughout Germany. In the latter part of the fifteenth century it was revived by Ferdinand and Isabella in their combined kingdoms in Spain and was used by them in getting rid of Jews and Moslems; it was then made into a permanent and active Spanish institution, ecclesiastical in principle but largely dominated by civil influence and used for political purposes, and as such it lasted until the nineteenth century. In some other parts of Europe it was revived in the sixteenth century and used against Protestants.

Most of what I write here pertains to the thirteenth century institution. The Spanish Inquisition is another story. The name Inquisition is applied both to the tribunal, or court, and to the method of its procedure. Its essential feature was that a number of judges were appointed directly by the Pope and sent out to various trouble spots to act in his name in dealing with heresy and other offenses

245

against the Faith. The methods employed by their courts were not new; they were based on canon law and incorporated some principles and procedures from civil law. In general the courts of the Inquisition were more just, humane, and lenient than the civil courts of that day.

The procedure went something like this: An inquisitor —very often a Dominican priest, but sometimes a Franciscan or a secular priest—would come into a city or an area in which there were known to be active heretics. He was supposed to establish contact with the local bishop and work in cooperation with him; and very often he relied on the help of the civil authorities too. They were generally eager to help; but if they refused they could be excommunicated.

The first thing the inquisitor did was to grant a "term of grace" of one month in which to permit his suspects to repent and confess. His primary purpose was to bring about their conversion. If they did confess they got off with a penance—perhaps a severe one, like a pilgrimage.

During that month of waiting the inquisitor had the opportunity to pick up much information from his contacts with local authorities and civilians. His list of suspects became more definite. At the end of the "term of grace" these suspects were cited to appear for trial. They were not imprisoned, but were made to take oath that they would appear when summoned, and sometimes they were put under bond. Violation of an oath created a strong suspicion of heresy, because many of the heretics despised oaths. When the suspects were called into court there was still time to confess, repent, and get off easy. But if they denied their guilt they were questioned diligently, under oath, and the testimony of witnesses was taken. If the suspicion remained strong but proof was inconclusive, every

246

effort was made to obtain an admission of guilt. Threats were used first; if that didn't work the suspect might be put in prison, and there he would be visited by friends or influential people who would try to persuade him to confess. If all that failed, the final recourse was torture.

The use of torture has generally brought the sharpest criticism against the Inquisition. In the beginning it was not permitted; it was first authorized by Pope Innocent IV in 1252. It had been rather generally used in civil courts before that time. The Inquisition was supposed to torture a suspect only once and not to break any of his bones, mutilate him, or endanger his life. In principle the suspect was to be questioned only after the torture was completed. Actually these restrictions were sometimes ignored; for instance the torture would be interrupted and the suspect questioned while he was on the rack, and if he still refused to confess the screws would be tightened again.

At least two witnesses were needed to convict a man, but usually the judge required more. Canon law had always excluded the "infamous"—heretics and excommunicated persons—from acting as qualified witnesses; however, the Inquisition accepted their testimony and left its evaluation to the judge. The theory was that the activities of heretics were carried on in dark secrecy, so that only other heretics could have information about them.

It was common practice to withhold the names of witnesses from the accused. He had no chance to confront them or cross-examine them. Seldom was he able to get any witnesses to testify in his defense; they were afraid of being suspected of heresy themselves. He had no legal advisor; lawyers were afraid to accept such cases, and sometimes they were forbidden to do so. This was later changed, and legal advisors were available.

247

Even at that time people realized that some of these rules were unjust, and attempts were made to protect the natural rights of the accused. For instance, he could tell the judge who his enemies were and if the accusation came from them it might be quashed. False witnesses were punished severely; in those days perjury was considered one of the worst of crimes. Another protection was a sort of jury —the "good men" who were asked to review the case. Sometimes the documents and testimony were submitted to several dozen of these "good men," who were wise and respectable, often learned in theology or canon law. Generally they reviewed the case without knowing the name of the accused. Their recommendations were not binding on the judge, but were usually followed.

Still another protection for the accused was that he could reject a judge because of prejudice; and another right permitted him was that of appeal to the Holy See at any stage of the trial. If appeal was made the documents were sent to Rome under seal; time was gained, and a lighter sentence usually expected.

In theory, the accused person was not presumed guilty until proven so. Once his guilt was established sentence was pronounced in solemn manner. The common punishments inflicted directly by the Church were certainly not inhuman; e.g. the building of a church, a pilgrimage, visiting a church, hearing Mass, receiving the sacraments, the offering of a candle, participating in a crusade, fines, whipping, the pillory, the wearing of colored crosses, etc. The most severe was imprisonment—sometimes in chains—and even that was often considered an opportunity for repentance. And when a change of heart came, the punishments were often remitted. However, with heretics who refused to recant, or with those who relapsed after apparent conversion, the penalty was often excommunication, after which they were delivered "to the secular arm"—the civil authority—to be burned at the stake. It is impossible to know how many were put to death in this way—a good guess might be one in fifty of those found guilty.

If we are to understand the Inquisition at all we must judge it by the standards, beliefs, and attitudes of its own time. Its procedures do not conform to our modern concepts of justice and human rights. On the other hand, in comparison with some modern master-violators of human rights, like the Nazis and the Communists, the Inquisition was a puny piker.

Up until that time and for many subsequent centuries, intolerance was taken for granted. It was not a product of the Church, or of the Middle Ages. It was inherited; it was common to all people. Men sincerely believed, in those days, that religious differences and conflicts were disruptive of society. The state, if it was to be strong and prosperous, needed unity in religious belief almost as much as the Church did. Consequently heresy was looked upon as treason. It was a crime against God and a threat to society.

Judged by our modern standards the Middle Ages were a time of cruelty. Since the people hated heresy it was natural that they should use their customary cruelty in efforts to stamp it out. The inquisitors were generally upright and honest men, inspired by zeal for the faith, devoted to the law, and intent upon justice. But they were children of their own times, sharing its concepts and its attitudes. Their first purpose was the conversion of the heretic, but if he refused to be converted, and was found guilty, their rules of justice demanded extreme penalties, and nobody was troubled by qualms.

Q. Is the Church opposed to freedom of speech?

A. The Church regards man's freedom of speech as his sacred right. She is opposed to sinful abuse of this right.

Speech is one of the greatest faculties God gave to man. It is uniquely human, not shared by any other creature. It is man's means of expressing the thoughts of his immortal soul, his means of fellowship with other immortal souls.

The speech of others—oral and written—is our means of learning. Most of what we know about God and our own soul comes from speech. It is something sacred which may well be the means of our eternal salvation. But like all God's gifts, it can be readily abused—and become the instrument of our damnation.

God gave us the power of speech—and with that power the right to use it. But the same God forbids the *abuse* of that power of speech. No man has a *right* to commit sin. Many are the sins which can be committed by speech:

1. *Lying* is always sinful. No man has a right to lie—especially if that lie does harm to someone.

2. *Blasphemy* is turning God's power of speech against its Giver.

3. *Cursing* turns speech against our neighbor.

4. *Scurrility,* foulness, indecency, and suggestiveness are abuses of speech—whether in the parlor or on the stage.

5. *Defamation* of character—ruining another's reputa-

250

tion—is a sinful abuse of speech, even if we say nothing but the truth.

6. *Charity* is often violated by speech; deep wounds are inflicted, men are provoked to *anger or hatred,* led into sin, counseled falsely.

Speech is the means of false propaganda, of inciting to revolt, of leading to heresy, of inciting to lust and enticing to sin.

All these things are forbidden by God's laws, and he who does them sins.

Sometimes human laws are needed to protect society and individuals against abuse of speech.

In times of war, particularly, our nation must guard against treason and sedition, against sabotage by speech, against false propaganda and the betrayal of secrets necessary to security.

In times of peace we must protect our people from libel and from fraudulent misrepresentation in advertising or selling.

The Church finds it necessary to protect her children from the snares of heresy in speech or writing—from the hidden pit-falls of error and malicious misrepresentation. Thus she exercises censorship of books and supervises the teaching of religion.

These things are done not to restrict the *right* of speech, but to guard innocent bystanders against its abuse.

The right we highly prize. That right is best protected by encouraging its proper use and avoiding its abuse. No one need fear that the Church will destroy freedom of speech; but they can be sure that she will always strive to educate and guide her children to speak rightly, as well as freely.

251

Q. I was struck by a statement of Dr. James M. O'Neill, quoted in The Catholic Messenger *recently. He asked Catholics to disavow any connection with the slogan that truth has rights, but error has no rights. He contended that rights belong to persons, not to abstractions like truth or error. Applied to the Spanish view of religious tolerance, this seems to me a forceful criticism of that position. Can you explain the philosophical premises of Dr. O'Neill's statement?*

A. Dr. James O'Neill did a thorough and satisfying work a few years ago in refuting Blanshard's pack of documented lies. I recommend that you read his *Catholicism and American Freedom* and pass it on to any of your friends who have been deluded by Blanshard—who does seem to have gone quite out of style ever since he maligned the Irish. Doctor O'Neill's argumentation in this book is a thing of beauty, his logic clear, and his documentation a work of exactness. His temper is one of charitable restraint, in pleasing contrast to his opponent's irascible hatred.

Doctor O'Neill begins his book by admitting that he is not a philosopher; but don't let his humility on this point entice you to engage him in debate. His dialectic is deadly. Besides, the authority for the statment which you quote is evidently a well-known Jesuit philosopher, who is cited on page eighty-nine of the book. Here is my analysis of your quotation:

1. What Doctor O'Neill says is true.
2. What he evidently implies is false.
3. His practical conclusion is not far wrong.

1. Error has as much right as truth, because neither has any right. This is entirely true if you take the statement merely as so many words, without reference to connota-

252

tions. Only persons have rights. Rights come from God and inhere in the dignity of human personality. They are a moral claim to some personal good. Inanimate things have no rights; even plants and animals have no rights, since they are not persons.

2. If Dr. O'Neill's statement has any real meaning, it must imply that man has as much right to believe error as truth, or as much right to teach error as truth. This is false. Objectively and strictly speaking, man has no right to believe error, no more than he has a right to commit sin. He has no more right to teach error than he has to lead another man to sin.

3. Dr. O'Neill is a liberal making a plea for tolerance. His point is well taken. He means that we should recognize the sound dogmatic basis of tolerance and not apologize for it. His practical conclusion is not far wrong. But the eminent dialectician seems to have erred in his own domain. He has omitted an important step in his deduction. Every man has a *right to follow his own conscience,* even though that conscience be false. He is, indeed, obliged to follow his conscience. "He who acts against his conscience loses his soul." Man has a right to the freedom necessary to fulfill his obligation of conscience.

Most rights of man are limited, circumscribed by the rights of other men. The accurate determination of these border-lines, or the failure to respect them, causes most of the serious conflicts in human relations.

Usually, if men are to live happily together, a certain measure of compromise is necessary. In strict justice no man has a right to teach error. Yet each man has a right to his sincere beliefs and a right to follow the obligation, dictated by his conscience, to impart his beliefs to others. We

253

may call this a subjective right. It arises from man's general right to follow his conscience.

How far must subjective rights be respected? At least to the point where they come into conflict with definite objective rights of others. That point is often hard to determine with fairness.

It is perfectly evident that if a man believes himself obligated in conscience to cut off another man's ears, his right to follow his conscience in this matter should be restrained. His subjective right to follow his conscience is in conflict with my objective right to keep my ears on my head.

A man has a certain right to believe, profess, and teach false doctrines, in accordance with his conscience. The point of conflict of this right with the objective rights of other men is not always clear. Failure to respect subjective rights in this matter has been the cause of most of the persecutions of history. However, in looking back over some of these persecutions, we wonder if zeal for the glory of God has been the inspiration, or rather man's natural resentment at having someone disagree with him and his natural frustration at failure to convince his opponent.

In the United States, and in much of the world in modern times, we do not believe that a man's profession of error, or even his teaching of it, is sufficient danger to our rights to justify our forceful interference with him. We have the right to argue, refute, and even revile, in a measure. But we have no right to hinder, oppress, or punish. We do not consider the suppression of error as a usual means of obtaining the public welfare.

Catholics in a few other nations do not agree with us. The late Cardinal Archbishop of Seville believed that the open teaching of Protestant errors in his country was a
254

subversive and destructive menace to be suppressed, like our friend's efforts to detach ears. In this His Eminence was adhering to the Spanish tradition developed in mediaeval conflicts with the Saracens, strengthened against the Jews, and crystalized in the Inquisition.

Most American Catholics did not agree with the Cardinal, and with due reverence for his eminent dignity, some Catholic journalists took cracks at his righteous rigidity. We don't so much care what they do in Spain; we don't like to be embarassed before our non-Catholic friends here in America by having our own attitude misrepresented.

The whole question is one of tolerance. We cannot accept or encourage error. We cannot recognize it as equal to truth. We cannot become indifferent. But we can tolerate error in others, as we can tolerate sin in them. To tolerate means "to put up with." Freedom of religion is not protection of error, but protection of the erring man, who should not be hindered from serving God in accordance with his conscience. It is a just and charitable recognition of the sound dogmatic principle that even an erring conscience imposes duties and confers corresponding rights.

Bigotry forgets all virtues but that of faith. Its zeal for truth obscures charity, and even justice. Religious tolerance exercises many virtues; besides justice and charity, it demands prudence, fortitude and patience. "If I have faith sufficient to move mountains, and have not charity, it profits me nothing."

Q. As a Protestant, I have learned many things about your Church, and many doubts have been resolved. My most central question (like that of many other Protestants) is this: If the Catholic Church regained such ascendancy as it enjoyed in the days of Philip II of Spain, would it not again resort to force and terror to make men accept it as the only true faith?

You preach that God is Love, and that your Church is Christ's kingdom on earth, and must therefore bring love to all men. You never cease to remind your people that the individual human being is of infinite worth, and must be respected accordingly. And I know you teach that the best government is the one which most abhors the breaking down of any man's conscience, in the manner of the Communists, who say, "Do as I tell you, and believe as I say, or else suffer all the torture we can heap upon you!"

Ever-increasing doubt and fear prevail throughout every nation. And in these times of travail, your Church offers much that the world needs. So much, indeed, that if you clear up this one point made in my question, I am certain the result will be a turning to her on a vast scale.

A. You have given me a very difficult question. The answer is rather clear to me and to the average Catholic; my difficulty is in presenting it in such a way that you and your non-Catholic friends will believe me. This question seriously perturbs many of them, and their fears regarding it
256

have been exploited by bigots and agitators, who claim that the Church is by nature, doctrine, and history an authoritarian and intolerant institution.

Her enemies sometimes assert that she accepts our American Constitution with tongue in cheek, squirms uncomfortably under our separation of Church and state, and pleads for tolerance from her minority position, trying to hide her own ancient fangs of persecution until she can gain that numerical ascendancy which will give her power.

Another reason your question is difficult is that its answer must predict a contingent, hypothetical future. You are naturally skeptical of prophets. Reliable predictions of the future must be firmly based on past and present. The doctrine and history of the Church, and the discernible attitudes and convictions of American Catholics should give us the key as to what to expect.

Here again we encounter difficulty; both the doctrine and the history of the Church in this matter have frequently been presented to the American people in a distorted manner. Professional bigots have warned Americans not to trust the friendly, tolerant attitude of their Catholic neighbors, because these poor, well-meaning people are only the blind tools of a horrible hierarchy which shares nothing of their naive justice and charity.

Your mention of Philip II is only by way of comparison, but it will help keep our discussion clear and to the point if we confine ourselves to the United States and to American Catholics. It only confuses the issue to bring up arguments about what the Church is doing in Spain or South America. The immediate Catholic reaction is to counter with arguments about what the Protestants are doing in Sweden or Switzerland, and we are off on a tangent.

We Catholics in the United States are not Spanish Catholics. We do not have the Iberian temperament, traditions or attitudes. We are thoroughly American, with a keen sense of personal liberty, human rights, and freedom of conscience.

First of all, as regards the Constitution and its precious Bill of Rights, any American Catholic will tell you with truth and vehemence that he accepts it completely, with no reservation. Catholics are proud of the part they had in helping to design it, in accepting it, and in signing it. We prize it and revere it; and we know that as a result of it we have the best government the world has ever seen. And various recent experiments, from Moscow to Buenos Aires, have made us thank God fervently and frequently for the wisdom of our forefathers.

As regards the principle of separation of Church and state, we Catholics have been in an excellent position, throughout the history of our country, to appreciate its practical advantages. If there were any union between Church and state or any establishment of a Church in the United States, it would be a Protestant union or establishment, naturally. We believe that we have sufficient sense of fairness and justice, and have learned enough from our own happy experience, to give a Protestant minority equal breaks—should that day ever come.

It is no mere lip service which we pay to separation of Church and state in this country. Frankly, we could imagine a more ideal situation in which people entirely Catholic would live together in a Catholic state, which would work in perfect harmony and cooperation with the Church. And just as frankly, we are not in agreement with that extraneous principle interjected as a dictum in some Supreme Court decisions, which would erect a "wall of separation" between Church and state—making the state

258

entirely secular, practically irreligious, and completely un-cooperative with any church. It is one of the benefits of our system that our government has never been like that. It is generally helpful and friendly towards all religions, and manifests respect and concern for religious things.

To sum up the Catholic attitude, we believe that as long as there remain various religions in this land of ours, no matter who is in the majority an attitude of separation and impartiality is the only fair and just one that can be adopted by our government. In 1948, the late Archbishop McNicholas, speaking for the bishops of the United States, expressed this attitude forcefully and officially: "We deny absolutely and without qualification that the Catholic bishops are seeking a union of Church and state. If tomorrow Catholics constituted a majority in our country they would not seek a union of Church and state. They would then, as now, uphold the Constitution and all its amendments."

Now even if you completely believe me that American Catholics accept our democratic form of government with love and reverence and adhere firmly to the practical separation of Church and state, I have only begun to answer your question. If we Catholics were running the government, would our government remain tolerant towards non-Catholics? That is really your question. To answer it, we should consider briefly the Church's teaching on public, or political, tolerance.

Pope Pius XII, in a talk to Catholic jurists on December 6, 1953, recalled for us the traditional teaching of the Church on this matter, making it clear that the suppression of error is not the ultimate norm for the action of public authority. While this is an objective, certainly, it must be subject to higher and more general norms; and, in conse-

259

quence, the state, even the Catholic state, must often tolerate a variety of beliefs and practices.

The first duty of the state is to seek the common good, the general welfare of its citizens. This common good cannot be achieved in the midst of religious strife, rivalries, hatreds, injustices. Where several religions are firmly established in the same territory there is only one reasonable course for the state: complete religious freedom, with liberty and equality for all. Religious liberty is absolutely necessary in America, and always will be, as far as we can possibly foresee; and it matters not who is in the majority. It is required by wisdom and justice; without it the state could not realize its purpose.

Even the most Catholic state in the world must, in justice, recognize and respect: 1) the sincere and honest convictions of its people; 2) the inviolability of their consciences; 3) the injustice of trying to force them against their consciences; and 4) the violations of charity which are involved in disturbing the honest consciences of people to no purpose.

The Catholic Church in our country has spoken out strongly against the social, economic, and racial injustices which make second-class citizens of many in our nation. She would be turning back against her own teachings if she were to make non-Catholics second-class citizens once she came to power.

Tolerance in society is as much a matter of civilization as of religion. It expresses a general refinement of morals, an advancing maturity of concepts, and a deepening of ethical culture. For that reason it is not fair today to hold Catholics responsible for the actions of generations long vanished. The cruelties of former centuries disgust the modern Catholic as well as the modern Protestant. And it
260

should be noted that the ancestors of both were about equally guilty in those fratricidal struggles which followed the Reformation and make the ugliest pages in Christian history.

To sum it up, I am sure that if the United States became strongly Catholic tomorrow, there would probably be more encouragement of Catholic schools, stricter laws on divorce, and maybe, more censorship of movies; but there would be no restriction of that traditional American freedom of believing, worshipping, and practicing religion in accordance with the dictates of conscience.

Now again, even if you accept that statement, I have not fully answered your question. Real tolerance does not result from government guarantees; it proceeds from an attitude of the people, of society in general. The remaining question, then, is this: If we Catholics were in the majority would we be personally and collectively tolerant towards those in the minority who disagree with us? Official freedom under the Constitution would not make you happy if your Catholic neighbors all treated you with cruelty or condescension.

There is, I believe, a fairly widespread suspicion that basic Catholic teachings do not really permit tolerance, or at least do not encourage it. We are thought to be driven by a pervading fervor to conquer men's minds and wills, because it is contrary to our conscience to let error exist untrammeled.

This suspicion may be encouraged by Catholic firmness on the rightness of truth and the wrongness of error. The Church is a teacher of religious truth, and she is intolerant of religious error, even as the teacher of mathematics is intolerant of error in addition. Can you imagine a mathe-

261

matician being tolerant of the proposition that two plus two equals five?

By its very nature, truth is intolerant, even as goodness is intolerant. Goodness will not accept evil and call it good. Truth will not accept error under its own emblem. It would be ridiculous for the Church to accept truth and error on the same plane and hold them equal. She would run herself out of business as a teacher of the truth. She would agree that all religions are equally true, and therefore equally false. Consequently she would admit that she teaches a false religion. What a teacher!

The Church is careful not to encourage that prevalent indifference which has us all going to the same heaven by different routes, all comparably good. She is anxious to avoid that confusion on the subject of tolerance which would attribute to rational men an inherent natural right to be wrong. She recognizes that we have the capability and the psychological freedom to be wrong, just as we have the ability to sin. But we have no more right, before God, to be wrong than we have to commit sin.

If we are to keep clearly to the subject, we should define the meaning of tolerance. It is "patient forebearance in the presence of an evil which we are unable or unwilling to prevent." It does not mean that we accept the evil as good, or that we close our eyes and ignore it. We recognize it for what it is, but deliberately choose to let it run its course.

In religious tolerance we make a clear distinction between the error itself, and the person who is in error. The basic reason for religious tolerance is that we love and esteem the erring person, and even as we condemn his error, we recognize his sincerity and respect his conscience.

Real tolerance does not look down on the erring person

with pride or pity. We accept such a one as a man with convictions firm and reasoned as our own—but wrong. We know that innocent error can produce firm certitude; and experience teaches us that good faith should be presumed.

We are tolerant because God alone is the judge of a man's conscience; and it well behooves man's fellow man to give him the benefit of doubt.

We are tolerant out of a sense of fairness, on the sound basis of give and take. We demand and hope that other people will respect our religious convictions. We must do unto them in like manner.

We are tolerant that our charity may reflect the immeasurable love of God, who tolerates countless evils in the world.

We are tolerant in imitation of Jesus Christ, whose love led Him to forgive the sinner, and who advised that the cockle be allowed to grow with the wheat until the harvest.

Tolerance is the exercise of fundamental Christian virtues: love, justice, patience, kindness. We love our neighbor for the love of God. We love him even though he is a sinner—or a heretic. And usually we should love the heretic before the sinner, because he is more sincere and honest and well-intentioned—a better person.

Tolerance reflects a mature soul, with wisdom, charity, nobility, and benevolence. The person of wide experience, who knows the world and the ways of men, and has acquaintance with the finer things of life, is not inclined to be intolerant. It is the narrow, prejudiced, small-minded person who hunts heretics.

Jonathan Swift spoke contemptuously of those who have "enough religion to make them hate one another, and not enough to make them love one another." A person such as this is religiously immature. His intellect has not developed enough for him to appreciate the prevalence of error and the lucidity of its arguments. His emotions have not matured enough to leave his intellect free. Fears, prejudices, and hates plague him. He dares not project himself in sympathy into the other man's position; he is too insecure in his own faith. He is selfish in demanding that everyone agree with him; and he secretly fears that diversity will undermine his own convictions.

Intolerance is a matter of personality rather than of religion. We readily condemn hatred and narrowness in others. But even if we were to recognize these traits in ourselves we would find good rationalizations to justify them. Envy, greed, jealousy, and fear foment intolerance; and these vices feed on ignorance and prejudice. Catholics have no monopoly on these defects.

Catholics and Protestants in America share the same civilization, education, moral ideals, and social background. We should expect as much tolerance from the one as from the other. For that reason I firmly believe that if proportions were reversed overnight the Protestants would be at least as free and equal in Catholic America tomorrow as the Catholic is in Protestant America today.

6. The Church and Modern Problems

Sex. What's Wrong About Birth Control? The Legion of Decency. Is the World Over-Populated? Priests and Labor-Management Relations. Public and Parochial Schools. What is Co-Instruction? Catholics and Racial Justice. Is Segregation Sinful? Interracial Marriage. Correcting the Sinner. Feeding the Hungry. Should Women Work? Work on Sunday.

Q. Does it seem that the Church in this century, and especially in America, gives disproportionate attention to "sex"? Has this been for nineteen centuries the number-one topic of Church concern, or is it even today the number-one topic outside the United States?

A. The Church is inclined to give her concentrated attention to the number-one problem of each time and place. If she seems to insist on sexual morality in twentieth-century America that is because sexual problems have become paramount in our country today. If you need proof, glance quickly at the corner newstand or the movie marquee, stop in at any theater, put a dime in any juke box, drive by any lovers' lane, inquire at the drug store, or visit any court room.

Never before the present century has the Church been confronted with problems of widespread birth-control, general youthful promiscuity, blatant public huckstering of sex, and frightening marital instability. She would be neglecting her duty as moral teacher and guide if she did not give attention and forceful effort to these matters, especially in the face of a growing attitude, fostered by frank teaching and organized propaganda, that all these things are OK—simply the modern, mature, sane and uninhibited, normal human attitude.

The Church has to be doubly insistent in the United States because she is left quite alone to fight the cause of morality in these fields. Until the present century she had strong Protestant support in this, as in all other fields of morality. But during the past fifty years Protestants have gradually retreated from the common front. Most of them had always admitted divorce in principle, but generally they maintained strong opposition to it in practice. That opposition has weakened. They once opposed birth control strongly; now nearly all accept it, and many openly advocate it. Certainly they do not approve promiscuity, or filthy literature, or Hollywood's follies, but their opposition to these evils has so weakened that it can seldom be heard clearly; and by their sniping at the Legion of Decency and Catholic "censorship" they often appear to be on the opposite side.

In trying to hold that firm moral front—once a united front—Catholics now find themselves frequently condemned for their courage and constancy by the very ones who deserted them.

Sexual problems are only slightly less public in other countries of the modern world, and we are led to believe that under certain aspects they are even more critical in Sweden, Germany, France, and England. So the Church has to stand strongly on her principles everywhere today. And to make the task harder she often finds the principles themselves undermined by relativism in morality and deterministic theories of human conduct.

Man has not changed basically, of course, and the Sixth Commandment has always been a difficult one to keep. The Church has always found it necessary to preach an occasional sermon on the subject, to encourage, teach, and reprimand. But in the nineteen previous centuries it was a sort of routine problem, an acknowledged part of human nature, a result of original sin. Nothing to get upset about.

By contrast, sex seems to be an obsession of modern society. Frank Sheed, in *Society and Sanity,* sums it up with a striking statement:

"The typical modern man practically never thinks about sex.

"He dreams of it, of course, by day and by night; he craves for it; he pictures it, is stimulated or depressed by it, drools over it. But this frothing, steaming activity is not thinking, picturing is not thinking, craving is not thinking, dreaming is not thinking . . ."

Mr. Sheed concludes that upon sex as upon other matters we must use reason. Instinct is a good guide for the lower animals; but reason is the only safe guide for men. The Church has thought these problems out, and she tries to get modern man to think along with her. But too often he just continues to drool. So she keeps harping on the subject when she would much rather turn her attention to the great moral issues involved in the economic and social problems of our time, the issues presented by atom and hydrogen bombs, and cold wars and segregation.

Q. After listening to Margaret Sanger on Mike Wallace's TV program, I want to know just why the Church forbids birth control.

A. First, let me ask you a question: Just what do you mean by birth control? It is a rather ambiguous term; there are many ways by which birth might be controlled. Old maids have a foolproof system. The young couple who put off getting married until they can afford a home control birth by staying apart. Heroic spouses might conceivably control conception by abstaining completely from marital relationship; and many couples, most of them quite conscientious, watch carefully the days which are believed to be less fertile for their intercourse. There are peasant mothers in some countries who nurse their babies for years, hoping that they will not conceive during lactation. Sterilization is a very thorough and radical means of birth control; and today there are a variety of drugs and instruments to substitute for Onan's early and fatal method. Even abortion could be a method of birth control.

Second, let me make a technical correction: The Church does not forbid birth control; she has made no explicit law on the subject. But she does teach very forcibly that contraception, or *artificial* birth control, is a serious sin because it is contrary to the natural law of God. There is a big difference, you know. If the Church made the law she

269

might change it or repeal it. But since it is a law of God she cannot touch it, only teach it.

You will probably offer no argument when I say that the sexual organs of man and woman are designed by nature for reproduction and that the primary purpose of sexual relationship is the conception of a child—primary because it is to that end that the act is directed by its nature, by the design and plan of God. It need not be the primary purpose in the minds of the people engaged in the act; they may not even think about it, or may hope it won't happen. Nature takes care of its own primary purpose as long as men do not interfere, and often it finds a way of retribution when they do.

In presuming that you will offer me no argument I remain aware that there are many people who would. Margaret Sanger denied definitely that conception was nature's purpose in the sexual act. You heard her. And she went on to make it clear that you would argue with her in complete futility about this point, because she leaves you no grounds on which to base your arguments. She does not believe in God, or the moral law, or any divinely conceived plan or purpose in man's living. I hate to be ungallant, but I would be forced to classify her as a frustrated hedonist. The philosophy of the hedonist is that pleasure is the highest goal of life, and that sensation, thrill, and sensory satisfaction are the means of all human happiness. No use to speak to such a person of sin.

It is very true that sexual activities have other purposes than the begetting of children: they are an expression of love and an attraction of love; they are the emotional cement of marital union and the motive force for the sacrifice required to establish and maintain that union; they give physical relaxation and emotional normality; and they

270

add immeasurably to the zest, pleasure, purpose and enthusiasm of natural living.

These things are good. The Church is aware of their goodness. But she insists that man is not mere animal; he is a rational animal. Beasts have no power of reasoning; so their instincts control their sexual life. In man the mind is the highest faculty, and it should dominate over all the other powers of man and control them. In other words man should be reasonable. His sexual life should be ordered by reason, not coldly and calculatingly but in accord with its natural purpose, as designed by the Creator.

To perform an act and at the same time directly frustrate its primary purpose is to act unreasonably. To perform the marital act and positively interfere with its generative effects is to change the essential nature of that act. It is no longer the good and purposeful act that is in God's plan of creation, but an act which man has devised in his own scheme of cross-purposes.

Morality simply requires that husband and wife be reasonable in their relationship. A reasonable person understands the nature of things and treats them according to their nature. The nature of the sexual act is to procreate. So if they perform the act they must respect its nature, not distort that nature.

Sexual relationship does not always result in conception; so the evil of birth control does not lie essentially in the fact that conception is hindered, but in the positive action which is directly contrary to the purpose of the primary action. It would be just as wrong if it were ineffective and if conception took place in spite of it.

Pope Piux XI in his well-known encyclical on Christian marriage sums up the Catholic teaching clearly: "Any use whatsoever of matrimony exercised in such a way that the

271

act is deliberately frustrated in its natural power to generate life is an offense against the law of God and of nature, and those who indulge in such are branded with the guilt of grave sin."

This question of birth control is one which sharply, and often bitterly, divides Catholics from non-Catholics today. Not only hedonists favor the practice, but also good sincere Christian people, who are convinced of the desirability of the secondary purposes of sex for their own sake, and refuse to go along with our philosophical reasoning about the true nature and essential primary purpose of the marital act. They argue that sex is so powerful and essential that man cannot live without it, and on the other hand that reasons of health, economics, education, and social standing often make prolific propagation positively immoral.

These good people have been sold on the widely-advertised benefits of contraception in protecting the health of women and children; in reducing mortality, abortions, and defective children; in creating happier homes and lowering the divorce rate; in elevating the standard of living, providing educational and social advantages, reducing juvenile delinquency, and avoiding a frightening famine-plagued overpopulation of the world. Some of them are also attracted by the lure that contraception is the modern, mature method of controlling life instead of being controlled by it, of planning your family and getting the children you want when you want them, rather than taking them as they come. It makes man master of his own destiny.

Some of these arguments have value to them; others are a deception, like the reduction of abortions and divorce. And even the sound arguments can be countered with arguments equally valid and powerful. For instance, there

272

is no doubt that the wide-spread knowledge and availability of the means of contraception has increased pre-marital immorality and sexual promiscuity frighteningly—even to the point that our modern society finds a "reasonable" amount of this sort of thing acceptable, has dropped the notion of immorality, and speaks of pre-marital *experiences*. Along with this, in spite of prevention, is an increase in illegitimacy, abortion, and forced marriages. Furthermore, the will for sterility which often invades marital life through contraception takes half the natural meaning and purpose from that life and makes it selfish and unsatisfying. This probably accounts for the fact that two-thirds of the people who get divorces have no children.

All these arguments about the benefits or evils of birth control have no direct bearing on the essential immorality of contraception in itself. Good purposes or good effects do not justify a sinful act. It is this consideration alone which determines the Church's attitude on the subject. She does not propose mere numbers as the basis of the ideal family. She simply tells us we must not commit sin.

Q. Our daughter claimed that the movie she attended was "OK for adults." But mother claimed that she should not attend this particular movie house, and referred her to a recent article in The Catholic Messenger *which stated that this theater was "off bounds." The daughter's defense was, "There were four priests there."*

Is it not better to deny one's self the aesthetic pleasure of a movie that is OK than to assert one's academic freedom and patronize a theater that has had a record of frequent violations of the moral code in its showings?

There is much confusion in this area concerning the workings of the Legion of Decency, and it stems from the assertion of academic freedom. When our bishop indicates to us that there is danger of serious sin in attending movies shown by a certain theater manager, do not priests and laymen alike bear the responsibility of heeding our bishop's warnings? And where our bishop indicates that a certain manager has been guilty of violations and deserves the boycotting contained in the Legion pledge, should we not follow the lead given us by our bishop?

A. Any person with normal practical prudence would avoid this question like poison. It offers the answer-man three possibilities:

1. Take an unfraternal crack at those cinema-minded clerics, realizing that they are probably my close friends,
274

and that there with them, except for the grace of prior engagement or diverse interests, might have been I.

2. Take a low and liberal view of the whole business of censorship, giving loose rein to my own innate tendencies to rebellion, and thus tend slyly to undermine the bishop's authority in his own paper, taking ungracious advantage of his own liberal attitude towards those who work with him.

3. Try to please two factions, conciliate opposing attitudes, compromise a few principles, and thence end up thoroughly drenched in self-disdain from my slopping efforts to carry water on both shoulders.

The unpleasant results of any chosen course might be easily avoided by simply throwing this question into the waste basket. But my guilt complex warns me of the incongruity of conducting a question box with the right hand and rejecting honest questions with the left, just because of a few inherent booby-traps. I have a persistant theory that if I am careful about my principles and honest in my answers I will not get into serious trouble, even though I do tread passingly on a few bunioned toes. The theory needs persistence because it meets with jolting reversals.

We will partially clarify the conflicts involved in this problem if we consider, in broad outline, the nature of the Legion of Decency, and the implications of obedience.

As I understand the Legion of Decency, without technicalities, it was established for two purposes:

1. To provide incentive for cleaning up the movies, by pressure at the box office;

2. To protect you and me from personal harm in our movie-going, by providing a reliable guide to decent, questionable, and objectionable films.

275

Unless I misunderstand it, the Legion was not intended to be a medium of censorship or an instrument of organized and directed boycott. It seems to have become both, on occasion; and I personally believe that this misuse of it has greatly weakened its support in liberal Catholic circles, stirred opposition to it among non-Catholics, and created general confusion as to its nature and obligation. There are many, cleric and lay—and I do not exclude myself from their number—who have lost enthusiasm for the shining ideal of the Legion pledge, because they see it so frequently involved in embarrassing back-alley fighting with gutter-type films, which welcome the publicity; because it has, on occasion, been used as a ready and fairly subservient instrument of organized and picketed boycott by certain "militant" Catholic organizations, and because there is occasionally injected into its own voluntary bloodstream the virus of assumed authority.

Let us restore the Legion to its pristine purity of purpose and method and it will once more become a forceful means of expressing Catholic attitude and a useful guide to the conscientious cinema addict. If there must be occasional censorship, and we ardently hope that it may seldom be needed, then let it be exercised under direct authority of the bishop in his own diocese, without implications of some supra-episcopal, national authority, which does not exist.

What was that original purpose? To enlist the enthusiastic cooperation of faithful Catholic people in a crusade for decency in films. What were its pristine methods? The enlistment of individual action through voluntary pledge, without new obligation, and without any watch-dog to supervise the keeping of the pledge. It did not confuse consciences by seeming to enact a law; it simply stressed

276

the natural obligations we have under the Fifth, Sixth, Ninth, and a few other assorted Commandments. It simply asked us to avoid sin and serious dangers of sin; and benignly accepted our pledge that we would do so.

Your complaint of the "assertion of academic freedom" seems a barb aimed at professors; but they are not the only ones in our country today who writhe and tend to revolt under restrictions and censorship. Though we complain loudly of lack of subservience in our American society, our complaints will echo hollowly. The spirit is there, and it is deep, and it may well be, in large part, good. At least it will not be uprooted. And any leader who hopes to influence the American people—Catholic or non-Catholic—knows that he must lead them, not try to drive them. Even the armed forces explain to recruits the reasonableness of their regulations.

Do I seem to plead for the right of priests to ignore the directives of their bishop? They wouldn't want me to. The entire issue regarding the status of *that* theater has been pretty confused. I am sure that they did not consider that the bishop had ever formally forbidden anyone to go there. At least I did not. I must admit that I paid little attention to the original action, since I had no intention of attending that theater or any other. But it was my impression that the bishop merely reminded Catholics of their Legion of Decency pledge, urged observance of it, and indicated this theater as one which made a practice of showing Class C pictures.

I feel confident that the incident to which you refer took place before that "out of bounds" statement in *The Catholic Messenger*. Consequently I am sure that these four priests, and other members of the clergy and laity who frequented this theater, did not believe that they were

277

guilty of disobedience towards their bishop. If priests were to go to that theater now they would probably be guilty of impertinence, disrespect, and scandal, but still not directly disobedient; because no formal law calling for obedience has been given. That "out of bounds" statement was a forceful episcopal reminder that we should observe our Legion of Decency pledge, and an authoritative interpretation that this particular theater is showing Class C pictures as a matter of policy.

You will tell me that my defense of those priests is still wobbly; that, even though there was no order demanding obedience, they were still obliged to stay away out of respect for the bishop's earlier interpretation, and as an example for the people. I have not talked to any of them; I don't know who was there; but I suspect that their reasoning was similar to what mine would have been: that theater had not shown a Class C picture for a long time, but on the contrary had shown a string of very good ones (or so I am told). Might it not properly be judged to have purged itself of its blight? You have to give a man a chance to reform; and you don't ordinarily demand years of sinlessness to prove his reform. The force of this reasoning is heightened by another bit of cogent rationalization: may it not well be that a theater which shows habitually a superior type of film, even though it occasionally comes up with a Class C stinker, is more worthy of our patronage than one of those respectable joints which dishes out a steady diet of Class B trash? Many of us feel, deep down in the unexpressive regions, that we never meant this type of theater when we pledged to withhold our patronage from those houses which show objectionable pictures as a matter of policy.

The priests of this diocese do not need to reassure their
278

bishop that they are thoroughly obedient, and that if he gives a clear and definite order they will obey it, as they solemnly promised to do at the time of their ordination. On the other hand the bishop does not need my hint that many of his priests exercise a certain independence of thought and are jealous of their freedom. He knows this and has never made gestures to restrict them. And I am confident that any of us, priests or laity, after reading that official statement about "off limits" a couple of weeks ago, will thoroughly respect his judgment and follow it, until we honestly judge that the theater has again purged itself . . . and we will be more careful in our judgment this time.

After reading this over I want to express the hope that nothing I have written will lessen respect for the Legion of Decency ratings, as the best guide we have, or probably can have, to good and decent movies. And, even more, I hope that it will not serve to dull the conscience of anyone as to the personal obligation of avoiding harmful or dangerous movies. My point is that the following of ratings should be spontaneous and voluntary, not organized or forced; that its classifications should remain guides to us in determining our personal obligations and not directives seeming to emanate from pontifical authority. The Legion has episcopal sponsorship and papal approval, but it has not derived therefrom any measure of supra-episcopal jurisdiction.

Q. In a recent issue of **The Catholic Messenger,** *Father William J. Gibbons, S.J., stated that the world does face the "danger of over-population." Is not this Malthusianism? Are we not to believe that when God ordered man to "increase and multiply" He would give man enough resources to sustain human life in a decent manner?*

A. The Reverend Thomas Malthus was an English clergyman of the late eighteenth century. He was very gloomy about man's prospects, predicting that human beings would soon all be starving to death because population was increasing much faster than the food supply. He made it mathematical: the increase of humans is geometrical—2, 4, 16, 256, 65536; the best food increase to be hoped for is arithmetical—2, 4, 8, 16, 32. So in fifty years—by mid-nineteenth century—disaster would be upon us.

The mid-nineteenth century saw an industrial boom and more food per mouth than Malthus had known. While events made his dire predictions ridiculous, he has not lacked disciples who find much truth in his general theories. They are called neo-Malthusians. Their favorite proof is India, where the starving population increases five million a year and the food supply increases hardly at all. And usually their favorite facile remedy is birth-control.

The subject is much too vast and complicated for me to have even an opinion on the facts. The world's population
280

is certainly increasing rapidly, and yet we are constantly finding new sources of energy, supplies, and food. In the industrial areas of the world the standard of living increases with the population. There are tremendous opportunities for the improvement of farming methods, increasing soil fertility, and utilizing new areas, to say nothing of the food supply which comes from the sea. If these advances were made, the world might feed many times its present population. But prophets of doom warn us that the population growth, led by India and China, will overwhelm us and starve us before we can make these advances.

My faith in God gives me assurance that He knows all the answers and has it all planned out; He is constantly on the job, looking after the world, noting each sparrow which falls, and is constant in His love for the man He created in His own image, redeemed with His own blood, and adopted as His own son. God has never promised man that he will be free of want, suffering, or catastrophe. But He has promised him eternal happiness if he keeps His laws. He never claimed that His universe was perfect. It couldn't be; it is created. But He has demonstrated considerable ingenuity in solving its problems as they arise. Among living things on earth there seems to be a system of balance and compensation. Let one increase out of proportion and a parasite comes along to reduce it to its place, and then something else handles the parasite. When man disturbs the balance he usually runs into problems. God wants him to use his ingenuity and to work, but if he starts trying to solve his own population balance contrary to God's law, his problems will be eternal.

The thermonuclear bomb might be the instantaneous solution to the problem!

Q. What right do priests have to interfere in labor-man-agement relations? Aren't they a little out of their field? I think that these matters should be left to men who are working in that field, i.e. Chamber of Commerce, NAM, etc.

A. Your question looks like a "plant" to me. Else why didn't you include the Communist Party and the WCTU in your list of competent agencies? Who ever accused the Chamber of Commerce of competence in the field of labor relations? Who ever suspected the NAM of lack of preju-dice? Ever hear of the NLRB?

The Question Box does not dodge questions because they are "plants" or issues because they are hot. We are quite willing to help grind axes, and we prefer a double-bitted one. Then, watch out for the chips!

The Church is vitally concerned with the moral aspects of labor-management relations, in which justice and char-ity are directly involved. The Church is the divinely ap-pointed teacher and arbiter of justice. Christian charity is her primary field of activity.

The Church has similar vital interests in various secu-lar fields where ethics and morality are involved, e.g. in medicine and surgery, where the Fifth Commandment often rules; in family relations, where the Fourth and Sixth Commandments are concerned; in law and business, which are particularly regulated by the Seventh Command-ment.

There are secularists galore who would try to drive the Church from all such fields, and take from her other prec-ious rights which have been her own for centuries, e.g. education. There are those who demand, "What right do priests have to interfere in problems involving abortion, or

282

birth control, or euthanasia, or fraud, or delinquency?" It is the same as asking, "What right do priests have to preach the moral law of God?"

The Church is concerned with men as individuals created by God and endowed by Him with spiritual and immortal souls. The Church was established by God to save those souls. It is her task to lead men to God. Labor is not a commodity; labor is men. Jesus Christ died for those men. By sanctifying grace He raises them to the dignity of sons of God. He makes them His brothers, members of His Church, part of His Mystical Body.

The Church is concerned with the divinely-given rights of men; their right to life and liberty, and to the means of salvation. She is interested in their right to property and to security in the necessary means of earthly existence. The assertion and protection of these basic rights is the duty of the Church. These rights involve moral principles and spiritual truths.

Bishops and priests, as shepherds of the flock of Christ, are necessarily concerned with all those things which directly affect the welfare of the flock. It is well-known that economic injustice carries a long train of evils, not only physical and social, but also moral and spiritual: poor nourishment, bad housing, ragged clothing, troubled family relations, juvenile delinquency, sin and crime.

The Church is properly interested in labor-management relations. So, too, the priest is interested. No one can rightly question that. But you evidently propose objection, by your question, to the priest's direct intervention in labor disputes, strikes, picket-lines, and disturbances. You want to use the axe, which we help you grind, on opponents in local controversy.

So we proceed to sharpen both bits of the axe. We are

283

out of the field of principle now. We are discussing means and methods. Here there is room for argument and disagreement. Much depends on the priests's qualifications, his ability to really help settle the dispute. Much depends on his acceptability to both management and labor. Can he do any good? Or will he only aggravate the antagonism? Is he fair in his judgment, and well informed of the matters in dispute? Does his presence help calm violent tempers and lead to reasonable discussion? Or is his very collar inflammatory? Does he really contribute to justice and charity? Or does he stir up prejudices? Does either side really want him there?

There is no doubt of the priest's right to act in such matters. That right is clear and we must defend and uphold it. Sometimes it may be a duty. But you and I have a right to disagree about the advisability or propriety of some particular priest's action in some particular dispute. We are free, and should feel free, to express our opinion on actions which are public and controversial. But let us not question motives or sincerity. We simply disagree. Either one of us could be wrong. Maybe we are both partially wrong.

The priest must always be conscious of his responsibilities to his parish, to the community, and to the Church in general. How will his actions be interpreted? That very consciousness can make a coward of him. It can make him afraid to sponsor right and justice in the face of ingrained prejudice. Forceful action on controverted issues will always stir antagonism. Should the dormant canine be left to slumber? Or should he be roused and vanquished?

Most of us like things to be peaceful and friendly. We have to defend our Church so often against prejudiced attack that we resent having any issue raised which further burdens our apologetics—however much we may be right.

284

Priests on picket-lines are controversial. But so are labor disputes. Sometimes good sharp controversy clears the air and lets justice and charity emerge from the smoke.

Most of us are as prejudiced in labor-management issues as we are in religion. We judge according to our prejudices. One of us sees all capitalists as greedy, grasping, grinding grafters, who never give a worker a break, if they can first break the worker or his union. To this partisan only the laboring man can be right, however red his union bosses, however selfish and short-sighted their demands. Another of us sees all unions as guilds of gangsters, every strike as Communist sabotage, and every picket as a bright red hoodlum or a sadistic goon. This one naturally asks: What part have priests with gangsters, Communists, hoodlums and goons? The question is loaded.

Q. 1. How do public schools and Catholic schools compare? Are the children doing the same work outside of religion?

2. Can a child who is attending vacation school and catechism classes every Sunday receive approximately the same training as a child attending the parochial school?

3. Do you not agree that in learning to live with other people one must learn to be tolerant of all religions?

Certainly a child attending parochial schools and meeting only Catholic children will be very narrow-minded.

I am not opposed to parochial schools but I do want my children to have a well-rounded education.

A. First let us glance at what the Church has to say on the subject of Christian education:

Pope Pius XI in his encyclical on the Christian Education of Youth (1929) declares "that the so-called 'neutral' or 'lay' school, from which religion is excluded, is contrary to the fundamental principles of education. Such a school, moreover, cannot exist in practice; it is bound to become irreligious . . ."

After referring to his predecessors, Popes Pius IX and Leo XIII, the Holy Father declares: "We renew and confirm their declarations, as well as the sacred canons in which the frequenting of non-Catholic schools, whether neutral or mixed, those, namely which are open to Catholics and non-Catholics alike, is forbidden for Catholic
286

children. Neither can Catholics admit that other type of mixed school in which the students are provided with separate religious instruction, but receive other lessons in common with non-Catholic pupils from non-Catholic teachers."

The law of the Church is clear and emphatic, as expressed in the Code of Canon Law.

Canon 1372 states that the parents have the right and the most grave obligation of giving a Christian education to their children. Nothing shall be taught them which is contrary to Catholic religion or morality. Religious and moral instruction shall hold first place in the curriculum.

Canon 1373 says that religious education shall be given in every elementary school. In secondary and higher schools, a more thorough religious training shall be given.

Canon 1374 is particularly to the point: "Catholic children shall not attend non-Catholic, neutral, or mixed schools."

This is the law. Mixed schools are those open to both Catholics and non-Catholics.

The Canon goes on to say that only the bishop can decide the circumstances which might permit an exception to this law, and he must follow instructions of the Holy See in the matter, and see that every care and caution is used to prevent harm to faith or morals. At most, attendance at such schools (i.e. public schools) can be tolerated only by way of exception. (Canon 1374).

Canon 1379 imposes on the bishop and pastors the *duty* of establishing Catholic schools wherever possible.

The same Canon stresses the duty of the faithful to do their part in building and maintaining the schools.

The three Plenary Councils of Baltimore laid down particular regulations for the United States. They emphasized

287

the obligation of the bishops and pastors to establish a school in every parish which could possibly support one. (The failure of the pastor to build a school should be reason for his removal from the parish.)

The Third Council particularly stresses the bitter conflict of the day (1884) between the Church of God and the spirit of the world (secularism) over the education of children, and the Fathers did then solemnly proclaim: "Catholic parents, we not only exhort you with fatherly love, but command you with all the authority we possess, that you give your children a Christian and Catholic education exclusively, that you protect them from the dangers of secular education, and that you send them to parochial, or other Catholic schools, unless the bishop should permit otherwise in a particular case."

This particular case is unquestionable in the absence of a Catholic school.

If that doesn't answer your questions, here are my answers by number:

1. In all secular subjects Catholic schools compare very favorably with public schools. They teach the same curriculum, frequently excelling, occasionally falling short. What they lack in material facilities, the parochial schools frequently compensate for in the devotion, training, and experience of their teachers.

2. Vacation and Sunday school can never compensate for the parochial school. They are only inadequate substitutes. See the concluding sentence of the quotation from Pope Pius XI above.

3. I certainly agree that we must be tolerant of the sincere beliefs of other people (but not tolerant of the errors themselves, as you suggest). We must understand the meaning of the word tolerance—and not let it become indiffer-
288

ence. Tolerance is the charitable act of putting up with something we know to be wrong.

As regards the alleged narrow-mindedness of parochial school children, I would only remind you that excessive broad-mindedness sometimes become flat-headedness.

If you really want your children to get a well-rounded education, send them to the parochial school by all means. They can't get it in a public school, which must of necessity leave out entirely the spiritual and supernatural side of their education—making it decidedly flat.

Q. I have been hearing talk about co-instructional schools. Just what are they, and how do they differ from co-educational schools?

A. Co-instruction is a compromise between segregation and integration.

Complete segregation of the sexes in school is an old European custom, still much in force in many countries over there, in State or public schools as well as Catholic schools.

In 1929 Pope Pius XI wrote an encyclical on the Christian education of youth in which he labeled co-education "false" and "harmful." He condemned such close and equal association between the sexes and pointed out that nature had formed boys and girls quite differently in organism, temperament, and ability, with the result that common and equal training cannot take care of their different needs. The two sexes are destined to complement each other in the family and in society, and the differences between them ought to be maintained and encouraged during their formative years.

Educators following the lead of His Holiness point out the differences in content and method required for the best education of boys and girls, differences which must be neglected in co-education. They refer also to a loss of mutual respect through familiarity, and hint strongly at moral problems arising from too close association.

290

We have no intention of showing lack of reverence for papal teaching, but there are certain cold facts of Catholic education in America which cannot be ignored, and which make the unquestioned ideal of separate education impossible or impractical in most of our parishes and cities.

First is the factor of cost. It is more expensive to maintain two institutions than one. And anyone even remotely in touch with Catholic education knows that we have a heroic financial struggle on our hands to maintain our Catholic schools, to expand them to meet rapidly increasing needs, and to improve them in emulation of the constantly advancing material standards of our public schools. To try to split them by sexes would be to commit voluntary educational suicide. More than one Catholic high school in my own diocese has already given up the struggle during the past twenty years.

Sexual segregation would often double administrative problems, along with costs. In the average parish in our diocese the effort to maintain two separate schools would be simply ridiculous. No one has thought seriously of trying it.

Where separate schools exist in this country, they are usually private institutions which do a selective job of education, ignoring the needs of the masses, who consequently end up in public schools.

Separate schools for boys and girls are not in accord with our American customs. These customs present glaring defects in rightness and holiness, and I am not trying to canonize them. But we do have to live with them, and our boys and girls must be educated with that purpose in mind. Efforts to ostracize ourselves only multiply problems.

Complete segregation, in the face of our American customs of dating, company-keeping, and mate-selection, would be an artificial thing which would ill-prepare our youth for factual living. It would be like raising a plant in a hot-house and then suddenly setting it out to face the rigors of a wintry climate. There is ample evidence that in the past this artificial marsupialism has resulted in a disproportionate number of old maids and bachelors. And there are present indications that it makes boys and girls ill at ease in the frequent presence of each other which our social customs demand. It creates false glamor, silly idealization, giddy desire, and an untrained gullibility for coping with wolves and vampires of the actual American wilds.

Here is what a Sister-principal of a high school with 1500 students, which has recently gone co-educational, says:

"Priests, sisters, and lay teachers, all agree that the boys are less boisterous if there are girls in the classes, and the girls tend to be less giddy if there are boys present. The opportunity of seeing the failings and shortcomings of others in class helps them to develop a truer picture of the opposite sex. You might be interested in this example. During the summer session conducted at our school we have students from approximately twenty-five different schools. The teachers said repeatedly that they could detect the boys from an all-boys school by their loud and boisterous conduct and likewise could pick out the girls from the all-girls schools because of their 'boy-crazy' attitude."

Do we seem to be arguing against Pope Pius XI? The point is rather that the ideal upon which he insists is not generally practical in the hectic turmoil of our American social customs. Nothing in home or neighborhood prepares the children for segregation; and the separate education does not prepare them adequately for home and neighbor-hood.

Co-instructional schools are an effort to avoid the extreme results of both systems. It has been called a synthesis. More plainly, it is a compromise. Boys and girls are usually separated for study and instruction, permitting that distinct type of education adapted to the character and needs of each sex. But boys and girls are not made total strangers to each other; they are together at lunch, for recreation and social functions, and in a variety of common activities, in a manner which accords with American living, to which they are otherwise accustomed, and for which they are being trained.

Let me quote from literature from Bishop O'Dowd high school in San Francisco, which was dedicated early in 1955:

"The purpose of the co-instructional high school is . . . to recognize the vast differences in boys and girls and to 'maintain and encourage them' particularly in adolescence, and in additional ways to foster, according to age and circumstance, 'with due regard to time and place . . . the legitimate association of the sexes.' (The quotes are from the encyclical of Pope Pius XI).

"Mixed faculty . . . boys and girls taught all academic subjects in separate classes . . . to meet the requirements of educational psychology in recognizing the intellectual and emotional differences between the sexes.

"In other school-functions boys and girls cooperate in joint activities. Choral groups, featuring four-part harmony . . . dramatics, student council, school paper, the rooting section, sodality, and other countless activities. In going to and from school, boys and girls are not separated or segregated. At lunch time they may eat together as befits ladies and gentlemen.

"Perhaps here is a real solution to the parental dilemma, one that does not sacrifice the advantages of academic segregation of the sexes, nor on the other hand forego the many advantages of co-education, particularly in social and recreational life."

Co-instruction is an effort to obtain the advantages of separate education at the reduced cost of co-education.

Q. Why do we have so much discrimination among our own Catholic people? There are Catholics in our own parish who think it is tragic about the Negro priest in the South not being allowed to say Mass for white people, yet these same persons are the loudest in their criticism of the Mexican element in our own parish. Why? Isn't this one world we live in and aren't we all God's children?

A. If we Catholics really try to be just and charitable in these days of conflict and controversy, maybe we can arrive at a better understanding of the true teaching of Christ: that we love one another.

We have good reason to know what prejudice is; we have been its frequent victims. But while condemning others for their prejudice against us we have turned right around and developed prejudices of our own, just as bad, just as unreasonable, just as unChristian.

Any time I hear a Catholic say: "Yes, I know he is a human being, with a soul like mine, but—" I know he is butting into some inane rationalizations to excuse his prejudices. He is violating charity and looking for the opportunity to be unjust.

According to our Catholic moral principles, men have natural rights given to them by their Creator. These rights inhere in their human personality, not in their color, race,

295

nationality, or social status. Discrimination violates these rights, and a violation of a man's rights is an injustice.

The virtue of justice seeks to protect every man's rights. It imposes on each one of us the obligation of respecting those rights—just as we want others to respect our rights.

Suppose that your fellow townsmen wouldn't let you live anywhere but beyond the tracks simply because you are a Catholic—or an Irishman. Suppose that there were seats at the back of the bus marked "For Catholics." Suppose that you had to call every Protestant "Sir" or "Mister" and had to know how to keep in your papist's place. Would you like it? Would you feel you were being treated right? And just suppose that the barbers in your town were to adopt a rule that they wouldn't cut an Irishman's hair. Can't you imagine the bricks through the windows?

If it is unfair and unjust for them to treat you that way as an Irishman and a Catholic, then it is unfair and unjust for you to treat Negroes and Mexicans and Jews in similar manner.

We Catholics have a stake in the protection of human rights in this country. We are a minority group. We have to fight for our rights and we don't get them all. But we do a lot better than the Negro in Mississippi—or in Iowa City. And we do a lot better than the Mexican in Texas— or in Davenport.

Whenever human rights are attacked or endangered anywhere in this country, we Catholics should bristle. It is a violation of that justice and charity for which we stand. And it is an indirect attack on our own rights.

"Our rights we prize and our liberties we will maintain" —but not by violating the rights of minority groups, or the guaranteed civil liberties of those we dislike or suspect.

296

Q. I read in the local paper that you have had difficulty in securing off-campus housing for Negro students (in Iowa City). I intended to call you and tell you that I would gladly help out and rent a room to a Catholic Negro student. But since I have not been long in town I first asked several people (good Catholics) for their opinion. Their answers were unanimous: don't be foolish and ask for trouble. I dcided not to try to change, single-handed, the tacit agreement in this town regarding segregation. But I am deeply puzzled by this attitude on the part of Catholics. How can they possibly reconcile it with the teachings of the Church?

A. Some Catholics do not try to reconcile their attitude in this matter with the teachings of the Church. They simply are prejudiced because they were brought up that way, or because people around them are prejudiced. They don't subject their sentiments to the light of reason, or seriously ask themselves whether they fit in with their faith.

Other Catholics reconcile their attitude to the teachings of the Church by an involved series of mental gymnastics called rationalization. This is a process of finding plausible excuses for something we want to do. Its excuses are pretty flimsy to an unbiased observer, but they serve to salve the rationalizer's own conscience. You have seen these worn clichés: the Negro is just naturally inferior; he is lacking in virtue, honesty, intelligence, and social grace; he is dangerous and not to be trusted; his presence in a neighborhood lowers property values; and besides, you wouldn't want your daughter to marry one of them.

Many of us Catholics are not really prejudiced at all, but simply afraid to speak our own mind or act out our own

297

convictions. We are afraid to go counter to traditions and social customs, afraid that we will be criticized by those who really are prejudiced. We take for granted that prejudice is general, normal, and socially respectable, and that we may be considered a bit queer if we fail to conform. We don't want to be radicals, do we?

Probably in no field of Catholic morality is there greater disparity between doctrine and practice. The doctrine is clear and definite: there is absolutely no philosophical or dogmatic basis for discrimination. All men are essentially equal. Differences are only incidental. All have human, immortal souls. All are loved by God, and destined to eternal life. Jesus Christ died for all equally, and all are called to membership in His Mystical Body.

Our Lord Jesus Christ has commanded that we love Almighty God above all things, and that we love our neighbor as ourselves for the love of God. We must love all men. The true Christian makes no distinction of race or nationality in his love. But sometimes it seems hard to find a true Christian. There were so-called Christians who fell for the racism of Hitler. There are nominal Christians who support the flagrant injustice of South Africa's desperate government. And there are mis-named Christians who support the cynical injustice of Mississippi juries and Arkansas governors. There are even Louisiana Catholics who refuse to let a colored priest—another Christ—offer the Holy Sacrifice in their church.

We Christians who chisel on the love of our fellow men fail equally in our love for Christ. Recall the judgment scene which Our Lord described in Matthew 25, 31-46: "And when the Son of man shall come in his majesty . . . And all nations shall be gathered together before him, and he shall separate them . . . the sheep on his right hand,

298

but the goats on his left . . ." You remember it well, or if you don't I would suggest that you read it over carefully, and then see if it can't be paraphrased something like this:

"I was a poor black boy, and you wouldn't let me into your homes, or even into your neighborhood, or your schools, or theaters. I was hungry, and not only did you refuse to give me anything to eat, you wouldn't even let me into the restaurant. Amen, I say to you, as long as you did it not to my dusky brethren, neither did you do it to me. So depart from me you cursed . . ."

That is not sentimentality. It is clear and evident application of the meaning of our Lord's words. If we refuse to see Christ in His brethren, we refuse to see Christ.

Thus far we have been talking about the virtue of charity. The fundamental virtue violated in race discrimination is justice, that virtue which seeks fairness and equality among all men in all things. Justice would give every man his right and his due. It is best expressed by the golden rule: "Do unto others as you would that they should do unto you."

There is a simple question which we can ask ourselves to find out if we are unjust in a particular situation: How would I like it if someone treated me that way? We must answer honestly. How would I like it if I were considered inferior by all my neighbors, if I were rated a second-class citizen, denied fair opportunities of employment, decent housing, educational opportunities, the right to vote, and a hundred other basic human rights? How would I like it? The Negro has feelings just as keen and sensitive as my own coddled ones.

There are two types of justice to be considered in this matter of discrimination:

Distributive justice requires that every citizen have equal

rights guaranteed by the government, equality in voting, in jury duty, military service, taxes, and public services; equal protection under the law and in the courts; equal enjoyment of those things which are provided for the public at public expense, such as schools, parks, streets, transport and public housing. There is evidence that our federal government is recognizing this type of justice; and some of our states are officially in line too. Others are way out of line, and proud of it.

Commutative justice regulates our personal relations with individual Negroes. It requires that we pay a just wage and use fair employment practices. It requires fairness in personal associations and business dealings. Justice has to do with honor, respect and personal dignity. When you patronize or look down upon someone you are apt to violate justice. You can be unjust by hurting someone's feelings. Justice is an exact and demanding virtue.

That man is a hypocrite, bad as the Pharisee, who calls himself a Christian and denies to any race or group of people their God-given natural rights. Yet the history of Catholics relative to race prejudice in the United States is not inspiring. In only one respect can we loudly boast of being better than other Christians; we did not belong to the KKK.

In recent years, however, we have come awake. We can point with pride to the courage and foresight of Archbishops Ritter in St. Louis and Rummel in New Orleans; and we thank God for the exemplary leadership of Bishop Waters in Raleigh. The Congregation for the Propagation of the Faith has published an enlightening report, and the Catholic position, once obscured by lethargy and evasion, has been made clear by the American bishops and by our
300

present pope and his predecessor. It remains only for you and me to fall in line.

To feel the full measure of discrimination you should become interested in a family like the one whose plight prompted this question: some of the finest people we had in our parish, faithful, honest, devout, friendly, refined, and sincere, entirely respectful and inoffensive. Yet practically no decent apartment in the city was available to them. Housing is difficult for anyone in this town; but these people never had a chance. Finally their baby came along and made them eligible for university housing. There is no discrimination there. Our distributive justice functions well. It is commutative justice which is defective in our elite city.

The South African fights from fear (his frightful days are numbered). The Southerner acts from deep ingrained prejudice and entrenched social custom. What excuse do we have in Iowa? Especially we Catholics, who claim to be just and charitable.

Q. I assume there is no challenge to the statement that the Church has for a good long time tolerated the separation of the races in matters religious in the South.

That being so, the parishioners of the segregated congregations certainly have had reason to think such conditions were not in conflict with the position of the Church, haven't they?

If the above is true, why does the Church suddenly threaten or invoke excommunication for adherence to what it has itself so long permitted? Could it not more charitably use a gradual approach?

A. How gradual should the approach be? It is probable that the snail's pace of the past century has served to create the false impression you point out.

Can even a gradual approach be without incident amid the turbulent hatreds and fears now being fanned by demagogues in certain areas of the South?

I had opportunity to visit a little corner of the South some time ago and to talk to serious people who discussed objectively the problems ahead. No thinking person should try to minimize those problems, which are rooted deeply in tradition, social custom, and passionate conviction mingled with fear. But I carried away the impression that if spouting politicians and professional hate-mongers could be capped like gushers, there would be hope for eventual and fairly peaceful solution.

302

The Church has been proceeding with gradual force for some time in various parts of the South. The progress has flamed incidents, but in time the embers hardly glow. How many years ago is it that the Archbishop of St. Louis had his faithful followers swarming violently about his head seeking his scalp? They have long since been peaceful. The Bishop of Raleigh, a forceful Southerner, had to personally confront a rebellious congregation a few years ago to bring about integration at Mass. Archbishop Rummel's interdict was far from the first flame he had kindled, and his progress has been notable. And the Bishop of Lafayette apparently achieved his purpose with a little temporary and salutary excommunication.

Your point is well taken, but I fail to see that the Church is going too fast. Her progress is usually characterized by an oft-quoted motto: *festina lente*—make haste slowly. She has often been too slow in the past, but her pace, already increasing in recent years, has been abruptly accelerated by the Supreme Court. Would you now have her lag behind and let civil authority teach her the message of Christ? Before, she might silently tolerate without scandal. Now that the question is sharply raised she must speak clearly or seem to side with error.

Q. In the list of sins which you gave recently you made no mention of discrimination like that in Louisiana. Against which commandment does this come? It must be a sin, or people could not be excommunicated for it.

A. It certainly is a sin, and it fits under various commandments. It breaks at least five of the ten:

The First Commandment requires that we exercise the

virtue of charity by loving God above all things, for His own sake, and our neighbor as ourselves, for the love of God. Those who bar a Negro priest from the altar certainly have a strange way of showing their love for Christ's personal representative. Those who try to bar little black children from catechism class and beat up their teachers should listen again to the gentle words of Jesus: "Suffer the little children to come unto me, and forbid them not, for of such is the kingdom of heaven!"

The Fourth Commandment obliges us to respect and obey the authority of Holy Mother Church. It was contemptuous violation of authority which was the immediate cause of Archbishop Rummel's interdict on the parish at Jesuit Bend. A similar spirit of contempt and revolt caused Bishop Jeanmard to impose his excommunications. Both these penalties were medicinal or remedial in purpose. As soon as they had accomplished their purpose of correction they were removed.

The Fifth Commandment deals generally with the virtue of justice in matters of personal rights, such as life, health, liberty and equality. When you deny a man that measure of equality demanded by human dignity you kill him, at least in part, in his spirit.

This commandment also forbids scandal, and those Catholic people in Louisiana gave nationwide scandal, which the prompt action of their bishops largely repaired, with a good lesson taught.

The Seventh Commandment demands, among other types of justice, that which we call distributive. It demands that all the members of society participate fairly in the common goods, benefits, and facilities of society. Discrimination violates distributive justice and the Seventh Commandment most flagrantly.

304

The Eighth Commandment demands respect for a man's honor and standing in the community. Discrimination debases him, insults him, dishonors him.

There are five other commandments. It is quite possible that revolt against Church authority may induce serious danger to faith and religion, thereby violating the First Commandment. I am quite sure that racial strife leads to cursing, and possibly even to blasphemy, both of which are against the Second Commandment. Even the Third Commandment was drawn into the matter when the Catholics at Jesuit Bend refused to go to Mass on Sunday because a Negro priest was saying it. I think we can pass over the Sixth and Ninth, though I am sure the problem does not leave them untouched. The Tenth is violated, at least indirectly, by those who put property values above human values.

So I think we can say without exaggeration that racial prejudice and discrimination are apt to shatter all ten Commandments.

Q. Can you help me straighten out my thinking on racial integration? Until the recent Supreme Court decision I never gave it a thought. It had seemed to me a social problem rather than a religious one. Since the Church has become involved in it, I find myself wondering what view she takes on various aspects of the situation. For instance, what is the view of the Catholic Church on interracial marriage—which might be one of the results of complete integration. Also, in social gatherings for young people, such as dances, etc., does the Catholic Church believe that integration should be complete and unbiased? Should white and colored boys and girls mix in dances, as escorts, etc.?

A. Your questions are the ones which drive our Southern friends frantic. Their favorite rationalization against permitting Negroes into white schools is that it will be a step on the way to interracial marriage. And when that dirty word is mentioned they start shooting in defense of Southern womanhood.

Basically, you are right in believing that this is a social problem rather than a religious one. But no aspect of social relations can be completely divorced from moral principles. Furthermore, the Church lives in society and is made up of the same human individuals who constitute society. She brings people together in churches, conducts schools and hospitals for the members of society. So she is constantly called upon to put her own principles into practice.

The same rules of justice and charity which regulate your individual relations with your neighbor apply to the complicated relations of millions of you's with millions of neighbors. We each have rights and duties. But they are human rights and human duties; not white rights and white duties, or Negro rights and Negro duties. Our rights are inherent in our human personality, not in our color.

The Church is usually in no great haste to change established social custom. She has a long history of tolerating abuses rather than stirring up conflict. But when the issues come out in the open and her sound principles are challenged or denied she must speak up loudly and firmly.

Right now there is in our country sharp, and often bitter, controversy as to what rights a colored man has. What would you have the Church do? Pussyfoot? Hedge? Both doctrine and morality are involved in this controversy, and on the basis of both doctrine and morality the answers are very clear and certain. The only possible controversy among Catholics would involve means and methods, speed or delay. In these circumstances, even though it heighten the conflict, the Church must speak out firmly. She must fulfill her divine mission of teaching the truth of Christ, even though some of her stubborn, hard-headed members get sore and leave her.

So the Church insists on the equality of all men before God, and their equal rights before the law. In our modern society this implies that there can be no distinction, on the basis of race or color, in the fair and equal use of public facilities, such as schools, streets, parks, and the voting booth. It means that equal protection must be provided human life and liberty regardless of color: fair police action, just and equitable procedure in the courts, and free-

307

dom from mob threats and violence. It means equal economic opportunity, freedom of speech and assembly, freedom of worship, opportunity for decent housing, opportunity for education and self-development, and all those other rights and privileges which we prize so highly as American citizens.

The Church is not committed to undue haste in solving problems which are rooted deep in social custom and prejudice. She does feel that she should lead the way cautiously. But she knows that you can't force men against their perverse will in matters of this kind. She can teach and admonish, however, and pray that grace will mellow perversity.

In your individual personal relations, justice and charity seldom dictate your choice of friends and companions. Social equality demands that we show people the courtesy, respect and consideration which they deserve by reason of their personality and behavior, without regard to color. It does not demand that we ask any particular person, or group or class of persons, into our home, or make them our drinking companions. You don't consider yourself guilty of sin if you refuse to date Protestants, Jews, or pagans. On the contrary, your pastor urges you to keep company only with your own lest you run the danger of a mixed marriage.

Interracial marriages are not forbidden by the law of the Church. Some moralists believe that in our actual American society they are forbidden by general moral law because of 1) the dangers to matrimonial harmony which result from diversity of background, tradition, and social attitudes; 2) the tensions that are produced between families and friends; 3) the social ostracism which will be a
308

burden on marital life; and 4) the problems which will be created for the children.

So while interracial marriage remains basically a matter of personal choice, it is in our society highly inadvisable, and any priest will feel in duty bound to point this out to you, if you consult him. And if marriage is inadvisable, then the type of association which would lead to marriage is likewise inadvisable—and the objections are just as strong for the Negro as they are for the white person. To see it from the other side: Protestants should not keep company with Catholics; Negroes should not keep company with whites—for their own good. And there are always exceptions to every general rule.

Q. Your reply to the letter on interracial marriages raises new questions, or leaves a couple of questions unanswered. If interracial marriages are morally, as well as socially, inadvisable, then the races should not mix socially, because such associations may lead to love, courtship, and marriage. Are you not back, then (however involuntarily), to the primitive racism of white Southerners who say they will fight for segregation of the races until their dying day? And how can this be reconciled with what several Catholic bishops in the South have said against segregation?

Second: how will the climate of opinion opposed to interracial marriages ever become congenial, or at least tolerant towards such marriages, if Negro-white couples are forever discouraged (by sociologists and moralists) from marrying? Most bigots begin to lose some of their prejudice as they become more familiar with the thing they hate. At the same time that Negro-white couples are

309

being properly told of the hardships their marriage will bring, couldn't they also be praised, if they are determined to marry, for doing some very necessary pioneering for future generations when interracial wedlock will be "acceptable"?

A. You people are trying to maneuver me into a position which I refuse to occupy—a simulated either-or position, which would make me choose between my convictions as a marriage counsellor and the demands of justice and charity in human relations. I refuse because the position is unnecessary and unrealistic; it results from faulty logic, based on assumptions unproven.

When a person seems to be backed into a corner and wedged there between the horns of a dilemma, he is apt to look around for reassuring company to console him in his predicament. My search is quickly and happily rewarded. Right beside me I find Father John LaFarge, S.J., and he has been there a long time without suffering discomfort. When one needs company a man like him beats a crowd. He is the valiant pioneer of Catholic campaigners for racial justice, against segregation, and for social equality. But on the subject of interracial marriage he has this to say:

"There are *grave reasons* (italics are his) against any general practice of intermarriage between the members of different racial groups. These reasons, where clearly verified, amount to a moral prohibition of such a practice." (*The Race Question and the Negro,* p. 196).

Sometimes a pragmatic test is a good way to try out the validity of our deductions. Now I know beyond any question that interracial marriages are strongly inadvisable under present social conditions in this country; I can adduce valid arguments and quote outstanding authorities. I have in mind, particularly, a noted and liberal non-Catholic marriage counsellor who states simply that the odds against such marriage are insurmountable: "Marriage does not occur in a vacuum; it occurs in a social milieu. Irresistible social pressure may be brought to bear upon it and upon the persons in it. In some societies, Negro-white marriage may be made to succeed; but in ours, where attitudes are highly seasoned by tradition and where prejudice runs rampant, it becomes scarcely short of impossible . . ." (Bowman, *Marriage for Moderns*, p. 181).

This author is from Missouri; so maybe we should tone down his pitch, even though his book shows no signs of personal prejudice. His attitude is typical of writers on the subject.

On the other hand, I know with absolute certainty, from the firm principles of my Catholic faith, and the sound teachings of moral theology, that all men have from their Creator equal rights, inherent in their personality, irrespective of their color; and that we all have a mutual obligation in justice and charity to respect these natural human rights. Segregation as it is practiced in this country, and racial discrimination of any kind which supposes one race to be superior and would force another race into a position of inferiority, is patently subversive of these human rights, and consequently immoral.

Now those two things I know for certain, and when you tell me that I cannot hold them both at once, or that I must derogate the one or compromise the other, then I know that there must be something wrong with your argument. So I start looking for the holes in it.

The biggest hole shows up where your argument proves too much. If interracial marriage is to be avoided, and

311

desegregation with its resultant social contacts between the races leads to interracial marriage, then we must keep segregation completely intact. That's the way the Southerner's argument goes, and it leads to logical conclusions like "keeping the Negro in his place," keeping him in separate waiting rooms, schools, and public conveyances, keeping him off "white" playgrounds, never speaking to him as an equal, always patronizing him, preventing him from voting, etc. It's all very logical, but very unreal, because the minor premise is simply an assumption.

I am going to throw the burden of proof back to you. Establish your premise. Show me the evidence that establishment of equality, friendship, just and charitable relationships between the races, leads to interracial marriage. Actually I believe there is evidence in the opposite direction. As the status of the Negro is improved, and as he is freed from fears, insecurity, and a constant reminder of inferiority, he is in a better position to find a similar and suitable partner from his own race. Seldom has the average Negro shown much interest in marriage to a white partner.

Actually, I think that the question of intermarriage has very little relevance to the problem of racial justice and desegregation. It is a red herring drawn across the line of argument to divert attention from the real issues; it is a red flag waved in front of Southern prejudices to inflame them; it is the shibboleth of the Southern superman; the catchword of a cliché which substitutes for thought. Out with it.

By argument equally lucid and fallacious I might prove to you that we Catholics should create ghettos for ourselves, burrows or warrens in which we would segregate ourselves from all our non-Catholic neighbors, avoiding

312

all social contacts with them, accepting an inferior status so that we would not associate with them on terms of equality (we would have to accept inferiority, because we are unable to subjugate them to inferior status). Our reason for all this would be that we might thus avoid mixed marriages. Surely marriage between members of different religious groups is less desirable than marriage between people of different races. So if you would advocate "keeping the Negro in his place," segregated and inferior, to avoid interracial marriage, then by more cogent argument we as Catholics should be willing to accept segregation, inferiority, and social ostracism that we might thus avoid mixed marriage.

Maybe you object that my argument is not parallel, since the Negro does not voluntarily accept his segregation. All right, let us put it another way. Many Protestants are as strongly opposed to mixed marriages as are Catholics. Suppose the Protestants of the country were to band together in a campaign to prevent the flower of their evangelical youth from being sullied, perverted, and degraded by predatory papists in the unpreventable pregnancies of irrevocable nuptials. To accomplish their purpose they would relegate all us Catholics to segregated status, patronizing us as credulous inferiors, barring us from all equality in social contact, and depriving us of many of our civil rights. And to all our objections their reply would be that they must prevent mixed marriages at all costs.

My argument is as good as yours and my conclusions just as ridiculous—but hardly more so. My conclusion strikes you as ridiculous, because it is so impossible—we hope. Your conclusion doesn't seem ridiculous, because we are used to seeing it in practice.

If I have not squelched your argument as completely as

313

I think I have, and must still choose between the prodding horns of your dilemma, then I must, of course, choose interracial marriages. They are not wrong in themselves; the big objection to them is that social circumstances provide dangers to their permanence and happiness. And before interracial marriages become a problem on any considerable scale, these social circumstances will have to change greatly, and with that change the problem will diminish. On the other hand discriminatory and enforced segregation is morally wrong—a sin—and certainly I cannot choose that.

And now briefly to the second part of your question. The choice of a partner in marriage is a personal choice. Another person's choice need not concern you or me. If I am called in for consultation I will give advice according to my conscience and convictions. But if I am called upon to assist at the marriage of a Negro and a white person I will assist whole-heartedly and hopefully. I will hope that they know what they are doing and that they realize the problems they will encounter. But I assure you that they will never encounter a problem from me as their pastor; and if they encounter any problem in my church, it will immediately become my problem. They will have my blessing on their marriage, my encouragement and special concern for their family life and their social acceptance. I will admire and commend their courage at the same time that I question their wisdom.

Q. A Catholic friend of mine entered into a youthful and hasty marriage, was divorced, and is now married out of the Church. Recently our pastor appointed her chairwoman of a very important parish committee. She will undoubtedly do a wonderful job for the Church—perhaps better than a Catholic in good standing. She was thrilled when Father called her. She is my very good friend and I am happy for her. But some of my Catholic friends, who are very charitable and sweet people, are wondering about it. Couldn't it serve as an impetus, in borderline cases, to cause those pondering the idea of marriage outside the Church to decide that it isn't so bad after all? It could be that the priest didn't know her position.

(Questions on this subject come in frequently. I have several on hand now. I shall try to combine them and make one answer do for all.)

We have several friends and business associates (non-Catholic) who have been divorced and remarried. Is it wrong to be close friends with these people? How wrong?

What about being close friends and visiting a Catholic person who has been divorced and remarried?

My brother had been divorced, and several years ago he married a non-Catholic girl. They seem to be very happy together, and now have two children. Recently my brother has talked about going to Mass again. What should my attitude to him and his family be? We are all so confused about this at home. Could you please help us?

A. I wish I knew the exact answer to each of these questions. No, I don't either, because exact answers would not be correct. At one time or another I have read some very exact answers and found myself fuming about their dogmatic attitude and lack of understanding. And yet if we are too tolerant we run the danger of sentimentality—the danger of scandal and encouragement to sin.

All that I shall say here applies to bad marriages already in existence—those which have established a status—those which are evidently not going to be broken up by anything less than an earthquake, spiritual or material. Our attitude towards persons entering into such marriages presents quite different problems. It has been previously discussed in this column and is not at issue now.

We shall try to stick to sound principles, but to avoid the glib and ready answers which these principles might inspire. We shall try to keep the natural, human problems in mind without becoming maudlin about them. We shall not try to simplify a question which is very complex, very personal, and widely variant. Our answers will probably be vague and inconclusive. But such are the only truthful answers I know.

First of all, we must never become insensitive to sin. We are apt to, when we live in the midst of it, see our best friends and close relatives doing it, and find it quite respectable and socially accepted. We must remember the Sixth Commandment, no matter how lovely its violations may appear, no matter how thoroughly rationalized. Adultery is mortal sin however much it be love-impelled, or stabilized by circumstance.

Secondly, we must never be intolerant or uncharitable towards sinners—even unrepentant sinners. We are led to believe that the woman taken in adultery (John 8, 3) was repentant, but those words of the Master are not re-stricted: "He that is without sin among you, let him first cast a stone at her."

We must be careful lest we encourage sin. Moralists call this giving scandal. In these marriage problems we might encourage sin in two ways:

1. Encourage those who are living in sin to continue as they are. Maybe we give them too much sympathy in their problems, which are often very real and deeply human, involving the happiness, welfare, love, and security of many people—especially children. Maybe we give them false hopes for an ultimate favorable solution, or forlorn hopes for death-bed repentance. We encourage them to pray for a miracle, or help them to gloss over any consciousness of guilt.

2. Encourage others to imitate them—as in the border-line cases you mention. If our social attitude were strongly intolerant such attempted marriages would be few. But what can we do to change a social attitude, especially when it is largely formed by non-Catholics?

To condone is to encourage. We must be careful lest we indicate by our words, our actions, or our attitude that the status of these people is all right, or nearly so. "At least it is really not so bad. God will understand! After all, they do love each other so much! And then there are the children!"

Cooperation in sin is sinful. Relatives and very close friends might find this principle applicable—if they help to provide the means for the sinful union.

Charity and justice both permit us to do business with sinners, to be friends of sinners, and very often associate socially with sinners. And I don't know where you can

317

draw the line. Each case is different, influenced by personalities and circumstances. Here are a few indications:

In our business and social contacts with divorced non-Catholics we can generally ignore their irregular situation. It is almost an integral part of their heresy. They are apt to be in fairly good faith about the whole matter. And if we were to manifest any criticism or reproach it would only offend and antagonize, and serve no good purpose. Unless these people are relatives, or were close personal friends in happier days, we should be careful not to develop too close friendship or association. This will be for our own good, and will avoid scandal to others.

When Catholics are involved in bad marriages our attitude should be stricter. The only good faith they can have is that which they have painstakingly rationalized for themselves, and it is a very tenuous and unsound faith, which we must never encourage. Mostly they know that they are living in sin, and it is not charity to soften their realization of that fact. On the other hand we accomplish nothing by being harsh, or unpleasant, or offensive to them. Charity generally forbids such an attitude. It rather encourages kindliness and helpfulness as long as these do not condone the sin or give scandal to others. And this is where the personal angles come in. So much depends on circumstances, personalities, and various intangibles, that general rules are apt to fail.

When the situation occurs in your own family the problem becomes more complicated, and is usually resolved by feelings and emotions rather than by principles. Sometimes it is hard to be just and charitable towards a sinning loved one. There is too much that hurts inside us. We become hard in manner to cover up that hurt and fend off further wounds. Emotions are so mixed up that they

318

express themselves gruffly or with harsh restraint. Sometimes, on the other hand, we find the mother-hen attitude, ready to fight all comers in defense of the weak member of the brood.

My own attitude towards solutions of this problem within the family is this: Let them solve it as befits their own family relationships and emotional involvements, as long as they do not condone, or encourage, or cooperate in sin; and as long as they are not needlessly cruel and uncompromising, uncharitable or unjust. What moralist can give mothers a set of general rules on how to treat a sinful son? Who can legislate the attitude of affection or estrangement between brother and sister?

Laws and principles deal with generalities, and with possible future events. Prudent judgment deals with particular cases, present here and now. It can not ignore personalities, emotions, and complicating circumstances. It does well if it can avoid excessive influence from loves, hates, tensions, and prejudices.

Prudence is a practical judgment in a particular case. As practical men we must sometimes accept a bad situation for what it is. Frowning sternness will not change it. Smiling friendliness need not encourage it. We don't want the sinners to think that we hold them blameless; but we are not required to make a career of showing our blame. We don't want our sympathy to mislead others who might consider it approval; but we need not constantly display our righteous disapproval.

I believe that the only real danger is that we become infected by the prevalent social attitude. We are surrounded daily by these adulterous arrangements which result from frequent divorce. They are generally accepted with a knowing nod or a tolerant smile. As we get used to them we are inclined to accept them as inescapable—to condone them with kindly tolerance. "Separation would be unthinkable." Thus we help the sinners to shrug off all thoughts of heroism in preference to hell. Often we priests are the first to counsel them to keep the faith, attend Mass, say their prayers, commit no more sins than necessary, and so keep themselves ready to live right if it should later become easy for them to do so. What else can we say?

I have said so little that is definite that I want to keep on saying it. Kindness, politeness, friendship, and sympathy proceed from the beautiful virtue of charity; and they should characterize our relations with our neighbors —even though some of them seem to be worse sinners than we are. Prudence must restrain us, however, from condoning sin, or encouraging it, or glossing it over. Humility should keep us from sanctimonious disdain; yet habit and custom must not blunt our awareness of sin. We must guard against infection from the false social conscience which surrounds us; and guard even more lest we spread that infection.

If your questions have not been answered they have, at least, been volubly evaded. Personally, I would be slow to criticize the practical answer found in a particular case by either you or your pastor, or by a mother or sister or neighbor or friend.

Q. In recent times the extent of the hunger and misery of the world has come to the notice of everyone. Bishop Sheen in his magazine Mission *has cited the fact that two-thirds of the world's population goes to bed hungry. Abbé Pierre deplores the misery of the slums of France, and the Catholic Press describes the needs and hunger of the DP's of the world. What is the obligation of the individual Catholic toward the needy of the world? Is it enough for him to give occasionally to the Bishops' Relief Fund, or are more generous measures necessary? Must he give up all his surplus wealth? Or part of it? Or even some of his necessary income? It seems incongruous that we have so many luxuries in America while so many in other countries lack the necessities.*

A. It is hard to place a limit on the obligation of charity. The virtue is best exercised when it is spontaneous—a generous expression of love without thought of obligation. Too much concern for duty in the matter may result in either of two evils: 1) niggardliness, which counts its donations carefully, and gives grudgingly as it feels obliged, or 2) a sense of compulsion, which makes us ill at ease with the proper enjoyment of our material possessions.

Yet we must know the general rules, of course. Even a spontaneous virtue must be prudent; and a lagging virtue needs to be prodded by a sense of duty.

The law of charity requires that we love our neighbor,

without exception, for the love of God. Beneficence—charitable giving—is a practical application of charity; so it must extend to all our neighbors, friends and enemies, Americans and foreigners, good and bad, in accordance with our means and their need.

It is evidently impossible for you and me to help each and every one who is in need throughout the world. We should be disposed to help all as occasion offers. But we can only do our fair share. How much is that?

The extent of our obligation of beneficence is determined by three simultaneous considerations:

1. *Propinquity.* We have a greater obligation to those who are near to us. That nearness may be family relationship, friendship, personal contact, residence in the same neighborhood, city, state, or nation. We still have an obligation to help our enemies in need, or those on the other side of the world. But the obligation thins out a bit as distance intervenes.

2. *The urgency and seriousness of the need.* In disaster, when lives are critically threatened, our obligation may be very great indeed. In ordinary day-to-day routine needs you feel the bee put on you, but you hardly know how firmly or righteously.

3. *The means we have at our disposal.* The rich man is obliged to do more than the poor man. We are obliged to give from our surplus goods much more than from those funds essential to our life or status.

Juggle those three considerations together to fit each case, and you have your answer. But there is leeway in each of them; and when you get the cube of that, it may be difficult to pin down any particular obligation. However, let us make no mistake, the obligation of charity is by nature grave. Our Lord, Himself, left no doubt of that:

"Depart from me, ye cursed, into everlasting fire . . . because I was hungry and you did not give me anything to eat." (Matt. 25, 41).

How much do you have to give? St. Alphonsus liked to make things exact. He suggested two percent of your income to help those in need. I don't know how that figure stands up today. It should certainly be higher for those with bigger incomes. But I imagine that if the average person gives that much he can find in it a salve to sooth the prickings of conscience, even if he is not sublimely charitable or notably generous (N.B. Church dues are not included in that percentage.)

Who should be the beneficiaries of our beneficence? Today, in the inscrutable generosity of Almighty God, critical needs in our own country are not common. So our obligation extends out farther than it might otherwise—into lands where the need is dire and extensive. Then too, as you say, we have more; so it should naturally go farther.

How measure our obligation in a practical way? I believe that if we are really generous in our response to the annual appeal of our bishops, to Bishop Sheen's appeal for the missions, and to various special pleas that are addressed to us, we can feel that we have done our share as far as alms-giving is concerned. (N.B. Be critical of appeals. Don't respond to every letter you get; check up to see if it is deserving.)

Charity imposes upon us a wider obligation than that of alms-giving. Hand-outs will never solve the problems of a hungry world. Efforts are being made, on a wide scale, to increase production by application of scientific methods and mechanical aids. Some of these efforts are sponsored by the United Nations. More of them result from cooperation between nations; and we can be rather proud of our own nation in this regard, e.g. the Point Four program. Charity requires that we support efforts of this kind and do our part to encourage them. Their motives may not always be pure love of God or neighbor; but they do promise to be vastly beneficial. And our personal motives in supporting them can be as sublime as divine charity can make them.

Q. Could you please discuss in your column the views of the Church regarding the status of women, particularly in matters of job-holding. It seems to me that there is something wrong with feminine "emancipation," but I want to be sure my ideas are in accord with those of the Church.

A. Happy and holy would our thinking be if we were all careful to make sure that our ideas accord with those of the Church—in every field in which the Church officially expresses definite ideas, e.g. education, social and economic righteousness, racial prejudice, public morality, international peace, and domestic virtue. When the Church speaks out in these fields it is usually because doctrinal teachings or moral principles are directly involved. And Jesus Christ appointed the Church to teach faith and morals with authority like His own: "As the Father has sent me, I also send you . . . He who hears you hears me; and he who despises you despises me . . . and Him who sent me." (John 20, 21; Luke 10, 16).

The ideas of the Church regarding the position of women in the modern world have been clearly set forth by our Holy Father, Pope Pius XII, in public utterances. I have at hand two of his talks, the first to the women of Italian Christian Societies, on October 21, 1945; and the second to the International Union of Catholic Women's Leagues, on September 11, 1947. I shall try to interpret for you the meaning of these talks, as I understand them.

325

The expressions I use here are mine, however; so if there are errors don't blame them on the Holy Father.

In judging any questions involving social change we should be careful of prejudice. The modern is not necessarily wrong; the traditional is not inherently sacred. Principles are permanent, but the mode of their application varies. We should not embrace the new without restraint, simply because it is new, and up-to-date, and à la mode. But neither need we reject it out of hand merely because grandmother would not have liked it.

We should also keep in mind that seldom is social change all white or all black. It has both good and bad in it. In a complicated question like this we should not expect a flat answer that the emancipation of women is good or bad. We should try to figure out whether there is more good than bad in it.

If our thinking is to be practical in matters of this kind we must sometimes give due recognition to the *fait accompli*. Certain changes are so firmly established and certain trends so inexorable that no amount of pressure or shouting will change them. Our problem is to make the best of them; accentuate the good in them and eliminate the evil. Neither angry polemics nor nostalgic yearning for the good old days will turn back the wheels of time. We can only help them roll to a better position ahead.

If our thinking is to be clear and accurate we must never lose sight of basic truths. Almightly God created woman, just as He created man, with an immortal soul fashioned in His own image and destined to eternal happiness. The souls of man and woman are equally precious in the sight of God, equally recipients of His love and grace. Jesus Christ died as much for one as for the other.

While man and woman are spiritually equal, there are

evident physical and psychic differences between them which determine their mutual relations and differentiate their roles in life. The primary purpose of both man and woman is to give glory to God and attain the happiness of heaven. But each one accomplishes this according to his or her nature. Woman is by nature a wife and mother first, and it is her first duty to be a good wife and a good mother. Anything which prevents her from the proper performance of these first duties is bad, and anything which hinders her in them is undesirable and is only to be tolerated for sufficient cause.

In former days women could devote themselves to their primary duties without distraction. Their place was in the home, and it was a sacred and fruitful place. They established the ideals of the home and maintained its sanctity, and from their own quiet place they exercised a tremendous influence upon society.

Now things have changed. The Holy Father points out that whether she likes it or not, woman is often forced out of the home, drawn out into the business world by economic necessity, pushed into the social arena, entangled in political strife. In vain, he says, would we preach a return to the hearth. Emancipation was a word for idealists. Necessities of life dictate these modern changes.

His Holiness accepts the situation as fact, with only a regretful glance at the past, and a pause to point out the evils and abuses which may follow; equal rights mean equal weight of work; woman leaves the home where she was queen and enters the factory where she finds no respect; her house is often neglected, her children unkept and uneducated, growing up without love or example; she is no longer mistress of a happy home, but an assembly-line drudge, entitled to the same pay as a man, as long as she turns out equal production.

The Holy Father wastes no time bemoaning facts. Since women are out of the home by necessity, let them make the most of their opportunities in the world. He would not have them merely resigned, as patient victims of their situation. He urges them to be active, alert, and positive. Leadership in women's activities is too often left to those whose aims are secular and material, who demean the dignity of their own sex, often by their own notoriety. Good women should make their influence felt on behalf of social needs, education, and the care of the sick; to protect the dignity of daughter, wife, and mother; to preserve the sanctity of the home, the integrity of the family, and the welfare of the child; to guard liberty and religion and the rights of conscience.

The Holy Father points out that there are three vocations for women. He gives due praise to the religious life, but he is evidently not concerned with that in his talks to women active in the world. The matrimonial vocation is evident and natural, and manifestly intended for the great majority. But there are many women who find their vocation in the very impossibility of marriage, accept the situation, and devote themselves to the love of God, the service of others, and works of charity and zeal. It is with special emphasis that His Holiness calls upon this third group to take an active and forceful leadership in public life.

I see that I have not answered your question. But I don't think the Holy Father gave an answer either. He evidently regrets that woman is so often forced from her proper domain where she should rightly reign as queen and that respect for her is often lowered in her equal contacts with man; but the facts demand that we make the most of it! Since women must be in the world, they can help bring the influence of the Church into public life, to make its force felt in the civil, social, and even the political order, to bring the errant currents of public life into harmony with the law of God, and inspire in it the spirit of Christ.

But all this requires faith that is deep and firm, and a religious life which expresses that faith in humility, prayer, and sacrifice. We are fighting the forces of secularism, and we do not conquer them by walking in their wake. There must be intimate union with Christ, so strengthened with prayer and sacrifice that it will remain firm to the point of heroism.

Q. Is it, as a general rule, a venial sin for the majority of people to knit, crochet, sew, or work on their car or garden on Sunday?

The enclosed article concerns a point that is vital to a majority of Catholics. It disagrees with what I had previously understood to be the rule, namely that such recreation, or "servile work" was permissible if it were not for profit.

A. The article which you send is by Father Donald F. Miller, C.SS.R., a sound spiritual writer of wide popularity. It appears in *The Liguorian*. Father Miller deplores the growing tendency to disregard Sunday as a day of rest. He says that there is considerable confusion and misunderstanding among Catholics as to the kind of work forbidden on Sunday. And it is the stated purpose of his article to try to straighten out some of this confusion.

The part which causes you trouble arises from Father Miller's definition and examples of servile work: "This is any kind of work that is ordinarily done by manual laborers, that primarily taxes the body and not the imagination or the mind, and that has traditionally been considered a kind of work forbidden on Sunday." And he expressly mentions gardening, washing or working on the family car, crocheting, and sewing, as examples of servile work. (I believe we should read "knitting" for "crocheting" in the article. The context indicates that it is some-

330

thing the girls do to sox, sweater, and mufflers. Crocheting is usually considered an "artistic" work, permissible on Sundays. But this is only a technical error in the field of feminine fancy-work.)

Father Miller's article agrees thoroughly with all my moral books, and he presents his subject clearly and logically. I have no argument with him. I am simply dissatisfied with the traditional notion of servile work, as handed down from the Middle Ages with little change. It does not fit modern conditions of work and life. This dissatisfaction is not mine alone; it is manifested in the customs of our Catholic people, and has been expressed by many writers during the past fifty years. Among them is Father Miller's fellow-Redemptorist, Father Vincent J. Kelly, of Boston.

If we are going to have a little theological argument here in this column we had better start by clarifying the topic in dispute. It is simply this: What is servile work?

You know that the law of the Church forbids servile work on Sundays and holydays. But what is servile work? The law doesn't define it; it simply forbids it. Who does make the decisions as to what servile work is?

The traditional moralists say that servile work is determined by its own intrinsic nature. It is a type of work. Period. It is the work once done by slaves or servants, whence it gets its name. It is the work done in overalls, with a plow or an axe or a shovel. It is the work done in an apron, with dish-cloth or dust-cloth, and a bit of smudge on the nose.

By contrast, the works which are liberal, or not servile, are those of the scholar, the artist, and the gentleman: the works of mind and imagination—creative efforts.

If there seems to be snobbery or class consciousness in that division of work, let us recall that one of the early

331

purposes of this law of the Church was to keep the master from making his servants work on Sunday. It should be a day of rest for them. No need to worry about the master's rest; he didn't much need it. Neither was there special need in those days to protect the scholar or the artist from exploitation.

Your idea that "servile work" is permissible if it is not done for profit is ridiculous to the traditional moralist. If it is servile by its nature, then it is servile. Period. The fact that you may do it for pleasure or recreation makes no difference. If it is *liberal* by nature then you can earn a million dollars by doing it on Sunday and yet not break the law of the Church.

The traditional moralist is not the least interested in your intention or the effort you expend. Servile work remains servile no matter how charitable or generous your intention in doing it; but you can paint dirty pictures all day and only break the Sixth Commandment. Knitting is servile work even though it tire you little; but you can walk forty miles with full hunter's field-pack, blister your feet, and come home half dead, and not a lick of servile work have you done.

It used to be that this traditional norm of servile work was quite practical. But now there are many thousands of different kinds of work never dreamed of in past centuries. Who is going to say whether the work of a laboratory technician is servile or liberal? What about an electrical engineer? The answer is apt to be arbitrary, and your guess as good as mine. Many of the new jobs are half brainwork and half manual labor. But you can't say they are half permitted on Sunday and half forbidden. They must be either servile or liberal. Who fits them in which slot?

According to our traditional moralists the work of the

stenographer, bookkeeper, accountant, and the like, is not servile. So it is not forbidden on Sunday. Consequently, if we adhere to the old traditional norms, we must tell people in our big city offices that it is perfectly all right for them to work on Sunday, full blast, same as any other day. About half of our modern commercial world could carry on business as usual without breaking the law of the Church. No servile work is done; it is not public buying or selling in the traditional sense.

Fortunately for Sunday observance the good sense of our people is much stricter than the traditional moralist would be if he remained logical. Custom is the best interpreter of the law (Canon 29) and custom is not necessarily stagnant. It changes with the times. And if moralists keep their noses so close to their books that they can not observe the changes of times and customs they are apt to become impractical.

Maybe St. Thomas Aquinas foresaw that things would be different in the atomic age. Anyway he indicated that "types of work, considered in themselves, may change according to place and time."

Some of the old categories of servile work have not changed, and never will, e.g. plowing your field, laying bricks, and stoking a furnace. Some will always remain liberal, whatever the purpose or pay, e.g. reading and writing. But the classification of others must depend on common estimation and custom—that custom which results from the Catholic conscience, from the common sense of priests and people.

This standard of custom has made servile work a relative thing, within certain limits. Unconsciously it takes into consideration extrinsic factors like profits, intention, and fatigue. Work is more apt to be held licit if it is done

333

for fun, without hope of pay, or if it is done for pious purposes, or if it doesn't require much effort or tire you greatly.

A similar tendency for relative interpretation achieved success regarding the law of fasting. The traditional rules of moralists concerning full meals and collations, and so many ounces of this and that, were quite foreign to our modern American customs of eating. Consequently the law was often observed in the breach. Now the relative norm has been made official in most of the United States; and far more people are observing the fast. A relative norm for servile work might have similar happy results.

This common-sense norm would define servile work as that labor which we put out during the week to earn a living or turn a profit. Servile work is the week-day's work—the exercise of your trade or profession.

Sunday is the day of rest, and if you do your regular week-day work on Sunday you are not resting. You are defeating the purpose of the Sabbath, even though your work be entirely liberal, mental and imaginative. You are making Sunday the same as any other day. You are not taking time to serve the Lord on that day, or preparing yourself to serve Him better on other days.

On the other hand, if your favorite recreation—from the liberal and mental work of every day in the office—is puttering with your roses, or with your do-it-yourself kit, and if the work you are doing is not strictly menial, then common sense and custom are apt to tell you to go ahead—quietly, so as not to disturb your neighbors. That's the idea of many of our best parishioners, who can be found puttering around lawns, gardens, and automobiles on Sunday, without idea of committing sin.

Modern interpretation, as expressed in popular custom,

334

puts this puttering on a level with golf, hunting, fishing, and bird-watching. It is your hobby, your recreation; it is not servile work. Your servile work is keeping books, or selling insurance, or juggling radioactive isotopes.

Now look what you made me do: foul up all Father Miller's nice logical clarification and create more of that confusion he deplores. Go on and do your bit of crocheting on Sunday, or even your knitting, if it is not for profit. But don't get me started on subjects like this. I just get everybody mixed up. And someone is sure to jump on me.

INDEX